BOOK OF BOOKS

BOOK OF BOOKS

PEARLS FROM THE MEANDERING STREAM OF TIME THAT RUNS ACROSS CONTINENTS

James Mathew
Kent Bicknell

Libri Publishing

First published in 2021 by Green Frigate Books
Green Frigate Books is an imprint of Libri Publishing

ISBN 978-1-911451-10-5

A CIP catalogue record for this book is available from The British Library

Cover and Design by Carnegie Book Production

Libri Publishing
Brunel House
Volunteer Way
Faringdon
Oxfordshire
SN7 7YR

Tel: +44 (0)845 873 3837

www.libripublishing.co.uk

Shanti
A name and an invocation

Acknowledgement

Dear reader: I would like to take a moment of your time to thank those who helped prepare the manuscript of the *Book of Books.*

Kent Bicknell, second author of the book, also helped the T.G.M. Rare Book Museum with several acquisitions. Suresh Gopalakrishnan helped find verses in the scriptures relevant to R.W. Emerson's "Brahma". Rajan Mathew supplied the brief biography of T.G. Mathai.

Elizabeth Witherell transcribed the tipped-in manuscript leaves in *The Writings of Henry David Thoreau: Manuscript Edition.* She authenticated the author's handwriting in the copy of *A Week on the Concord and Merrimack Rivers*, and searched for copies of *A Week* containing corrections by Henry D. Thoreau.

Ashna Jacob, designer of the book, also edited all images for the book, with the technical assistance of Alan Jacob. Richard Mangan took the photos used throughout the book, and E.A. George created the illustrations.

Robert Pavlik, the chief editor, edited several iterations of the manuscript, and prepared the index. Anna Anil George has been my sounding board along the road.

The T.G.M. Rare Book Museum houses the treasures included in the *Book of Books.* Obeisance to thee, leading lights of East and West, where-unto they trace their origins!

Hats off to my friends and colleagues at Libri Publishing, UK, who transformed the manuscript into a book. You put your best foot forward, take your bow! Any misstep is mine.

James Mathew

Milwaukee, Wisconsin

10 September 2021

Reviews

This book on rare books, holographs and historical artifacts in a single collection is a treasure in itself. With generous portions of passages paired with pictures and tastefully spiced with comments, this book is a feast to the intellect. I commend this book as an *aperitivo* for starters and a *digestivo* for the sated. *Bon Appetit* to all guests!

Adoor Gopalakrishnan, India
Writer & Filmmaker
Recipient of India's highest film honour, Dadasaheb Phalke Award
British Film Institute Award
French honour: Commander of the Order of Arts & Letters

Books are inanimate friends, ready to challenge, comfort and inspire us. This *Book of Books* gathers examples of these various genres, offering the reader a glimpse into the minds of people who made their mark on previous generations. We profit as we read from the past which they recount, and we gaze into the future.

Father Michael Collins, Ireland
Author of *Books That Changed History*

Book of Books represents an original and needed contribution to understanding the very profound impacts that the Transcendentalists made to fostering important conversations across the world about how to understand the reality of global spiritual traditions. The attempts to find the language and conceptual paradigms for this comparative exploration resonate with us still. *Book of Books* will provide case studies in this complex and challenging undertaking, inspired by the dazzling originators of this movement who were, for the first time, beginning to read works of all the world's major religions.

Todd Lewis, United States of America
Edward G. Murray Distinguished Professor in Arts and Humanities
College of the Holy Cross

Contents

Foreword

A book on books might not be a brand-new idea, but this one on rare books, holographs and historical artifacts in a single collection with a theme that runs across cultures and centuries is a treasure in itself. With generous portions of passages paired with pictures and tastefully spiced with comments, this book is a feast to the intellect.

The book begins with entries from the intellectuals of a young nation in the West who gave birth to its literature, the transcendentalists of America – Henry David Thoreau's *A Week on the Concord and Merrimack Rivers* with his hand-corrections in which he extolls the *Hindoo Scriptures* and Ralph Waldo Emerson's signed holograph of "Brahma" that echoes a familiar voice among them. Then comes a serving of the sacred texts of an ancient civilization in the East from which the transcendentalists drew light – the *Gita* and the Upaniṣads, and more, such as *The Rubāiyāt of Omar Khayyām* and *The Buddhist Ray*. These entries are followed by courses from luminaries of a more recent past from the West, the East and in between who ushered in a new dawn of mutual respect with equal profit – Leo Tolstoy, Annie Besant, Swami Vivekananda, Rabindranath Tagore and Mahatma Gandhi, to name a few. I am particularly touched by the fragments of Gandhiji's hand-written notes of his prayer speech for 23 September 1947. There are some delights from the present at the end – author-inscribed volumes from Geevarghese Mar Osthathios, B. Sugathakumari and myself in them.

A brief biography of the namesake of this Collection, Thamaravelil Geevarghese Mathai, a self-educated scholar who was a role model for his village, complements this book.

I commend this book as an *aperitivo* for starters and a *digestivo* for the sated. *Bon Appetit* to all guests!

Adoor Gopalakrishnan

Thiruvananthapuram

3 July 2021

Preface

This book provides a guided tour of a museum of rare books, manuscripts and historical artifacts. The visitor is invited to explore pearls which are *not without their links*, that dangle on the strands of Time from the ancient to the present, stretched across the East and the West – treasures from the Thamaravelil Geevarghese Mathai Rare Book Museum.

This book contains descriptions and photos of classic and collectible books and manuscripts, often with excerpts from them – *the noblest recorded thoughts of man.*

A substantial portion of the "exhibits" in this "museum" pertains to poets, philosophers, prophets and reformers of mid-nineteenth century America and the luminaries of a much older period from the East who had enlightened them. Another considerable part pertains to those in the West who reignited interest in Eastern thoughts, and vice versa, in the late nineteenth to mid-twentieth centuries by their lives and by their voyages. This exchange led to a renewed mutual appreciation and application of ideas and ideals, and improved understanding among nations and peoples. A few entries have personal association with the curator of the museum.

Like the museum itself, this book is dedicated to its namesake, Thamaravelil Geevarghese Mathai. Both are offered to the kind-hearted who hunger and thirst in the pursuit of wisdom. A brief biography of T.G. Mathai is appended.

The authors, James Mathew and Kent Bicknell, and the chief editor, Robert Pavlik, strived to be accurate in facts and to attribute due credits. Any error or omission that remains is unintentional and will be corrected at the first available opportunity.

James Mathew

Milwaukee, Wisconsin

4 July 2021

Preface to the Biography

My father, Thamaravelil Geevarghese Mathai, started writing his autobiography in 1969. Ever since I came across this unfinished work soon after his death in 1987, I wanted to finish what he started. The publication of this brief biography is a fulfilment of that wish, albeit in part, for I had envisioned a longer one.

The initial impetus for writing this biography was to record the trials and tribulations of the patriarch of our family for the benefit of his descendants, who have spread to the far corners of the Earth as he had prayed for before any one of them was born, most of whom have not seen him but know him as the *great father* in a distant past and place. But if the legacy of a man born in a remote village under challenging circumstances, who lived deliberately according to the covenant he made with God at an early age, inspires other children and parents in similar stages, this biography will serve a larger purpose.

It is all the more proper that this biography is enjoined to the catalogue of a collection of rare books, manuscripts and historical artifacts named after its subject, a book of books, if you will, because throughout his life he taught himself new subjects while teaching others the value of learning.

I would like to thank the many people who helped me in writing this brief biography, but particularly my brother and sisters for filling in the gaps, and Kent Bicknell and Robert Pavlik for editing it.

Rajan Mathew

Bangalore

17 August 2020

T.G. Mathai (1914–1987)

Seedlings/Gleanings

Beginnings

Thamaravelil Geevarghese Mathai (T.G. Mathai) was born in the village of Nariyapuram, Kerala State, India (the Princely State of Travancore, British India) on 17 August 1914. The 17th of August is always the New Year's Day of the Malayalam Era (Chingam 1, 1090 ME). He was the son of Easo Geevarghese and Achiamma Geevarghese. Both parents had lineages from prominent early Christian families of Kerala that thrive to this day. The early history is mostly oral. Easo Geevarghese belonged to the Plavila Kandathil family in Arattupuzha, a village near Chengannur, Kerala. A descendent of one of the brothers of this family married from the Sankarathil family and the couple had a son they named Easo Geevarghese ("Easo" is Malayalam for "Jesus").

Soon after Easo was born, his mother died, and his father later remarried. In time, Easo would marry into the Mazhuvam Mannil family in Nariyapuram.

Easo Geevarghese, T.G.M.'s father
(1878–1958)

Achiamma Geevarghese, T.G.M.'s mother
(1886–1977)

1

The prominent patriarch of the Mazhuvam Mannil family was Korala, who was known as "Muthalupidikaran" (*wealth collector*) because he was a tax assessor and collector of the Kingdom of Pandalam as well as a landlord in lands reaching south to the River Achenkovil. He had five sons and two daughters. The sons lived in five family lands: Mazhuvam Mannil, Palladam Mannil, Uthickalil, Nediyavilayil and Thamaravelil (trans. *lotus court*).

Among these five brothers, the one at Thamaravelil was Mathen Iype. He married Aleyamma from the Pakkandathil family on the other side of the river. Mathen Iype died young, leaving Aleyamma Iype in dire straits with three young daughters, the middle one being named Achiamma.

Easo Geevarghese from Sankarathil married Achiamma Iype, inherited the Thamaravelil house and lived there along with Achiamma's mother, Aleyamma, who lived with them until her death at age 106. The principal of this biography, Thamaravelil Geevarghese Mathai, was the fourth of the six children of Easo and Achiamma Geevarghese. Young Geevarghese Mathai was particularly fond of his grandmother, Aleyamma, and called her "Valliammachi" (*great mother*).

Easo Geevarghese struggled with his health, and Achiamma became the sole bread-winner for the extended family. Unable to read or write, she was known for her skills in memorizing and mental arithmetic, which came in handy as a vendor of produce.

Rev. T.G. Kuriakose, T.G.M.'s brother
(1907–1985)

School/Education

Young T.G. Mathai loved going to school and learning. Born prematurely, he was small for his age. As he wrote in his unfinished autobiography,

> Not capable of spending idle time in bad company, it required no effort on my
> part to nurture virtues – obedience, discipline, truth and justice.[*]

Unfortunately, the boy could not attend school much beyond seventh grade, as his mother could not afford to send him. To educate himself at home over the next two years, he joined a library, read fiction and poetry, subscribed to notes from a language pundit by mail and participated in literary competitions. His knowledge continued to grow.

Slighted by his older brother for not labouring in the field and feeling unappreciated at home because of his "idle life", he left home determined not to return until he could stand on his own two feet. His father told him, "Do not be a slave under anyone's roof, nor wear any clothing that is not yours, and God will bless!"[†] Taking these words to heart, at age 16 he set out on foot to create his own life.

After a few twists and turns, and learning tailoring on the way, he arrived in Thirunelveli in present-day Tamil Nadu State. A stranger in town with a different dialect from other people, he searched for work. Starved, weak and at his wit's end, one day he thought it was time to quit. Suddenly a voice urged him, "Go out once more and try again!" He did, and secured a job at an Indian European tailoring shop by 4 p.m. that very day. In his autobiography, he shared his initial words to the skilled artisan who owned the shop:

> I said to the owner, "I hail from a lofty family; I have set out to realize self-
> reliance, to know how a man may live by his own effort. I have deliberately
> chosen a field not to be tainted by sin and corruption. Trust me with higher jobs
> and train me even more."[‡]

With nowhere to sleep but next to the shop itself, T.G. Mathai was threatened by rowdies as well as troubled by the police. At that point, he

---

[*] *Autobiography*, pp. 2–3, translated by James Mathew (J.M.)

[†] *Autobiography*, p. 3, translated by J.M.

[‡] *Autobiography*, p. 6, translated by J.M.

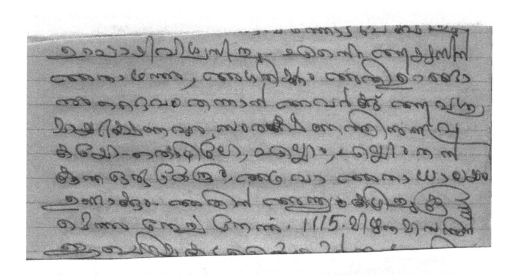

Clipping from T.G.M.'s autobiography, page 13

began to learn the martial art form Adi Thada (*Attack–Defend*).[*] Even decades later when there was no threat, T.G. Mathai continued to master the art of Adi Thada. He vowed to God that, given a chance, he would do his part to make things around him right.

> I prayed to God, firmly trusting in Him, that in my life, I will protect the orphan and the homeless, offer them a place to sleep; If God gives me the means, I will feed them or help them earn a living. I would create an orphanage, if you will, and there I would live the eve of my life.[†]

---

[*] World Heritage Encyclopedia, Adithada I, Project Gutenberg Self-Publishing – eBooks, Article Id: WHEBN0003572826, accessed 14 May 2021

[†] *Autobiography*, p. 13, translated by J.M.

Fearlessness

Even later in life, Thamaravelil Geevarghese Mathai had no fear of the physical. For example, after he returned to Nariyapuram and started his own tailoring shop and school, he was the only person in town who would not cower down in front of the notorious bully, Kuzhuvelil Kuttappan. All the other shop owners would close their shops when Kuttappan became intoxicated and literally took over the street. But T.G. Mathai would keep his shop open as he was not afraid.

One night when he was much older, he heard a series of eerie screams arise from the river, as if coming from a violent mob. Carrying a three-foot rod and a flashlight, he made his way quietly through the dark to the spot where the noise was coming from. He turned the flashlight on, only to find a group of youngsters who had had too much to drink and were playing, splashing and yelling in the water. The teenagers, caught in the spotlight of Thamaravelil Mathai-chan (as he was respectfully addressed) were ashamed. Heading back to his house with his flashlight on, he met with groups of neighbours who had gathered at safe distances from the "crime scene", too afraid to get to the bottom of the ruckus.

T.G.M.'s staff

Once, in his late fifties, a young lady from a group of bathers was swept away by the current of the swollen river as it stretched from bank to bank. A great wail went up from her companions, and many came running to see what had happened. None dared to attempt a rescue until Thamaravelil Mathai-chan arrived. Sprinting down the bank through the bushes, he overtook the victim as she was carried by the current. He jumped in, swam to midstream, caught her by the hair and brought her ashore.

Youth and Marriage

After about two years of working in Thirunelveli, T.G. Mathai mastered how to craft a gentleman's coat and trousers, a true rarity for village tailors. He returned to Nariyapuram for a visit. His intention was to go back to Thirunelveli and come back only after saving some money. His parents, however, wanted him to get married. A girl from the nearby Vallonnil family in Thattayil was proposed for him, and it is interesting that this family had a very similar background to his.

Baby (Mariamma) Mathew, T.G.M.'s wife
(1922–2016)

Neduvelil Aleyamma, Baby Mathew's mother
(1900–1990)

The patriarch of the Vallonnil family was Geevarghese, who married from the Poykayil family in Thevalakkara. They had six children, the eldest being a daughter. Geevarghese had a flourishing timber business, bringing wood from the Thenkasi forests in present-day Tamil Nadu and selling it in Kerala. During such a trip to Thenkasi, however, Geevarghese died. The family in Kerala got the news only after several days, and then the timber business died with him.

Geevarghese's sons were landowners and they all fared well. The only daughter was married to Poothakkuzhiyil Achen, a well-known and influential priest of the Orthodox Church, and a contemporary of Saint Gregorios of Parumala (1848–1902).[*] Poothakkuzhiyil Achen was the prominent first vicar of the prestigious St. George Orthodox Church in Trivandrum. His tomb stands outside the church today.

One of the five sons of Geevarghese was V.G. Mathai.[†] He was married to Aleyamma from the Neduvelil family in Thumpamon. They had three daughters and a son. Unfortunately, V.G. Mathai died very young and Aleyamma became a widow at the age of 27. She also lost her only son at the age of three. At age 14, her second daughter, Mariamma, affectionately called "Baby", was married to Thamaravelil Geevarghese Mathai, the subject of this biography, when he was 22.

> On Sunday Makaram 24, [1112 ME] the Rev. Fr. Abraham Poothakuzhy conducted my wedding at the Thumpamon Great Church.[‡]

Clipping from T.G.M.'s autobiography, page 7, recording his marriage

---

[*] Brief history of Saint Gregorios Chathuruthi, http://www.syriacchristianity.i/StGGBriefhistory, accessed 13 May 2002

[†] Vallonnil Geevarghese Mathai, not to be confused with Thamaravelil Geevargese Mathai, the subject of this biography.

[‡] *Autobiography*, p. 7, translated by J.M.

T.G.M. with his wife Baby Mathew, c. 1974

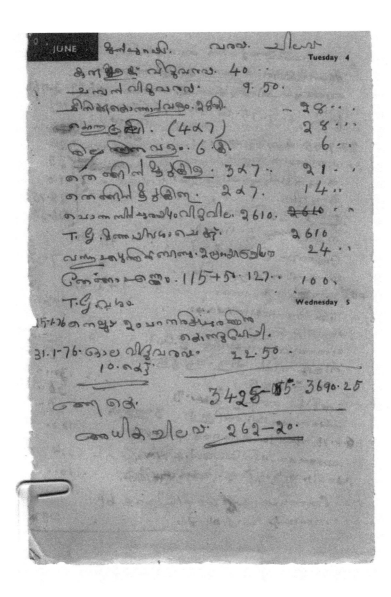

A page from T.G.M.'s journal showing book-keeping

A Covenant with God

The children of T.G. Mathai are fortunate to have discovered a draft manuscript of the beginnings of an autobiography along with a journal in which he entered events of the day, daily accounts and reflections.

In this unfinished manuscript, he wrote that he had prayed for eight children, and that the first four be daughters.

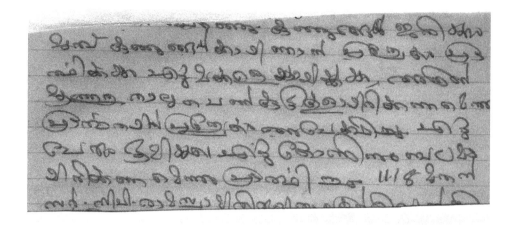

Clipping from T.G.M.'s autobiography, page 7, praying for children

> Before any children were born I prayed to God begging for eight children, and I especially begged in my prayer that the first four be daughters, and that all eight form pillars of strength to the earth in its eight corners.[*]

Once he confided in his older son that he had prayed to God that his wife and children should not depart from this world before him. He explained that he was certain his prayer had been heard and answered – and so he made a covenant with God. On his end, he promised to help the poor as much as he was able, and this at a time when he was struggling to make ends meet.

There are many outstanding instances of him trying to live up to this commitment. Once, a widow, a distant relative of his, came and wept before him because she had no money for her daughter's marriage. Without letting another soul know, he sold a small piece of land he owned and gave the money to the widow. After T.G. Mathai passed away, the woman who had been able to marry owing to his assistance shared this kind deed with his family, who had known nothing about it at the time.

One morning in the 1960s he was having tea in the village tea shop when a poor villager came in and asked for breakfast on credit. With unkind words, the shopkeeper turned down the request. T.G. Mathai opened his wallet, gave the shopkeeper its entire contents of 15 rupees (at a time

---

[*]   *Autobiography*, p. 14, translated by J.M.

when a cup of coffee was 25 paise). He instructed the shopkeeper to give the man breakfast every day, adding that he would settle the account each month.

Unto This Last

On his way to town from home, if he saw familiar faces who lived on daily wages but were idle for want of work, he would send them to his house. There, no matter how late the morning was, he would find some yard work for them to do. In addition to paying their wages, his wife also found means to cook meals for them, sometimes having to borrow both money and rice from neighbours. He often saw peddlers at day's end with unsold produce, withered and dry from the blazing sun. He would buy their vegetables at full price. If his wife chided him for bringing home fruits and vegetables that had gone bad and that nobody would purchase, he would gently respond that he had to buy them precisely because nobody else would.

The Sun Never Sets on His Family

Eight children were born to T.G. Mathai and Baby between 1939 and 1954, the first four of which were daughters. When T.G. Mathai died suddenly at the age of 72, he and his wife had 15 grandchildren, and two more would be born within three years. When his wife, Baby Mathew, died in 2016, at the age of 94, they had twenty great-grandchildren. The descendants of Nariyapuram Thamaravelil Geevarghese Mathai have spread across five continents: Oceania, Asia, Europe, Africa and North America. His covenant with God remained true, for none died while he lived.

When Shanti Mathew, James Mathew's daughter and the granddaughter of T.G. Mathai, was in junior high school in the United States, she was assigned to write an essay about a person whom she admired. She chose to write about her grandfather:

> I've never met the person I admire the most. He passed away on March 3, 1987, two months and 14 days before I was born. That man is my father's father, my grandfather. …

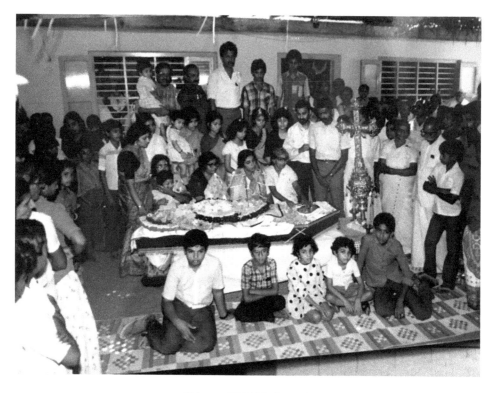

Taken at T.G.M.'s funeral

It is not hard to believe why he [my grandfather] is remembered with such fondness today. Fourteen years after his death, his 'life' is still being celebrated. On his last death anniversary, the largest of all occurred. The six of his children in India came and there was a huge gathering and service at church. Afterwards, a lunch was held at my grandmother's house, not only in honor of my grandfather, but another revered guest as well: The Bava Thirumeni. The Bava Thirumeni is to the [Indian] Orthodox Church what the Pope is to the Catholic Church. Needless to say, there was a great feast and everyone was very honored to have him come.

My grandfather is the person I admire the most. He was an amazing man, and human being. I not only look up to him, I respect him and hold him dear to my heart.

Equally High Education for Boys and Girls

In those days educating children, particularly daughters, beyond high school was rare in the village. In his later days, T.G. Mathai would say that his major regret in life was not sending his oldest daughter to college.

Instead, after completing high school she joined a newly started certificate course in primary health care at the Medical College, Trivandrum. Upon graduation, she got a government job as a primary health worker, rose through the ranks and retired as the district food inspector of her home district.

All the other children went to college. The second daughter graduated with a major in physics, specialized in radiation protection and retired a high-ranking officer in the Kuwaiti government; afterwards she earned a master's degree in law, which she practised. The third daughter earned a master's in physics from the University College, Trivandrum, and was a college professor for many years in her home state. Later she taught in schools in Africa, took another degree in education and, with her husband, founded a school in her home state. Today she continues to teach while serving as its senior principal. The school, the Holy Trinity School (K-12), is thriving with over 1,500 students.

The fourth daughter earned a master's degree in English language and literature and a degree in education, and taught grade school in New York, while the fifth child, a son, graduated in engineering and became a decorated officer in the Indian Navy. He held positions including superintendent of the naval ship yard in his home state, and retired as a commodore. The sixth, a daughter, graduated with a major in science prior to earning a BS degree in nursing from Christian Medical College, Vellore. The seventh, a daughter, graduated with a major in history and went on to earn a degree in law. The eighth child, a son, studied at the Medical College, Trivandrum and went on to become the chairman and program director of a major cardiology division and fellowship program in the US.

In an age when the education of girls was too often neglected in the villages, T.G. Mathai served as a role model for other parents as he provided an education for his daughters and sons alike. At the same time, he often directly counselled parents to give their children a higher education, and he encouraged (and supported) many boys and girls in this endeavour.

Once, a 17-year-old boy (T.P. –), the son of a friend, came and told him tearfully that while he had been admitted to college after graduation, his father was not sending him because he could not pay. T.G. Mathai sold

T.G.M.'s tomb at the cemetery of Emmanuel Orthodox Church, Nariyapuram, Kerala, India

furniture from his shop to raise money and gave it for the boy's college admission fee. At a time when his own children's education was putting him in debt, he graciously paid for the boy's entire college education over the ensuing four years. This person, whose education he financed, rose to become a general manager of the historic Grindlays Bank.

As late as November 2019, over three decades after T.G. Mathai's death, a well-to-do gentleman in his sixties (K.J. –) approached the sons of T.G. Mathai as they were walking down the churchyard steps after visiting the tomb of their father. The man explained to the sons that he owed his upward mobility and current social and financial standing to counselling he had received from their father. In an incidental meeting by the river, their father had encouraged the man to pursue his education, which he had done.

By Faith and on Credit

T.G. Mathai was often sending two-to-three children to college at the same time. With little more than his tailoring and small-scale textile shop for an income, he sold the bulk of the land he had inherited from his father to pay the various tuition fees. He also accumulated debt, mostly through chit funds.* Finally, the land his wife had inherited from her mother also had to be sold, mainly to clear the chit-fund debts.

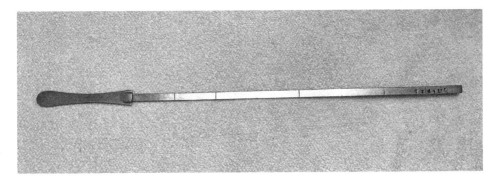

T.G.M.'s yardstick

Shortly after the death of T.G. Mathai, his younger son was at Kunjan Pappy's Store, a stationery shop in the town of Pathanamthitta. The shopkeeper, knowing who he was, introduced him to a gentleman as T.G. Mathai's son. The latter was apprehensive when he recognized that he had come face to face with Mr. Yohannan, a well-known chit-fund owner with whom his father had experienced some difficulty over a defaulted loan. Mr. Yohannan, however, appeared thrilled to be in the presence of "the son of Thamaravelil Mathai-chan" and proceeded to speak admiringly of his father.

---

*   Shailesh Menon, "Chit fund: how it works, red flags and your rights as an investor", *Economic Times*, E-Paper, 3 February 2020, accessed 13 May 2021

Self-education and Selfless Service

Throughout most of his adult life, T.G. Mathai continued to learn many other forms of art and science along with martial arts. For example, he learned astrology well, and in his journals are the astrological charts he created for each member of his family, indicating the position of planets at the hour of their birth. His astrological projections were highly valued by those who knew him.

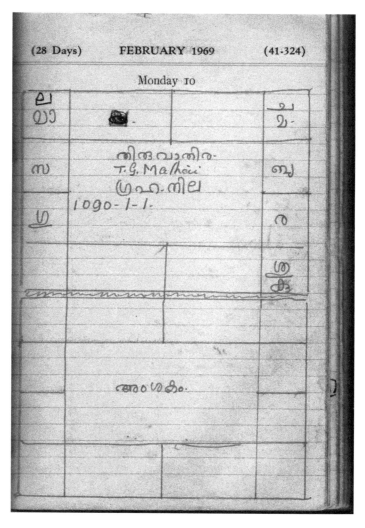

Astrological chart drawn by T.G.M. showing the position of planets at
the time of his birth

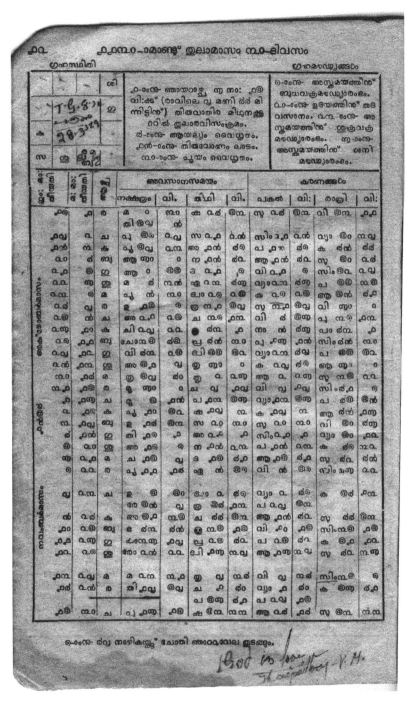

Astrological calendar marked with the birth of his eighth son in
T.G.M.'s handwriting

17

He also learned Marma Sastram, the science of the vital neurological points in the human body, which has defensive, offensive and therapeutic applications.* Later in life, he opened an Ayurvedic drug store at the same time that he learned Ayurveda (a science of indigenous medicine) from the careful study of books as well as from his oldest brother, a licensed Ayurvedic physician who received a government grant for his work.

As he learned these several arts and sciences, he also taught them to his disciples and helped many more. Everything that he passed on to others, he did for free, and even those who learned tailoring in his school never had to pay a fee.

Fishing: A Hobby and a Philosophy

Growing up near the river, he learned fishing at an early age, most likely from his father. His favourite method was by using a net called a "veesuvala" (*casting net*). The circular net is cast by a swift and wide swing, and is dragged back with the catch. First one strings a line of "confetti" for lures across the river at a strategic spot. In a wait-and-catch game, one stands on the river bank for hours – perhaps even the whole night – ready to cast the net in an instant, at the sight of a wrinkle in the water. This slight visual cue occurs when a fish turns around at the confetti and swims upstream. The whole process involves not only skill and stamina, but patience and hope. T.G. Mathai enjoyed knitting the net himself, an art rarely known to people except those who live in the coastal fishing villages. A veesuvala he knitted is still preserved.

Concern for the Environment

T.G. Mathai had several varieties of fruit and spice trees planted in the yard and he watered the young ones regularly. As he would carry two buckets full of water drawn from the well, he would pity the elder trees, which he felt were "watching", so he would water them as well. He cared for birds and they seemed to know it. When he sat for lunch, a flock of crows were his regular guests. If either the crows or T.G. Mathai were missing, they would call out for each other. T.G. Mathai's long-term close relationship with his friends, the crows, became the basis for a short story,

---

*   See, for example, http://lotusspace.com/marmashastra-sample.pdf

T.G.M.'s fishing net

"Remember the Crows", in a book of moral tales for children written by his sixth daughter, Valsamma.

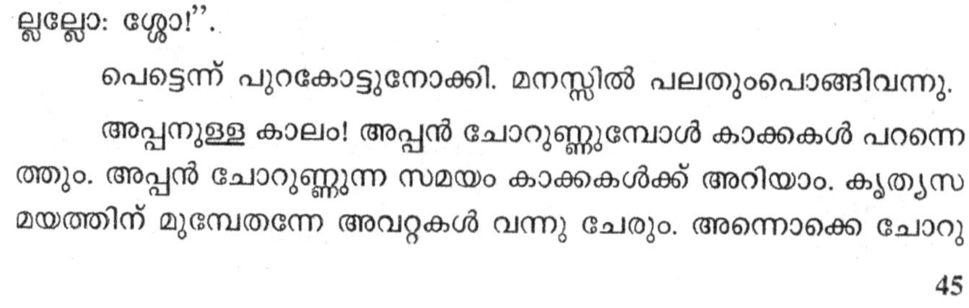

ല്ലല്ലോ: ശ്ശോ!".

പെട്ടെന്ന് പുറകോട്ടുനോക്കി. മനസ്സിൽ പലതുംപൊങ്ങിവന്നു.

അപ്പനുള്ള കാലം! അപ്പൻ ചോറുണ്ണുമ്പോൾ കാക്കകൾ പറന്നെത്തും. അപ്പൻ ചോറുണ്ണുന്ന സമയം കാക്കകൾക്ക് അറിയാം. കൃത്യസമയത്തിന് മുമ്പേതന്നേ അവറ്റകൾ വന്നു ചേരും. അന്നൊക്കെ ചോറു

45

Clipping from Valsamma Mathew's book of tales

The Days of Our Father! When Father sits down for lunch, the crows will fly in! They knew his lunch time, and will take their seats in advance.

From "Remember the Crows"
in *Come On Friends – I Will Tell You Stories*
by Valsamma Mathew, Nariyapuram*

A shrub planted by his room bloomed all year round, and was always abuzz with birds of different kinds. Alas, gone are those days, gone are the birds and their house.

The country road that led to T.G. Mathai's house and beyond would get so deep with mud in the rainy season that certain sections became impassable. Through his innovative methods, paid for from his own pocket, he would order truckloads of rubble to be dropped in the mud-pockets. Years after his death these roads were finally converted to asphalt by the Public Works Department.

* Translated by J.M.

Valsamma Mathew, T.G.M.'s daughter (1951–2014)

Chess

T.G. Mathai was an excellent strategist in the game of chess. Perhaps his only real competitor in Nariyapuram was a person known as "Illathu Thirumeni", addressed respectfully in that manner because he was a learned Brahmin priest. For years T.G. Mathai played with chess pieces he carved out of banana pith on a board he drew with chalk on the floor, until his daughter, returning home from Nigeria on vacation, brought him a neat portable chess set.

Bible and Church

Every day he would read and study the Bible. Whether heading to his daily work or out on a special mission, he never left home for work without reading the Bible and reflecting on what he had read. He attended the Orthodox church service every Sunday and on important holy days, and he observed the season of Lent. In his diary he recorded notes on both his daily readings and on the sermons that he heard. He did Christian missionary and gospel work with Deacon P.I. Mathews, known in later years as V. Rev. Mathews Ramban of Attachakal – a highly regarded monk of the Indian Orthodox Church (1904–1991) with whom he maintained a lifelong friendship.

T.G. Mathai taught regular classes on the Bible and the Orthodox faith, especially for the youth and the ladies' group meetings at the Nariyapuram Orthodox Church. Around 1985 he was invited to give the middle sermon for Good Friday, and as a topic he chose to speak on how Barabbas was spared. This was the last sermon that his younger son would attend in person.

The Conscience of the Village

After attending T.G. Mathai's funeral service, a friend of his older son (M.S. –) gratefully acknowledged that "Your father did a great favor to us soon before he left. He gave us a road to our house that our father had pursued for a long time." The facts behind this acknowledgement are that there was no approach road to their house to allow a vehicle to get through, as their house was behind the lot of a neighbour with no road on any side. Years of negotiations with the neighbour were unproductive, even though the family was willing to pay. T.G. Mathai persuaded the neighbour to provide for a road to the house through the neighbour's own property. He accomplished this with a few friendly words and a gentle reminder that, given the advanced age of his neighbour, he should not be in the way if there were an emergency that required a vehicle to have access.

Captain M.M. Raju (Rtd.) from Nariyapuram, now in his early 80s, recently recalled, "He used to come to our house from his Vallonnil house, which was quite far by the standards of the time. We called him Vallonnil Mathai-chan. In his knowledge and outlook, he was so far ahead of the townsfolk that I thought he might as well have been coming from Europe or America."

Diocesan Metropolitan Daniel Mar Philoxinos would seek T.G. Mathai's position on disputes in the church, addressing him as "Mr. Nariyapuram".

Thus It Came to Pass

Since the 1920s, there has been an annual three-day evangelical convention at Makkakunnu, Pathanamthitta, held during Nineveh Lent. From his youth onwards, T.G. Mathai regularly attended this convention. By the 1980s, however, his health would not permit him to attend all of the sessions (or even some of the conventions). In February 1987, as he

T.G.M., oil on canvas by artist Vasan, Kottayam, Kerala, India (1988)

left home determined to attend all three days of the convention, he remarked to his sixth daughter, "Who knows, if I will be able to attend next year …". Prophetically, it was to be the last convention of his lifetime.

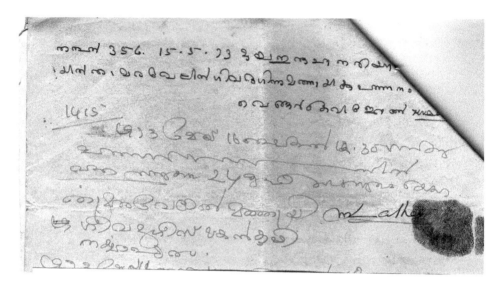

Signature of T.G.M.

Thamaravelil Geevarghese Mathai, the "great father" (*valliacha* or *big appacha*), entered eternity on the third day of the third month of 1987. This rare book museum offered to the world is a tribute to him.

Book of Books

Pearls from the Meandering Stream of Time
that Runs Across Continents

It would be worthy of age to print together the collected Scriptures or Sacred Writings of the several nations, the Chinese, the Hindoos, the Persians, the Hebrews, and others, as the Scripture of mankind. … This would be the Bible, or the Book of Books, which let the missionaries carry to the uttermost parts of the earth.

Henry D. Thoreau, "Monday" in A Week (1849), p. 149

HOLY BIBLE
Dictionary • Study Helps

Presented to

....

By

....

On the occasion of

....

....

....

The cover and title page with inscription of the *Holy Bible, King James Version*,
presented to James Mathew by his daughter

Holy Bible

Shanti Mathew, the daughter of James Mathew, inscribed this volume of the *Holy Bible, King James Version* when she was about eight years old. The publisher was World Bible Publishers.

> And the light shineth in darkness; and the darkness comprehended it not.
>
> John 1:5

This present from Shanti to her father marked the beginning of the Thamaravelil Geevarghese Mathai Rare Book Museum, which he now offers to the world as a tribute to his father.

America's Gift

This section pertains to the poets, philosophers, prophets, reformers and revolutionaries of mid-nineteenth century America – Henry David Thoreau, Ralph Waldo Emerson, Margaret Fuller Ossoli, Harriet Beecher Stowe, Frederick Douglass, Captain John Brown and Abraham Lincoln. Are they not different names for the same?

HENRY DAVID THOREAU

Why should I feel lonely? is not our planet in the Milky Way?

Henry D. Thoreau, "Solitude", in *Walden*

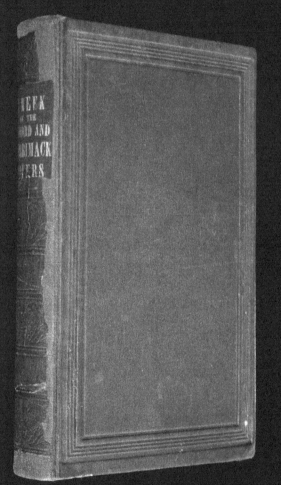

The cover and title page of *A Week* (1849)

1849 – *A Week on the Concord and Merrimack Rivers,* Thoreau's First Book with Corrections in His Own Handwriting

The first edition of Henry David Thoreau's first book, *A Week on the Concord and Merrimack Rivers*, was published by James Munroe and Company, Boston and Cambridge.

Henry D. Thoreau was born in Concord, Massachusetts, on 7 July 1817. In 1839, he and his older brother John built a 15-by-three-and-a-half-foot skiff and sailed on the Concord and Merrimack rivers from their home town to Concord, New Hampshire, and back in two weeks. In January 1842, his brother died in Henry's arms at the age of 27. Thoreau decided to immortalize in words the voyage with his brother. In 1845, he built a 15-by-10-foot house in the woods by himself and lived alone in it by the still waters of Walden Pond for two years. He "folded" the two weeks into a week, and wrote his first book.

> The Mississippi, the Ganges, and the Nile, those journeying atoms from the Rocky Mountains, the Himmaleh, and the Mountains of the Moon, have a kind of personal importance in the annals of the world. … I had often stood on the banks of the Concord, watching the lapse of the current, an emblem of all progress, following the same law with the system, with time, and all that is made; the weeds at the bottom gently bending down the stream, shaken by the watery wind, still planted where their seeds had sunk, erelong to die and go down likewise; the shining pebbles, not yet anxious to better their condition, the chips and weeds, and occasional logs and stems of trees that floated past, fulfilling their fate, were objects of singular interest to me, and at last I resolved to launch myself on its bosom and float whither it would bear me.

He named his first book *A Week on the Concord and Merrimack Rivers* and dedicated it thus:

> Where'er thou sail'st who sailed with me,
> Though now thou climbest loftier mounts,
> And fairer rivers dost ascend,
> Be thou my Muse, my Brother – .

The following letter from its publisher and entry in his journal by the author would have been interesting merely, if they were also not so deeply personal to Thoreau:

From James Munroe and Company
October 25, 1853

We send by express this day a box & bundle containing 250 copies of Concord River, & also 450 in sheets. All of which we trust you will find correct.

The Writings of Henry D. Thoreau: The Correspondence, Vol. 2: 1849–1856,
Robert N. Hudspeth, with Elizabeth Witherell and Lihong Xie (eds)
(Princeton University Press, 2018), p. 177

Three days later, when the pony pulled up at 255 Main Street, she knew no more than Munroe what a precious cargo she had been made to pull.

Thoreau carried the boxes marked "Henry Thoreau's Concord River" up to the attic, and took up his pen while his back was still raw.

The stairs to the attic of
Thoreau's Yellow House
Photo by James Mathew ©

The attic of Thoreau's Yellow House
Photo by James Mathew ©

Oct 28th

Rain in the night & this morning preparing for winter – …

For a year or 2 past – my 'publisher' falsely so called, has been writing from time to time to ask what disposition should be made of the copies of 'A Week on the Concord & Merrimack Rivers' still on hand, and at last suggesting that he had use for the room they occupied in his cellar – So I had them all sent to me here – & they have arrived today by express – filling the man's wagon – 706 copies out of an edition of 1000 – which I bought of Munroe 4 years ago – & have been ever since paying for & have not quite paid for yet – The wares are sent to me at last, and I have an opportunity to examine my purchace – They are something more substantial than fame – as my back knows which has borne them up two flights of Stairs to a place similar to that to which they trace their origin. Of the remaining 290 & odd 75 were given away – the rest sold. I have now a library of nearly 900 volumes over 700 of which I wrote myself – Is it not well that the author should behold the fruits of his labor? My works are piled up on one side of my chamber half as high as my head – my 'opera omnia'

This is authorship – these are the work of my brain. There was just one piece of good luck in the venture – The unbound were tied up by the printer 4 years ago in stout paper wrappers & inscribed H. D. Thoreau's

Concord River

50 cops

So Munroe had only to cross out River & write Mass – and deliver them to the Express man at once.

I can see now what I write for & the result of my labors –

Nevertheless, in spite of this result – sitting beside the inert mass of my works – I take up my pen tonight to record what thought or experience I may have had with as much satisfaction as ever – Indeed I believe that this result is more inspiring & better for me than if a thousand had bought my wares. It affects my privacy less & leaves me freer.

The Writings of Henry D. Thoreau: Journal, Vol. 7: 1853–1854,
N. Simmons and R. Thomas (eds) (Princeton University Press, 2009), pp. 121–3

Thoreau sold the remaining copies of the 1849 edition to Ticknor and Fields, Boston, who bound and issued them in 1862, after the author's death (*Bibliography of American Literature* [BAL] 20104. *Borst* A1.1.a).*

This volume in the T.G.M. Rare Book Museum has two important textual corrections in Thoreau's own hand:

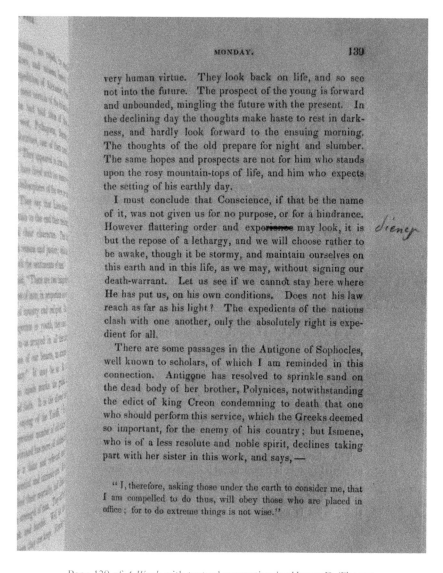

MONDAY.   139

very human virtue. They look back on life, and so see not into the future. The prospect of the young is forward and unbounded, mingling the future with the present. In the declining day the thoughts make haste to rest in darkness, and hardly look forward to the ensuing morning. The thoughts of the old prepare for night and slumber. The same hopes and prospects are not for him who stands upon the rosy mountain-tops of life, and him who expects the setting of his earthly day.

I must conclude that Conscience, if that be the name of it, was not given us for no purpose, or for a hindrance. However flattering order and experience may look, it is but the repose of a lethargy, and we will choose rather to be awake, though it be stormy, and maintain ourselves on this earth and in this life, as we may, without signing our death-warrant. Let us see if we cannot stay here where He has put us, on his own conditions. Does not his law reach as far as his light? The expedients of the nations clash with one another, only the absolutely right is expedient for all.

There are some passages in the Antigone of Sophocles, well known to scholars, of which I am reminded in this connection. Antigone has resolved to sprinkle sand on the dead body of her brother, Polynices, notwithstanding the edict of king Creon condemning to death that one who should perform this service, which the Greeks deemed so important, for the enemy of his country; but Ismene, who is of a less resolute and noble spirit, declines taking part with her sister in this work, and says, —

" I, therefore, asking those under the earth to consider me, that I am compelled to do thus, will obey those who are placed in office; for to do extreme things is not wise."

Page 139 of *A Week* with textual correction by Henry D. Thoreau

---

*   R.R. Borst, *Henry David Thoreau: A Descriptive Bibliography* (Pittsburgh: University of Pittsburgh Press, 1982)

On page 139 in line 12, Thoreau crossed out a portion of the printed word "experience" and added in pencil in the margin "diency" – so that the text may be read as "expediency" instead of "experience". This correction gives the critical impact Thoreau intended:

I must conclude that Conscience, if that be the name of it, was not given us for no purpose, or for a hindrance. However flattering order and ~~experience~~ diency may look, it is but the repose of a lethargy, and we will choose rather to be awake, though it be stormy, and maintain ourselves on this earth and in this life, as we may, without signing our death-warrant. Let us see if we cannot stay here, where He has put us, on his own conditions. Does not his law reach as far as his light? The expedients of the nations clash with one another, only the absolutely right is expedient for all.

than smooth and delicate in their finish. The workers in stone polish only their chimney ornaments, but their pyramids are roughly done. There is a soberness in a rough aspect, as of unhewn granite, which addresses a depth in us, but a polished surface hits only the ball of the eye. The true finish is the work of time and the use to which a thing is put. The elements are still polishing the pyramids. Art may varnish and gild, but it can do no more. A work of genius is rough-hewn from the first, because it anticipates the lapse of time, and has an ingrained polish, which still appears when fragments are broken off, an essential quality of its substance. Its beauty is at the same time its strength, and it breaks with a lustre.

The great poem must have the stamp of greatness as well as its essence. The reader easily goes within the shallowest contemporary poetry; and informs it with all the life and promise of the day, as the pilgrim goes within the temple, and hears the faintest strains of the worshippers; but it will have to speak to posterity, traversing these deserts, through the ruins of its outmost walls, by the grandeur and beauty of its proportions.

But here on the stream of the Concord, where we have all the while been bodily, Nature, who is superior to all styles and ages, is now, with pensive face, composing her poem Autumn, with which no work of man will bear to be compared.

In summer we live out of doors, and have only impulses and feelings, which are all for action, and must wait commonly for the stillness and longer nights of autumn and winter before any Thought will subside. We are sensible that behind the rustling leaves, and the stacks of grain, and the bare clusters of the grape, there is the field of a

Page 396 of *A Week* with textual correction by Henry D. Thoreau

On page 396, Thoreau added the missing 32 words. These three lines, omitted by the publisher, are significant. They talk about how when our senses begin to subside, we may become aware of a whole new field that lies behind the world of outer perception. Indeed, it might be argued that the lines carry the essence of the mystical core of transcendentalism. In the printer's proofs, Thoreau had asked that more space be added before the lines (he used visual space on the page to add emphasis) – which the printer accomplished by dropping three lines. Thoreau was very clear that he was writing for the ages, and he must have added these lines for those lucky enough to see them. Further, his handwriting, as opposed to that in his manuscripts, is very legible (similar to his hand on his surveys). He clearly did not want the reader to have to struggle with the words:

> In summer we live out of doors, and have only impulses and feelings, which are all for action, and must wait commonly for the stillness and longer nights of autumn and *winter before any thought will subside. We are sensible that behind the rustling leaves, and the stacks of grain, and the bare clusters of the grape, there is the field of a* wholly new life, which no man has lived; that even this earth was made for more mysterious and nobler inhabitants than men and women.
>
> [Thoreau's pencil insertion is in italics]

While first editions of *A Week* with corrections are not very rare, it is challenging to find a copy that has the additional lines on page 396 written in Thoreau's own handwriting. A search of institutions and booksellers as of 25 August 2020 yielded 212 copies of the 1849 and 1862 editions, of which 26 are known to have textual corrections on pages 43, 69, 120, 139, 157, 244 or 396. Of these 26 copies with textual corrections, only 10 are known to have the missing lines added on page 396 in Thoreau's handwriting. It is cautioned that perhaps not all copies have been examined for corrections and not all corrections have been authenticated to be in Thoreau's handwriting.

This volume came with a certificate from Gordon T. Banks of Goodspeed's Book Shop, Boston, stating that the addition on page 396 is in Thoreau's handwriting. Since then, it has been examined by more than one Thoreau scholar, and all agreed to its authenticity.

The first edition of *A Week* was usually priced $1.25, as is evident from Thoreau's letter:

Concord Ap. 10th 1861

Friend Pillsbury,

I am sorry to say that I have not a copy of 'Walden' which I can spare, and know of none, unless possibly, Ticknor & Fields have one. I send, nevertheless a copy of 'The Week,' the price of which is $1.25 which you can pay at your convenience.

The Correspondence of Henry David Thoreau,
Walter Harding and Carl Bode (eds)
(New York University Press, 1958), p. 611

On 5 September 2020, the median price for copies of the 1849 edition of *A Week* listed at biblio.com was $11,458.50, the equivalent of $344.95 in 1850.[*] If Thoreau had kept the 704 unsold copies of *A Week* in the attic of his house and retrieved them today, he could have sold them all for $8,066,784. He could buy the house at 255 Main Street, attic and all, for $2,479,000, and have a balance of $5,587,784 in hand.

But today, the world is so much richer because he chose not to *lay up treasures which moth and rust will corrupt and thieves break through and steal*!

---

[*] Ian Webster, Official Inflation Data, Alioth Finance, 5 September 2020, www.officialdata.org/us/inflation/2020?endYear=1850amount=11458.50

Thoreau's Yellow House, Concord, MA
Photo by James Mathew © 2018

WALDEN;

OR,

LIFE IN THE WOODS.

BY HENRY D. THOREAU,

AUTHOR OF "A WEEK ON THE CONCORD AND MERRIMACK RIVERS."

I do not propose to write an ode to dejection, but to brag as lustily as chanticleer in the
morning, standing on his roost, if only to wake my neighbors up. — Page 92.

BOSTON:
TICKNOR AND FIELDS.
M DCCC LIV.

1854 – *Walden,* First Edition of Thoreau's Second Book

The first edition of *Walden* was published by Ticknor and Fields, Boston. The official publication date of *Walden* was 9 August 1854, in a printing of 2,000 copies. The first copy was sold to the Unitarian minister W.R. Alger of Boston at the Old Corner Bookstore on Washington Street, home to Ticknor and Fields, on 1 August for $1.00.

See the entry for *A Week* in the T.G.M. Rare Book Museum.

> Near the end of March, 1845, I borrowed an axe and went down to the woods by Walden Pond, nearest to where I intended to build my house, and began to cut down some tall arrowy white pines, still in their youth, for timber. …
>
> I began to occupy my house on the 4th of July, as soon as it was boarded and roofed, for the boards were carefully feather-edged and lapped, so that it was perfectly impervious to rain; but before boarding I laid the foundation of a chimney at one end, bringing two cartloads of stones up the hill from the pond in my arms. …
>
> *Walden* (Boston: Ticknor and Fields, 1854), pp. 45–9
>
> Thus was my first year's life in the woods completed; and the second year was similar to it. I finally left Walden September 6th, 1847.
>
> *Walden* (Boston: Ticknor and Fields, 1854), p. 341

He "folded" the two years in the forest into a year and produced his second book. And he named it *Walden; Or, Life in the Woods.* On the day *Walden* was published, Thoreau wrote in his journal:

> Wednesday Aug 9th To Boston
>
> Walden Published. Elder berries XXX. Waxwork yellowing X
>
> *The Writings of Henry D. Thoreau: Journal, Vol. 8: 1854,*
> S.A. Petrulionis (ed.) (Princeton University Press, 2002), p. 259

Walden is an American classic, one of only two books of Henry D. Thoreau published during his lifetime. He would live to see the arrangements for the imminent publication of a second print of both *Walden* and *A Week* by Ticknor and Fields.

There is no purer "pond" in America than *Walden* – wade in and reflect, ye reader! Take a dip and be born again!

The cover, title page with ownership signature and page with portrait of
Henry D. Thoreau of *Excursions* (1863)

1863 – E. Rockwood Hoar's copy of Henry D. Thoreau's First Posthumous Book, *Excursions*

Excursions was first published a year after Thoreau's death. It was published by Ticknor and Fields, Boston. *Excursions* was the third of Thoreau's books and the first to be published posthumously, following *A Week on the Concord and Merrimack Rivers* in 1849 and *Walden* in 1854. The editors, his sister Sophia and Ralph Waldo Emerson, selected nine essays for the volume: "A Natural History of Massachusetts", "A Walk to Wachusett", "The Landlord", "A Winter Walk", "The Succession of Forest Trees", "Walking", "Autumnal Tints", "Wild Apples" and "Night and Moonlight".

Thematically, the essays blend Thoreau's passion for the natural world as discovered in his daily sojourns with his sense of history and place. The introductory essay is Ralph Waldo Emerson's short biography of Thoreau, which was previously published in the *Atlantic Monthly* in 1862 – modified from his eulogy delivered at Thoreau's funeral service on 9 May 1862. The frontispiece reproduces the crayon drawing of Thoreau by Samuel Rowse.

This copy has the ink signature of Ebenezer Rockwood Hoar on the title page: "E. R. Hoar/Oct. 1863", signed the month of publication. Ebenezer Rockwood Hoar was a member of what has been called Concord's "royal family". His father, Squire Samuel Hoar, was a successful lawyer and politician, and Hoar himself was a highly respected judge who later served as attorney general under President Ulysses Grant. He and his siblings were close friends of both the Thoreau and Emerson families. His sister, Elizabeth, was to marry Charles Chauncy Emerson, the brother of Ralph Waldo Emerson. The latter died unexpectedly in 1836. At that point, Elizabeth practically became a member of the Emerson family and was close to Thoreau as well. Judge Hoar's brother, Edward Hoar, was a frequent walking companion of Thoreau, accompanying him on longer trips to Mount Washington in New Hampshire and Mount Ktaadn in Maine.[*]

Judge Hoar was an early schoolmate of Thoreau, and they remained close until Thoreau's death. Hoar provided transportation for Thoreau's

---

[*] http://uudb.org/articles/hoarfamily.html

excursions when the latter was too weak to roam about on foot. Judge Hoar was one of the last to see Henry David Thoreau, bringing him a much-appreciated bouquet of hyacinths, just two hours before Thoreau passed away, on the morning of 6 May 1862.

Only 1,588 copies of *Excursions* were printed in the first edition, of which probably 1,500 were bound the first time around (BAL 20111 and *Borst* A3.1.a.) The T.G.M. Rare Book Museum has another copy of the first edition of *Excursions*.

1864 – *The Maine Woods,* First Edition of Thoreau's Fourth Book

Ticknor and Fields, Boston, published this first edition of *The Maine Woods*. According to BAL, the first edition consisted of 1,650 copies (BAL 20113) whereas, according to Borst, there were 1,450 copies (Borst A 4.1.a). Probably only 1,450 of the 1,650 were bound the first time around. The first part of this book, "Ktaadn", was previously published in the *Union Magazine* in 1848. The second part, "Chesuncook", was published in the *Atlantic Monthly* in 1858. The last part, "The Allegash and East Branch", was published for the first time in this book. (See 1858 – *Atlantic Monthly*, Vol. II, p. 68, for more on "Chesuncook".)

THE

MAINE WOODS.

BY

HENRY D. THOREAU,

AUTHOR OF "A WEEK ON THE CONCORD AND MERRIMACK RIVERS,"
"WALDEN," "EXCURSIONS," ETC., ETC.

BOSTON:
TICKNOR AND FIELDS.
1864.

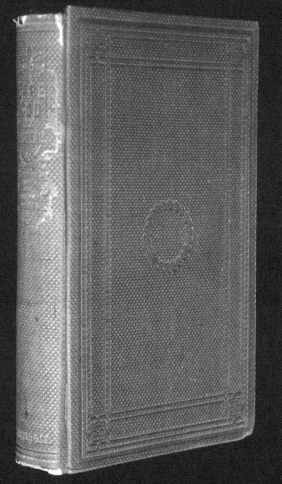

CAPE COD.

BY

HENRY D. THOREAU,

AUTHOR OF "A WEEK ON THE CONCORD AND MERRIMACK RIVERS,"
"WALDEN," "EXCURSIONS," "THE MAINE WOODS,"
ETC., ETC.

Principium erit mirari omnia, etiam tritissima,
Medium est calamo committere visa et utilia,
Finis erit naturam adcuratius adlineare, quam alius [si possumus].
Linnæus de Peregrinatione.

BOSTON:
TICKNOR AND FIELDS.
1865.

The cover and title page of *Cape Cod* (1865)

1865 – *Cape Cod,* First Edition of Thoreau's Fifth Book

Ticknor and Fields, Boston, entered the first edition of *Cape Cod* in the Clerk's Office of the District Court of Massachusetts in 1864. It was published in March 1865. According to BAL, 2,040 copies of the book were printed (BAL 20115). However, according to Borst, the first edition consisted of 2,000 copies (Borst A 5.1.a). Probably 2,040 copies were printed but only 2,000 were bound. This copy has a purple-coloured cover with golden-coloured ends. An advertisement page of books published by Messrs. Ticknor and Fields dated December 1864 is given at the end.

Thoreau visited Cape Cod three times between 1849 and 1855. When he visited Cape Cod for the first time in October 1849, it was the scene of a recent shipwreck. Arriving at the sea-shore in the nick of time, he contemplated the themes of sea and land, order and chaos, embrace and severance, life and death. The first chapter of *Cape Cod*, "The Shipwreck", had been previously published in *Putnam's Monthly* in January 1855.

> … but having come so fresh to the sea, I have got but little salted. My readers must expect only so much saltness as the land breeze acquires from blowing over an arm of the sea, or is tasted on the windows and the bark of trees twenty miles inland, after September gales. I have been accustomed to make excursions to the ponds within ten miles of Concord, but latterly I have extended my excursions to the sea-shore.

> I did not see why I might not make a book on Cape Cod, as well as my neighbor on 'Human Culture.' It is but another name for the same thing, and hardly a sandier phase of it.

pp. 1–2

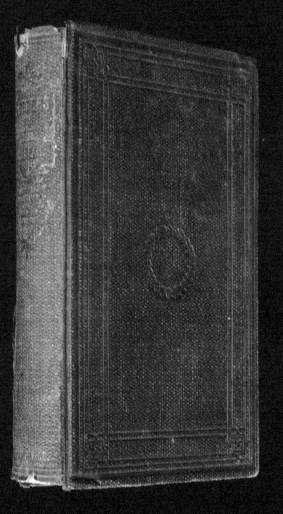

LETTERS

TO VARIOUS PERSONS.

BY

HENRY D. THOREAU,

AUTHOR OF "A WEEK ON THE CONCORD AND MERRIMACK RIVERS,"
"WALDEN," ETC., ETC.

BOSTON:
TICKNOR AND FIELDS.
1865.

The cover and title page of *Letters to Various Persons* (1865)

1865 – *Letters to Various Persons*, First Edition of Thoreau's Sixth Book

This first edition of *Letters to Various Persons* was published by Ticknor and Fields, Boston. It was edited by Ralph Waldo Emerson, who wrote:

> It may interest the reader of this book to know that nearly all these letters have been printed directly from the original autographs furnished by the persons to whom they were addressed. A few have been carefully copied, but without alteration, from the worn and torn originals.

1866 – *A Yankee in Canada*, First Edition of Thoreau's Seventh Book, Inscribed by Sophia Thoreau to Theophilus Brown

This is the first edition of *A Yankee in Canada with Anti-Slavery and Reform Papers*, which was published by Ticknor and Fields, Boston. The book was edited by Sophia Thoreau (Henry's younger sister) and William Ellery Channing. This book includes Thoreau's famous essays "Civil Disobedience" and "A Plea for Captain John Brown". 1,546 copies were printed and bound in three lots (BAL 20117; Borst A7.1.a). The chapter "Prayers" in this book was compiled by R.W. Emerson, and had previously been published in *The Dial* in 1842. "Prayers" contains a prayer written by Henry D. Thoreau.[*]

> Great God, I ask for no meaner pelf
> Than that I may not disappoint myself,
> That in my action I may soar as high,
> As I can now discern with this clear eye.
>
> And next in value, which thy kindness lends,
> That I may greatly disappoint my friends,
> Howe'er they think or hope that it may be,
> They may not dream how thou'st distinguished me.
>
> That my weak hand may equal my firm faith,
> And my life practise what my tongue saith;
> That my low conduct may not show,

---

[*] https://www.walden.org/our-collections/great-god-i-ask-for-no-meaner-pelf

A

YANKEE IN CANADA,

WITH

ANTI-SLAVERY AND REFORM
PAPERS.

BY

HENRY D. THOREAU,

AUTHOR OF "A WEEK ON THE CONCORD AND MERRIMACK RIVERS,"
"WALDEN," "CAPE COD," ETC., ETC.

BOSTON:
TICKNOR AND FIELDS.
1866.

The cover, the title page and Sophia Thoreau's
inscription page of *A Yankee in Canada* (1866)

Nor my relenting lines,

That I thy purpose did not know,

Or overrated thy designs.

The Dial, Vol. 3, No. 1 (1842), pp. 79–80

The essay that would become famous under the title "Civil Disobedience" was first delivered as a speech at the Concord Lyceum in 1849. Later in the same year, it was published in the literary magazine *Æsthetic Papers* under the title "Resistance to Civil Government" and in this book for the first time under the title "Civil Disobedience". (See 1849 – *Æsthetic Papers*, p. 58.)

Sophia Elizabeth Thoreau (1819–1876) inscribed this copy as follows:

Theo Brown

with kind regards

of S. E. Thoreau.

Theophilus Brown (1811–1879) of Worcester, MA, was a mutual friend of Henry D. Thoreau and H.G.O. Blake. In 1856, Henry D. Thoreau stayed with Theo Brown and his wife Sarah for four nights. It was during this stay that Brown arranged for the daguerreotype of Henry D. Thoreau to be taken by Benjamin Maxham.

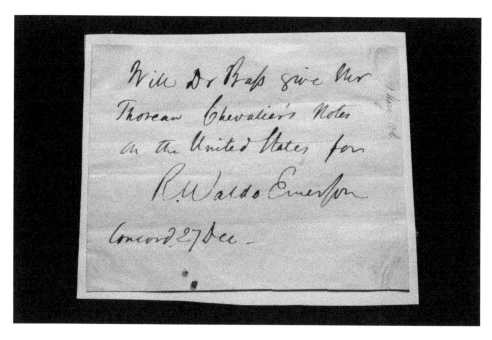

R.W. Emerson requests the librarian at the Boston Athenaeum to give Henry D. Thoreau a book for Emerson (1839–1847)

1839–1847 – Henry D. Thoreau Borrows a Book for R.W. Emerson

Will Dr. Bass give Mr
Thoreau Chevalier's Notes
on the United States for
R. Waldo Emerson

Concord. 27 Dec.

The note refers to Michel Chevalier's *Society, Manners and Politics in the United States*. The English translation of this book, in which Chevalier writes on the country in a series of letters, with a focus on the American economy, political system, infrastructure and various cultural aspects, was published in Boston in 1839. Dr. Seth Bass was the second librarian of the Boston Athenaeum, and he worked there from 1826 to 1847. This fact suggests that the note was written sometime between 1839 and 1847. It is likely that Emerson's friend and neighbour, Henry D. Thoreau, would have been interested in Chevalier's work as well, as his own work discusses many of the same subjects.

1842–1848 – Manuscript Fragment from Thoreau's Journal

This fragment of a leaf from Thoreau's journal is identified as belonging to W. Stephen Thomas (*The Writings of Henry D. Thoreau: Journal, Vol. 2: 1842–1848*, Princeton University Press, p. 470) and contains sections of the journal printed on pages 80, 82 and 83. (Portions also appear in *A Week*.)

Recto [p. 80]

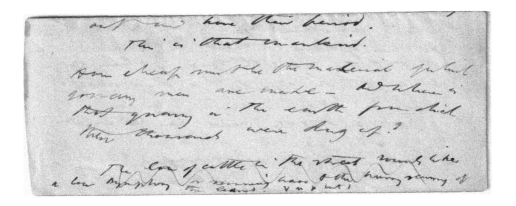

MS fragment from Henry D. Thoreau's journal, recto (1842–1848)

On attending a village fair, Henry D. Thoreau remarked on how he loved to see the "herd of men feeding heartily on coarse succulent pleasures – as cattle feed on the husks and stalks of vegetables."

> … out and have their period.
> This is that mankind.
> How cheap must be the material of which so many men are made – And where is that quarry in the earth from which these thousands were dug up?

> The low of cattle in the street sounds like a low symphony or running base to the hurry scurry of the leaves. V. in p but 1 [Thoreau seems to have crossed out these two lines]

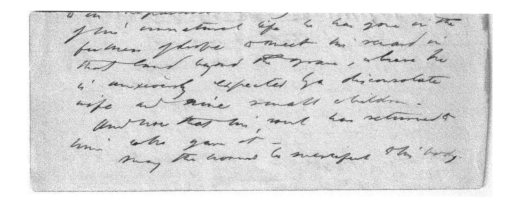

MS fragment from Henry D. Thoreau's journal, verso (1842–1848)

In reference to the death of Captain Jonathan Foster, Thoreau writes:

> Here rose the spirit of Capt. Jonathan Foster – the 19th day of May, and the 50th year of our independence. Such was his character on earth that even his nearest friends were reconciled to his departure. Having reached the term [a line of four words is unclear] of his unnatural life he has gone in the fullness of hope to meet his reward in that land beyond the grave, where he is anxiously expected by a disconsolate wife and nine small children.
>
> And now that his soul has returned to him who gave it – May the worms be merciful to his body.

1843 – Henry D. Thoreau's Copy of *The Vegetable Kingdom; Or, Hand-Book of Plants and Fruits*

This volume is Henry D. Thoreau's copy of Loring D. Chapin's *The Vegetable Kingdom; Or, Hand-book of Plants and Fruits.* This first edition was published by Jerome Lott, 156 Fulton Street, New York. This book is filled with lots of interesting information – from the amount of alcohol consumed in various parts of the US, to a map of plant types throughout north and central America and the qualities of hallucinogenic mushrooms around the globe.

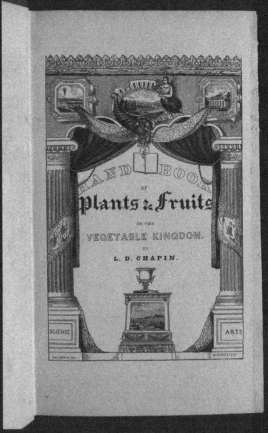

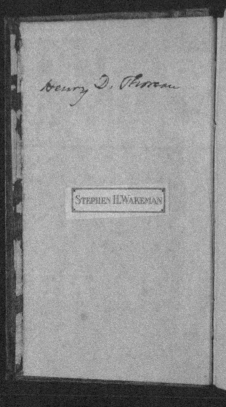

The cover, title page
and ownership
signature of *The
Vegetable Kingdom*
(1843)

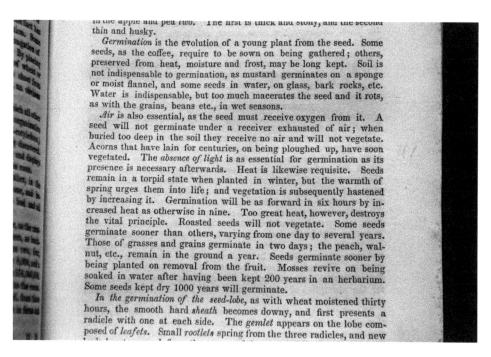

Germination is the evolution of a young plant from the seed. Some seeds, as the coffee, require to be sown on being gathered; others, preserved from heat, moisture and frost, may be long kept. Soil is not indispensable to germination, as mustard germinates on a sponge or moist flannel, and some seeds in water, on glass, bark rocks, etc. Water is indispensable, but too much macerates the seed and it rots, as with the grains, beans etc., in wet seasons.

Air is also essential, as the seed must receive oxygen from it. A seed will not germinate under a receiver exhausted of air; when buried too deep in the soil they receive no air and will not vegetate. Acorns that have lain for centuries, on being ploughed up, have soon vegetated. The *absence of light* is as essential for germination as its presence is necessary afterwards. Heat is likewise requisite. Seeds remain in a torpid state when planted in winter, but the warmth of spring urges them into life; and vegetation is subsequently hastened by increasing it. Germination will be as forward in six hours by increased heat as otherwise in nine. Too great heat, however, destroys the vital principle. Roasted seeds will not vegetate. Some seeds germinate sooner than others, varying from one day to several years. Those of grasses and grains germinate in two days; the peach, walnut, etc., remain in the ground a year. Seeds germinate sooner by being planted on removal from the fruit. Mosses revive on being soaked in water after having been kept 200 years in an herbarium. Some seeds kept dry 1000 years will germinate.

In the germination of the seed-lobe, as with wheat moistened thirty hours, the smooth hard *sheath* becomes downy, and first presents a radicle with one at each side. The *gemlet* appears on the lobe composed of *leafets.* Small *rootlets* spring from the three radicles, and new

Page 55 of Part I in *The Vegetable Kingdom,* with marginal pencil marking by Henry D. Thoreau

In this book, cited as one of the works in "the canon of American gardening",[*] Thoreau marked two passages. On page 55 of Part I, Thoreau marked a passage with three vertical lines in the margin in pencil. He cited this passage in "The Succession of Forest Trees":

> I have frequently found that in November almost every acorn left on the ground had sprouted or decayed. What with frost, drouth, moisture, and worms, the greater part are soon destroyed. Yet it is stated by one botanical writer that 'acorns that have lain for centuries, on being ploughed up, have soon vegetated.'[†]
>
> "An Address on the Succession of Forest Trees" in
> *The Writings of Henry D. Thoreau: Excursions*, Joseph J. Moldenhauer (ed.)
> (Princeton University Press, 2007), p. 179

On page 142 of Part II, Thoreau marked a passage with an "X" in the margin in pencil:

---

[*] http://lichen.csd.sc.edu/vegetable/about.php

[†] https://www.walden.org/work/the-succession-of-forest-trees, p. 200, accessed 3 August 2020

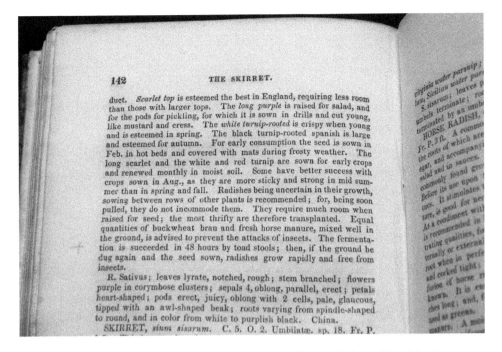

Page 142 of Part II in *The Vegetable Kingdom*, with marginal pencil marking by Henry D. Thoreau

Equal quantities of buckwheat bran and fresh horse manure, mixed well in the ground, is advised to prevent the attacks of insects. The fermentation is succeeded in 48 hours by toad stools; then, if the ground be dug again and the seed sown, radishes grow rapidly and free from insects.

James Mathew did not find that Thoreau cited this passage in any of his writings.

Toward the end of the book is a rather humorous description of the intoxicating qualities of a mushroom in Asia:

One of the largest and most beautiful of the agaric tribe is used in the north of Asia to promote intoxication, having the same effects as ardent spirits. It is the favorite drug, 'moucho-more,' used in Russia to intoxicate. The fungi are gathered in hot weather, and dried for this purpose. It is taken rolled up like a bolus and swallowed without chewing. When eaten fresh in soups it is not so intoxicating. One or two small fungi produce pleasant intoxication for a whole day; and if water be drunk after it, the narcotic effects are increased. The giddiness and drunkenness are like those produced by spirits. At first the recipient is cheerful and very active and talkative, and the effects are often ludicrous; so that in jumping over a stone, the person leaps as if to go over a fence. A talkative person withholds no secret, and others sing continually.

Part II, p. 224

This sounds like "flower power" and the psychedelic mushrooms of the 1960s!

This volume was sold as one of the books from Thoreau's library in the extraordinary auction of Stephen Wakeman's collection in 1924. It was listed as Item #1,062 and sold for $12.

1847 – *Graham's American Magazine* with Thoreau's Critique of Thomas Carlyle

This is an original issue of *Graham's American Magazine* for March 1847, published by George R. Graham & Company, 129 Chestnut Street, Philadelphia. The terms of subscription were as follows: three dollars a year, invariably in advance; five dollars for two copies. The lead article in this issue is "Thomas Carlyle and His Works" by Henry D. Thoreau (Vol. 30, No. 3, pp. 145–52). This essay is one of Thoreau's earliest publications.

This issue of the magazine also contains a review of *Poems* by Ralph Waldo Emerson, published by James Munroe & Company, Boston, under "Review of New Books" (p. 202).

1849 – *Æsthetic Papers*, with "Civil Disobedience" for the First Time in Print

The first issue of this literary magazine edited by Elizabeth Palmer Peabody is immortalized by the appearance in it, for the first time in print, of Henry David Thoreau's speech "Resistance to Civil Government". This essay was number X under "Articles" on page 189! This essay will become, arguably, the single most famous and influential essay of Thoreau, both in the US and around the world. It is more familiar under the title "Civil Disobedience", as it appeared in *A Yankee in Canada* in 1866. This essay would influence such revolutionaries as Leo Tolstoy, Mahatma Gandhi and Martin Luther King, Jr.

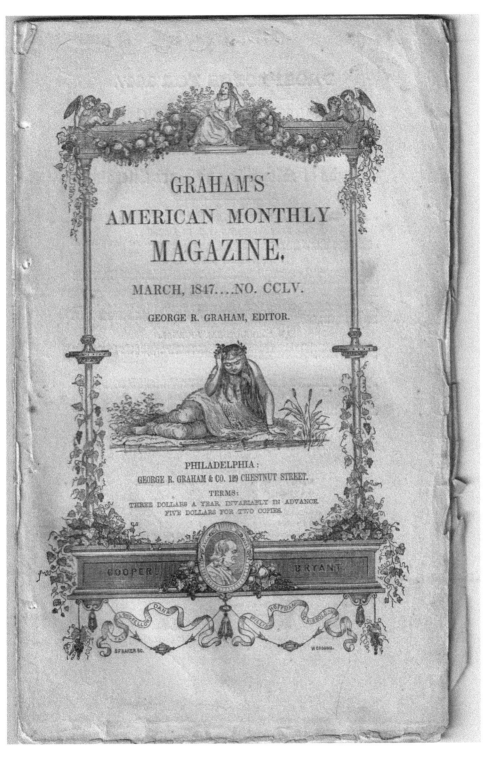

Cover of the March 1847 issue of *Graham's American Magazine*

Æsthetic Papers was intended to succeed *The Dial*, the transcendentalist magazine edited by Margaret Fuller.

> The plan of publication for this Work is like that of 'The British and Foreign Review,' which has been the model of its form, size, and type; namely, that a number should appear whenever a sufficient quantity of valuable matter shall have accumulated to fill 256 pages. This will in no case happen more than three times a year; perhaps not oftener than once a year.

p. iv

Alas, the first born was also the last, for no issues followed as Elizabeth conceived!

Elizabeth Palmer Peabody (1804–1894) was a pioneering educator, editor and activist who, in 1860, opened the first kindergarten in America for English-speaking children. In 1856, Margarethe Schurz had founded a kindergarten in Watertown, WI, for German-speaking children. Elizabeth's sister, Sophia Peabody, was married to Nathaniel Hawthorne and her other sister, Mary Tyler Peabody, was married to Horace Mann.

The *Papers and Proceedings of the 7th General Meeting of the American Library Association* held at Lake George, 8–11 September 1855, recorded this interesting announcement:

> The Treasurer has received for distribution, from Elizabeth P. Peabody, the unsold copies of the 'Æsthetic Papers,' edited by her, in the year 1849, and interesting from containing articles by Emerson, Hawthorne, and *others* in their earliest form. He has sent about sixty copies to libraries and librarians, members of the Association on application. If anyone knows of the remainders of editions of other books, to be had on similar terms, the Treasurer will be glad to attend to their distribution. They prove excellent baits. [Emphasis added]

Note that the treasurer of the American Library Association lumped Thoreau's name with "others"!

ÆSTHETIC PAPERS.

EDITED BY

ELIZABETH P. PEABODY.

> "Beautie is not as fond men misdeeme,
> An outward shew of things that only seeme.
>
> Vouchsafe, then, O Thou most Almightie Spright!
> From whom all gifts of wit and knowledge flow,
> To shed into my breast some sparkling light
> Of thine Eternall Truth, that I may show
> Some little beames to mortall eyes below
> Of that immortall Beautie, there with Thee,
> Which in my weake distraughted mynd I see."
>
> *Spenser.*

BOSTON:
THE EDITOR, 13, WEST STREET.
NEW YORK: G. P. PUTNAM, 155, BROADWAY.
1849.

INTRODUCTION. — The word "Æsthetic."

ART. X. — RESISTANCE TO CIVIL GOVERNMENT.

I HEARTILY accept the motto, — "That government is best which governs least;" and I should like to see it acted up to more rapidly and systematically. Carried out, it finally amounts to this, which also I believe, — "That government is best which governs not at all;" and when men are prepared for it, that will be the kind of government which they will have. Government is at best but an expedient; but most governments are usually, and all governments are sometimes, inexpedient. The objections which have been brought against a standing army, and they are many and weighty, and deserve to prevail, may also at last be brought against a standing government. The standing army is only an arm of the standing government. The government itself, which is only the mode which the people have chosen to execute their will, is equally liable to be abused and perverted before the people can act through it. Witness the present Mexican war, the work of comparatively a few individuals using the standing government as their tool; for, in the outset, the people would not have consented to this measure.

This American government, — what is it but a tradition, though a recent one, endeavoring to transmit itself unimpaired to posterity, but each instant losing some of its integrity? It has not the vitality and force of a single living man; for a single man can bend it to his will. It is a sort of wooden gun to the people themselves; and, if ever they should use it in earnest as a real one against each other, it will *surely* split. But it is not the less necessary for this; for the people must have some complicated machinery or other, and hear its din, to satisfy that idea of government which they have. Governments show thus how successfully men can be imposed on, even impose on themselves, for their own advantage. It is excellent, we must all allow; yet this government never of itself furthered any enterprise, but by the alacrity with which it got out of its way. *It* does not keep the country free. *It* does not settle the West. *It* does not educate. The

A plant specimen (of marsh rosemary) pressed by Henry D. Thoreau, labelled by
Sophia Thoreau and in pencil by Henry D. Thoreau

c. 1850 – Marsh Rosemary Preserved by Henry D. Thoreau

This unique botanical specimen is mounted in typical Thoreau-style and labelled in ink in his sister Sophia's hand, "Marsh rosemary". Underneath Sophia's label, in very faint pencil, Henry D. Thoreau wrote, "Marsh Rosemary". When Kent Bicknell showed the writing to Thoreau scholar Kevin MacDonnell, he confirmed that it was Thoreau's hand beyond doubt.* While the vast majority of Thoreau botanical specimens are at Harvard, this one slipped away in the late nineteenth century when it was given to a Thoreau enthusiast, Mary Fisher, by Ms. Hosmer of Concord who, in turn, received it directly from Sophia Thoreau after Henry's death. Mary Fisher was the author of *A General Survey of American Literature*, published by A.C. McClurg and Company, Chicago, in 1899, of which Chapter XV is devoted to Thoreau.

1848 – *Union Magazine*, Vols 3 and 4, July to December 1848 and January to June 1849

These volumes contain the first publication of Thoreau's essay "Ktaadn, and the Maine Woods" in five parts (pp. 29, 73, 132, 177, 216). This essay will later become part of *The Maine Woods*.

No. I – "The Wilds of the Penobscot"

The first paragraph of Part I begins thus:

> On the 31st of August, 1846, I left Concord in Massachusetts for Bangor and the backwoods of Maine, by way of the railroad and steamboat, intending to accompany a relative of mine engaged in the lumber trade in Bangor, as far as a dam on the west branch of the Penobscot, in which property he was interested. From this place, which is about one hundred miles by the river above Bangor, thirty miles from the Houlton military road, and five miles beyond the last log hut, I proposed to make excursions to Mt. Ktaadn, the second highest mountain in New England, about thirty miles distant, and some of the lakes of the Penobscot, either alone or with such company as I might pick up there.

---

*   Email to Kent Bicknell, 27 February 2016

No. II – "Life in the Wilderness"

The river ran both ways until:

> There were six of us, including the two boatmen. With our packs heaped up near
> the bows, and ourselves disposed as baggage to trim the boat, with instructions
> not to move in case we should strike a rock, more than so many barrels of pork,
> we pushed out into the first rapid, a slight specimen of the stream we had to
> navigate. With Uncle George in the stern, and Tom in the bows, each using a
> spruce pole about twelve feet long, pointed with iron, and poling on the same
> side, we shot up the rapids like a salmon, the water rushing and roaring around,
> so that only a practised eye could distinguish a safe course, or tell what was deep
> water and what rocks, frequently grazing the latter on one or both sides, with a
> hundred as narrow escapes as ever the Argo had in passing through the
> Symplegades. I, who had had some experience in boating, had never experienced
> any half so exhilarating before. … The Indians say, that the river once ran both
> ways, one half up and the other down, but, that since the white man came, it all
> runs down, and now they must laboriously pole their canoes against the stream,
> and carry them over numerous portages.

Part III is missing – pages 97 to 144 of this volume have been axed –
some lumberjacks must have cut them down and sent them down the
river. As if you could cut the trees without hurting the forest!

Interestingly, the T.G.M. Rare Book Museum has loose pages, apparently
lifted for jacks from a different copy of Volume 3 of the *Union Magazine*,
containing "Ktaadn, and the Maine Woods" including Part III (pp. 132–7).
This part, entitled "Boating on the Lakes", begins thus:

> It being about the full of the moon, and a warm and pleasant evening, we
> decided to row five miles by moonlight to the head of the North Twin Lake, lest
> the wind should rise on the morrow.

No. IV – "The Ascent of Ktaadn"

Transfiguration on Mt. Ktaadn:

> But soon my companions were lost to my sight behind the mountain ridge in my
> rear, which still seemed ever retreating before me, and I climbed alone over huge
> rocks, loosely poised, a mile or more, still edging toward the clouds – for though
> the day was clear elsewhere, the summit was concealed by mist, the mountain
> seemed a vast aggregation of loose rocks, as if sometime it had rained rocks, and

they lay as they fell on the mountain sides, nowhere fairly at rest, but leaning on each other, all rocking-stones, with cavities between, but scarcely any soil or smoother shelf. …

At length I entered within the skirts of the cloud which seemed forever drifting over the summit, and yet would never be gone, but was generated out of that pure air as fast as it flowed away; and when, a quarter of a mile further, I reached the summit of the ridge, which those who have seen in clearer weather say is about five miles long, and contains a thousand acres of table-land, I was deep within the hostile ranks of clouds, and all objects were obscured by them. … It was like sitting in a chimney and waiting for the smoke to blow away. It was, in fact, a cloud factory, – these were the cloud-works, and the wind turned them off done from the cool, bare rocks. Occasionally, when the windy columns broke in to me, I caught sight of a dark, damp crag to the right or left; the mist driving cease-lessly between it and me. It reminded me of the creations of the old epic and dramatic poets, of Atlas, Vulcan, the Cyclops, and Prometheus. Such was Caucasus and the rock where Prometheus was bound. Aeschylus had no doubt visited such scenery as this. It was vast, Titanic, and such as man never inhabits. Some part of the beholder, even some vital part, seems to escape through the loose grating of his ribs as he ascends.

Thoreau was alone. How could George and Tom have *looked him in the face*!?

No. V – "The Return Journey"

The last paragraph of Part V ends thus:

Twelve miles in the rear, twelve miles of railroad, are Orono and the Indian Island, the home of the Penobscot tribe, and then commences the batteau and the canoe, and the military road; and, sixty miles above, the country is virtually unmapped and unexplored, and there still waves the virgin forest of the New World.

No. I.   25 Cents.

Putnam's
Monthly

January,
1853.

NEW-YORK:
G. P. PUTNAM & COMPANY,
10 PARK PLACE.
LONDON—Sampson Low, Son & Co.

Entered according to Act of Congress in the year 1853, by G. P. Putnam & Co., in the Clerk's Office of the
District Court for the Southern District of New-York.

Cover of the January 1853 issue of *Putnam's Monthly*

1853 – *Putnam's Monthly*, with Part I of "An Excursion to Canada"

This is a single issue of *Putnam's Monthly* for January 1853 (Vol. I, No. 1), which was published by G.P. Putnam & Company, 10 Park Place, New York. The terms of subscription were: "Price $3 per annum or 25 cents per number. Single subscribers remitting $3 in advance will receive the work free of postage. Clubs of six, post masters and clergymen, will be supplied at $2. The postage will not exceed 7 and 1/2 cents per quarter to any distance in the United States." This issue contains the first of two parts of "An Excursion to Canada".

> I fear that I have not got much to say about Canada, not having seen much; what I got by going to Canada was a cold. I left Concord, Massachusetts, Wednesday morning, Sept. 25th, – , for Quebec. Fare seven dollars there and back; distance from Boston five hundred and ten miles; being obliged to leave Montreal on the return as soon as Friday, Oct. 4th, or within ten days.
>
> … In the midst of the crowded carts, I observed one deep one loaded with sheep with their legs tied together, and their bodies piled one upon another, as if the driver had forgotten that they were sheep and not yet mutton. A sight, I trust, peculiar to Canada, though I fear that it is not.
>
> "Concord to Montreal", pp. 54–9

1853 – *Putnam's Monthly*, with Part II of "An Excursion to Canada"

This is a single issue of *Putnam's Monthly* for February 1853 (Vol. I, No. 2) containing the second part of Thoreau's essay "An Excursion to Canada".

> I repeat these names not merely for want of more substantial facts to record, but because they sounded singularly poetic to my ears. There certainly was no lie in them. They suggested that some simple, and, perhaps, heroic human life might have transpired there. There is all the poetry in the world in a name. It is a poem which the mass of men hear and read. What is poetry in the common sense, but a string of such jingling names? I want nothing better than a good word.
>
> "Quebec and Montmorenci", pp. 179–84

1853 – *Putnam's Monthly*, Vol. I, with Conclusion of "An Excursion to Canada"

This is *Putnam's Monthly*, Volume I. The March issue (No. 21) contains the conclusion of "An Excursion to Canada". (This part did not have a subtitle.)

> In the morning when the mistress had set the eggs a frying, she nodded to a thick-set jolly-looking fellow, who rolled up his sleeves, seized the long-handled griddle, and commenced a series of revolutions and evolutions with it, ever and anon tossing its content into the air, where they turned completely topsy-turvey and came down t'other side up; and this he repeated till they were done. That appeared to be his duty when eggs were concerned. I did not chance to witness this performance, but my companion did, and he pronounced it a master-piece in its way.
>
> pp. 321–9

1858 – *Atlantic Monthly*, Vol. II, with "Chesuncook"

The *Atlantic Monthly* was founded by Moses D. Phillips and Francis H. Underwood in Boston, MA. It was dedicated to literature, art and politics. The first issue was published in November 1857 by Ticknor and Fields, 135 Washington, Corner of School Street, Boston. James R. Lowell was the first editor.

This volume contains the first appearance of Henry David Thoreau's essay "Chesuncook", which was published in three instalments: the first part is in the June issue (No. 8, pp. 1–12); the second part is in the July issue (No. 9, pp. 224–33); and the third part is in the August issue (No.10, pp. 305–17). "Chesuncook" would later become part of *The Maine Woods* (1864).

James Russell Lowell, the editor of the *Atlantic Monthly*, omitted a "sentiment" from Thoreau's manuscript of "Chesuncook" without the latter's knowledge. A furious Thoreau wrote him a letter excoriating him for altering the manuscript. This letter is a classic on the rights and responsibilities of an editor.[*]

---

[*] "Of Pine and Man: Reflecting on Henry David Thoreau's Sentiment in 'Chesuncook'", https://hekint.org/2017/03/04/ of-pine-and-man-reflecting-on-henry-david-thoreaus-sentiment-in-chesuncook

To James Russell Lowell   Concord June 22d 1858.

Dear Sir,

When I received the proof of that portion of my story printed in the July number of your magazine, I was surprised to find that the sentence – 'It is as immortal as I am, and perchance will go to as high a heaven, there to tower above me still.' – (which comes directly after the words 'heals my cuts,' page 230, tenth line from the top,) have been crossed out, … However, I have just noticed that that sentence was, in a very mean and cowardly manner, omitted. I hardly need to say that this is a liberty which I will not permit to be taken with my MS. The editor has, in this case, no more right to omit a sentiment than to insert one, or put words into my mouth.

The Correspondence of Henry David Thoreau,
Walter Harding and Carl Bode (eds)
(New York University Press, 1958), p. 515

True to his word, Thoreau would not give anything for publication in the *Atlantic Monthly* until James T. Fields took over as its editor in 1861.

The last paragraph of "Chesuncook" reads:

> The kings of England formerly had their forests 'to hold the king's game,' for sport or food, sometimes destroying villages to create or extend them; and I think that they were impelled by a true instinct. Why should not we, who have renounced the king's authority, have our national preserves, where no villages need be destroyed, in which the bear and panther, and some even of the hunter race, may still exist, and not be 'civilized off the face of the earth,' – our forests, not to hold the king's game merely, but to hold and preserve the king himself also, the lord of creation, – not for idle sport or food, but for inspiration and our own true re-creation? or shall we, like villains, grub them al'up, poaching on our own national domains?

Six years after Thoreau's call to action, but not until two years after his body was laid to rest at Sleepy Hollow, President Abraham Lincoln signed the Yosemite Grant (1864). The Yellowstone National Park would, however, not be established until 1872.

This volume also contains an interesting essay, "Asirvadam the Brahmin", without mentioning authorship (pp. 79–90). This essay was clearly inspired by the uprising, in 1857, of Indian soldiers under the British East India Company, against the company's rule of India. The British suppressed it by force, and dismissed it by calling it the "Sepoy Mutiny". But for the Indians, it was the first battle of the war for India's independence. This essay opens with the provocative question:

> Who put together the machinery of the great Indian revolt, and set it going? Who stirred up the sleeping tiger in the Sepoy's heart, and struck Christendom aghast with the dire devilries of Meerut and Cawnpore?

> Asirvadam the Brahmin!

The *Atlantic*, presently headquartered in Washington, D.C., traces its origin to the *Atlantic Monthly*.

1862 – *Atlantic Monthly*, Vol. IX, with "Walking" by Henry D. Thoreau and "The Battle Hymn of the Republic" by Julia Ward Howe

This volume contains Henry David Thoreau's essay "Walking", in the June issue (pp. 657–74). Thoreau first read this essay at the Concord Lyceum on 23 April 1851.

> I wish to speak a word for Nature, for absolute freedom and wildness, as contrasted with a freedom and culture merely civil, – to regard man as an inhabitant, or a part and parcel of Nature, rather than a member of society. I wish to make an extreme statement, if so I may make an emphatic one, for there are enough champions of civilization: the minister, and the school-committee, and every one of you will take care of that.

> … For every walk is a sort of crusade, preached by some Peter the Hermit in us, to go forth and reconquer this Holy Land from the hands of the Infidels.

> … If you are ready to leave father and mother, and brother and sister, and wife and child and friends, and never see them again, – if you have paid your debts, and made your will, and settled all your affairs, and are a free man, then you are ready for a walk.

It is in "Walking" that Thoreau categorically declared, "In wildness is the preservation of the world".

The February issue of the *Atlantic Monthly* in this volume also contains the first publication of Julia Ward Howe's "The Battle Hymn of the Republic" (p. 145).

THE

ATLANTIC MONTHLY.

A MAGAZINE OF LITERATURE, ART, AND POLITICS.

VOL. IX.—FEBRUARY, 1862.—NO. LII.

BATTLE HYMN OF THE REPUBLIC.

MINE eyes have seen the glory of the coming of the Lord:
He is trampling out the vintage where the grapes of wrath are stored;
He hath loosed the fateful lightning of His terrible swift sword:
    His truth is marching on.

I have seen Him in the watch-fires of a hundred circling camps,
They have builded Him an altar in the evening dews and damps;
I can read His righteous sentence by the dim and flaring lamps:
    His day is marching on.

I have read a fiery gospel writ in burnished rows of steel:
"As ye deal with my contemners, so with you my grace shall deal;
Let the Hero, born of woman, crush the serpent with his heel,
    Since God is marching on."

He has sounded forth the trumpet that shall never call retreat;
He is sifting out the hearts of men before His judgment-seat:
Oh, be swift, my soul, to answer Him! be jubilant, my feet!
    Our God is marching on.

In the beauty of the lilies Christ was born across the sea,
With a glory in his bosom that transfigures you and me:
As he died to make men holy, let us die to make men free,
    While God is marching on.

1863 – *Atlantic Monthly,* Vol. XI

This volume of the *Atlantic Monthly* contains an article "Sojourner Truth, The Libyan Sibyl" by Harriet Beecher Stowe, in the April issue (pp. 473–81). This article must be read in full! But on page 480, the author adds an anecdote, related to her by Wendell Phillips, which may be read as such:

> Describing a meeting in Faneuil Hall, where Frederick Douglass was one of the main speakers, Douglass ended his speech with 'It must come to blood; they must fight for themselves, and redeem themselves, or it would never be done.'

> Sojourner was sitting, tall and dark, on the very front seat, facing the platform; and in the hush of deep feeling, after Douglass sat down, she spoke out in her deep, peculiar voice, heard all over the house, –

> 'Frederick, is God dead?'

> The effect was perfectly electrical, and thrilled through the whole house, changing as by a flash the whole feeling of the audience. Not another word she said or needed to say; it was enough.

The January issue of the *Atlantic Monthly* in this volume contains "A Reply to the Address of the Women of England" by Harriet Beecher Stowe – signed Washington, 27 November 1862 (pp. 120–33). This reply by Stowe was in response to a letter signed by women from Great Britain and Ireland condemning slavery in the United States.

1863 – *Atlantic Monthly,* Vol. XII, with Two Essays by Thoreau

"Life Without Principle" was published in the October issue (pp. 484–95).

> If a man walk in the woods for love of them half of each day, he is in danger of being regarded as a loafer; but if he spends his whole day as a speculator, shearing off those woods and making earth bald before her time, he is esteemed an industrious and enterprising citizen. As if a town had no interest in its forests but to cut them down!
>
> p. 485

> Merely to come into the world the heir of a fortune is not to be born, but to be still-born, rather. To be supported by the charity of friends, or a

government-pension, – provided you continue to breathe, – by whatever fine synonymes you describe these relations, is to go into the almshouse.

p. 487

"Night and Moonlight" was published in the November issue (pp. 579–83).

> Of what significance the light of day, if it is not the reflection of an inward dawn? – to what purpose is the veil of night withdrawn, if the morning reveals nothing to the soul? It is merely garish and glaring.

p. 582

1864 – *Atlantic Monthly,* Vol. XIV, with Two Essays by Thoreau

"The Wellfleet Oysterman" appeared in the October issue (pp. 470–8).

> Nevertheless, we did not hesitate to knock at her door, when a grizzly-looking man appeared, whom we took to be sixty or seventy years old. He asked us, at first, suspiciously, where we were from, and what our business was; to which we returned plain answers.
>
> 'How far is Concord from Boston?' he inquired.
>
> 'Twenty miles by railroad.'
>
> 'Twenty miles by railroad,' he repeated.
>
> 'Did n't you ever hear of Concord of Revolutionary fame?'
>
> 'Did n't I ever hear of Concord? Why, I heard the guns fire at the Battle of Bunker Hill.' (They hear the sound of heavy cannon across the Bay.) 'I am almost ninety: I am eighty-eight year old. I was fourteen year old at the time of Concord Fight, – and where were you then?'
>
> We were obliged to confess that we were not in the fight.
>
> 'Well, walk in, we'll leave it to the women,' said he.
>
> So we walked in, surprised, and sat down, an old woman taking our hats and bundles, and the old man continued, drawing up to the large, old-fashioned fireplace, –
>
> 'I am a poor good-for-nothing crittur, as Isaiah says; I am all broken down this year. I am under petticoat-government here.'

pp. 470–1

This essay would become part of *Cape Code*, published by Ticknor and Fields (1865).

The other essay by Thoreau in this volume is "The Highland Light" in the December issue (pp. 649–59). Volume XIV also contains "Saadi" by R.W. Emerson in the July issue (pp. 33–7).

1856 – Original Land Survey of Tom Wheeler's Wood-Lot by Henry D. Thoreau

Do not hire a man who does your work for money, but him
who does it for love of it. …

The community has no bribe that will tempt a wise man. You may raise money enough to tunnel a mountain, but you cannot raise money enough to hire a man who is minding his 'own business.'

"Life Without Principle"
in *The Writings of Henry D. Thoreau: Reform Papers*,
Wendell Glick (ed.) (Princeton University Press, 1973), p. 159

For many years I was self-appointed inspector of snow storms and rain storms, and did my duty faithfully; surveyor, if not of highways, then of forest paths and all across-lot routes, keeping them open, and ravines bridged and passable at all seasons, where the public heel had testified to their utility.

"Economy" in *The Writings of Henry D. Thoreau: Walden*,
J.L. Shanley (ed.) (Princeton University Press, 1992), p. 18

A natural skill for mensuration, growing out of his mathematical knowledge, and his habit of ascertaining the measures and distances of objects which interested him, the size of trees, the depth and extent of ponds and rivers, the height of mountains, and the air-line distance of his favorite summits, – this, and his intimate knowledge of the territory about Concord, made him drift into the profession of land-surveyor. It had the advantage for him that it led him continually into new and secluded grounds, and helped his studies of Nature. His accuracy and skill in this work were readily appreciated, and he found all the employment he wanted.

R.W. Emerson
Atlantic Monthly, Vol. X, August 1862, pp. 239–49

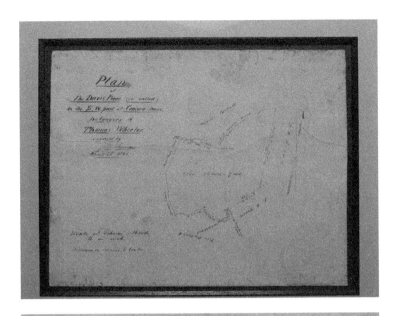

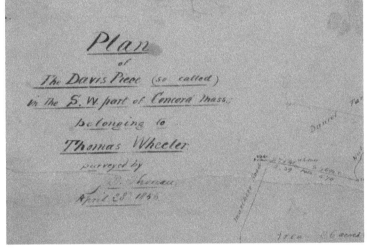

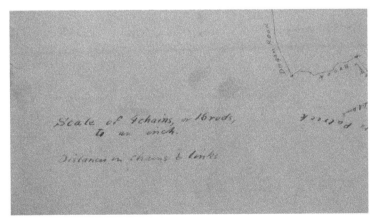

Survey of Thomas Wheeler's wood-lot by Henry D. Thoreau, Thoreau's
signature on the survey and the scale of survey, 1856

This document was signed in Thoreau's hand and dated 28 April 1856, with the hand-drawn integral survey still present. It states at top left, "Plan of Davis Piece (so called)/in the S. W. part of Concord Mass.,/ belonging to/Thomas Wheeler/surveyed by/H. D. Thoreau/April 28, 1856". The "H" in the signature has been torn away. At lower left, it reads, "Scale of 4 chains, or 16 rods,/to an inch./Distances in chains & links". The survey shows the Davis Piece to be 26 acres and 7 rods. The abutting properties are specified.

Thoreau did about 200 surveys in his lifetime, and most of those that survive are in institutions. The Concord Free Public Library in Concord, MA, has a number of them. A draft copy of this survey of Thomas Wheeler's lot resides in the Concord Free Public Library.

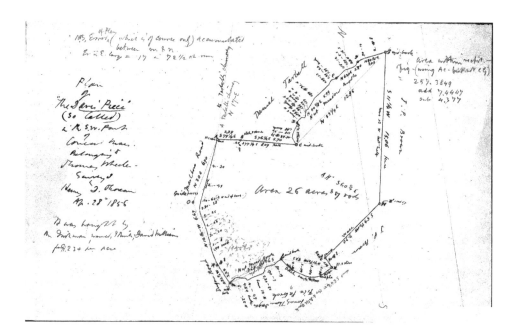

Draft of Henry D. Thoreau's survey of Thomas Wheeler's wood-lot (1856)
Courtesy of Concord Free Public Library

Tommy Wheeler's lot appears prominently in Thoreau's journal, 1851–1861:

28 December 1851

All day a drizzling rain – ever & anon holding up with driving mists – A January thaw – the snow rapidly dissolving, in all hollows a pond forming – unfathomable water beneath the snow. Went into Tommy Wheelers house – where still stands the spinning wheel and even the loom home made. Great pitch pine timbers overhead 15 or 16 inches in diameter – telling of the primitive forest here. The white pines look greener than usual in this gentle rain – and every needle has a drop at the end of it – There is a mist in the air which partially conceals them and they seem of a piece with it. Some one has cut a hole in the ice at Jenny's Brook – and set a steel trap under water, and suspended a large piece of meat over it for a bait for a mink apparently.

The Writings of Henry D. Thoreau: Journal, Vol. 4: 1851–1852,

L.N. Neufeldt and N.C. Simmons (eds)

(Princeton University Press, 1992), pp. 225–6

11 February 1855

P. M. – To J. Dugan's via Tommy Wheeler's.

The atmosphere is very blue, tingeing the distant pine woods.

The dog scared up some partridges out of the soft snow under the apple trees in the Tommy Wheeler orchard.

Smith's thermometer early this morning at – 22°; ours at 8 A. M. – 10°.

11 February 1855. Concord, Mass.

Journal, 7:179

THE THOREAU LOG.

Minott tells me of David Wheeler of the Virginia Road, who used to keep an account of the comings and goings, etc., of animals …

P. M. To Hill by boat …

The Great Meadows now, at 3.30 P. M., agitated by the strong easterly wind this clear day, when I look against the wind with the sun behind me, look particularly dark blue …

5 P. M. – Went to see Tommy Wheeler's bounds.

Warren Miles had caught three more snapping turtles since yesterday, at his mill, one middling-sized one and two smaller. He said they could come down through his mill without hurt …

25 April 1856. Concord, Mass.
Journal, 8:308-11
THE THOREAU LOG.

28 April 1856

Surveying the Tommy Wheeler farm.

Again, as so many times, I [am] reminded of the advantage to the poet, and philosopher, and naturalist, and whomsoever, of pursuing from time to time some other business than his chosen one, – seeing with the side of the eye. The poet will so get visions which no deliberate abandonment can secure. The philosopher is so forced to recognize principles which long study might not detect. And the naturalist even will stumble upon some new and unexpected flower or animal …

28 April 1856. Concord, Mass.
Journal, 8:313-6
THE THOREAU LOG.

30 April 1856

Surveying the Tommy Wheeler farm … About 3.30 P. M., when it was quite cloudy as well as raw, and I was measuring along the river just south of the bridge, I was surprised by the great number of swallows …

30 April 1856.
Journal, 8:318-20
THE THOREAU LOG.

1 November 1860

2 P. M. – To Tommy Wheeler wood-lot.

A perfect Indian-summer day, and wonderfully warm. 72+ at 1 P.M. and probably warmer at two.

The butterflies are out again, – probably some new broods. I see the common yellow and two Vanessa Antiopa, and yellow-winged grasshoppers with blackish edges.

A striped snake basks in the sun amid dry leaves. Very much gossamer on the withered grass is shimmering in the fields, and flocks of it are sailing in the air.

Measure some of the stumps on Tommy Wheeler's land, about that now frosty hollow, cut as I judge from sprouts four years ago.

Then Thoreau goes on to give the measurements of the stumps and estimates of their growths.

Journal, 14:203-8
November 1860
THE THOREAU LOG.

6 November [1860]

Sawed off half of an old pitch pine stump at Tommy Wheeler's hollow. I found that, though the surface was entire and apparently sound except one or two small wormholes, and the sap was evidently decaying, yet, within, or just under the surface, it was extensively honeycombed by worms, which did not eat out to the surface. Those rings included in the outmost four or five inches were the most decayed, …

The stumps of trees which were cut in the last century – oaks at least – must be not uncommon in our woods.

Looking from this hill, I think that I see considerably more oak than pine wood.

Edward Hoar's pitch pine and white pine lot on the south side of this hill is evidently a new wood. You see the green moss, the cladonia, and birches (which I think do not spring up within an old wood), and even feel with your feet an old cow-path and see an old apple tree inclosed in the wood. Are not birches interspersed with pines a sign of a new wood?

7 November [1860]

To Cambridge and Boston.

Journal, 14:219-20
November 1860
THE THOREAU LOG.

1860s – A Pencil from J. Thoreau & Co.

A pencil made by J. Thoreau & Co.

Once available for the ardent collector, a complete and stamped pencil made by Thoreau and his father at the family company is harder to find these days. The T.G.M. Rare Book Museum has two other Thoreau pencils which do not have the stamps. The latter came with the provenance, "This is one of a remainder lot of old pencils presented to the Thoreau Society in 1954 by Arthur W. Parke of Concord who purchased them many years ago from Herbert Nealey, late of Concord. Mr. Nealey vouched for them as 'genuine Thoreau pencils' secured by his father when the Thoreau pencil factory on Belknap Street closed." For more behind the pencil, see the New York Public Library blog, "The Ingenious Pencils of Henry David Thoreau", written by Nicholas Parker and published on 29 March 2017.*

1862 – *Atlantic Monthly*, with "Wild Apples"

The *Atlantic Monthly* for November 1862 (Vol. X, No. 61) was priced at 25 cents. This magazine devoted to literature, art and politics, and was published by Ticknor and Fields, 135 Washington, Corner of School Street, Boston.

This issue contains "Wild Apples" by Henry D. Thoreau as the lead article (pp. 513–26). "It is remarkable how closely the history of the

---

*   https://www.nypl.org/blog/2017/03/29/ingenious-pencils-henry-david-thoreau

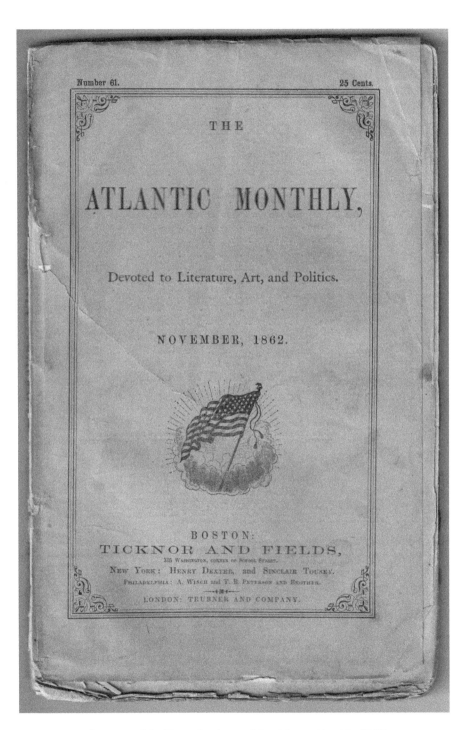

The cover of the November issue of the *Atlantic Monthly* (1862)

Apple-tree is connected with that of man", wrote Thoreau.

This issue also contains "The President's Proclamation" by Ralph Waldo Emerson (pp. 638–42).

proved by its penetrating power. Provide a number of pieces of seasoned white-pine board, one inch thick and say two feet long by sixteen inches wide. These are to be secured parallel to each other and one inch apart by strips nailed firmly to their sides, and must be so placed that when shot at the balls may strike fairly at a right angle to their face. Try a number of shots at the distance of one hundred yards, and note carefully how many boards are penetrated at each shot. The elongated shots are sometimes turned in passing through a board so as to strike the next one sideways, which of course increases the resistance very greatly, and such shots should not be counted; but if you find generally that the penetration of those which strike fairly is not over six inches, you may rest assured the gun cannot be relied on, except in a dead calm, for more than two hundred yards, and with anything of a breeze you will make no good shooting even at that distance. Nine inches of penetration is equal to six hundred yards, and twelve inches is good for a thousand.

A striking proof of the prevailing ignorance of scientific principles in rifle-shooting is afforded by the fact that it is still a very common practice to vary the charge of powder according to the distance to be shot. The fact is, that beyond a certain point any increase of the initial velocity of the ball is unfavorable both to range and precision, owing to the ascertained law that the ratio of increase of atmospheric resistance is four times that of the velocity, so that, after the point is reached at which they balance each other, any additional propulsive power is injurious. The proper charge of powder for any rifle is about one-seventh the weight of the ball, and the only means which should ever be adopted for increasing the range is the elevating sight.

In conclusion, I would impress upon the young rifleman the importance of always keeping his weapon in perfect order. If you have never looked through the barrel of a rifle, you can have no conception what a beautifully finished instrument it is; and when you learn that the accuracy of its shooting may be affected by a variation of the thousandth part of an inch on its interior surface, you may appreciate the necessity of guarding against the intrusion of even a speck of rust. Never suffer your rifle to be laid aside after use till it has been thoroughly cleaned, —the barrel wiped first with a wet rag, (cotton-flannel is best,) then rubbed dry, then well oiled, and then again wiped with a dry rag. In England this work may be left to a servant, but with us the servants are so rare to whom such work can be intrusted that the only safe course is to see to it yourself; and if you have a true sportsman's love for a gun, you will not find the duty a disagreeable one.

THE PRESIDENT'S PROCLAMATION.

In so many arid forms which States incrust themselves with, once in a century, if so often, a poetic act and record occur. These are the jets of thought into affairs, when, roused by danger or inspired by genius, the political leaders of the day break the else insurmountable routine of class and local legislation, and take a step forward in the direction of catholic and universal interests. Every step in the history of political liberty is a sally of the human mind into the untried future, and has the interest of genius, and is fruitful in heroic anecdotes. Liberty is a slow fruit. It comes, like religion, for short periods, and in rare

Page 638 of the November issue of the *Atlantic Monthly* (1862)

In so many arid forms which States incrust themselves with, once in a century, if so often, a poetic act and record occur. … He [Abraham Lincoln] has been permitted to do more for America than any other American man.

On 19 September 1862, the Union troops won a decisive victory against the Confederate forces near Sharpsburg, MD, in the Battle of Antietam. President Lincoln issued the Emancipation Proclamation on 22 September 1862. It was signed into effect on the first day of 1863. Henry D. Thoreau would have loved to live in this moment, but alas, he died on 6 May 1862.

Other articles in this issue of the *Atlantic Monthly* include "Kindergarten – What is It?" by Elizabeth Peabody, the founder of kindergartens for English-speaking children in the United States.

1870s – Cabinet Card of Henry D. Thoreau

The original of this last photograph of Henry D. Thoreau was an ambrotype taken by E.S. Dunshee in New Bedford, MA. According to concordlibrary. org (accessed 19 July 2021), Dunshee took two slightly differing ambrotypes of Thoreau on 21 August 1861. A cabinet card is an albumen print mounted on card stock. Are these two cabinet cards of Henry D. Thoreau the same, or are they slightly different? The T.G.M. Rare Book Museum has the lighter one on the right which, according to some observers, is different from the darker and more familiar one on the left!

Cabinet cards of Henry D. Thoreau (1870s)
The eyes look at the viewer … The eyes gaze into the distance …

c. 1849 – Aunt Maria's Daguerreotype

Daguerreotype of Maria Thoreau, Henry D. Thoreau's paternal aunt (c. 1849)

This is an original daguerreotype of Henry D. Thoreau's paternal aunt, Maria Thoreau (1794–1881).[*] It is possible that it was taken in the spring of 1849 at the same time that Henry arranged for a daguerreotypist to take his sister Helen's picture just before she died. If the portrait was taken in 1849, Aunt Maria would have been 55 years old at that time. Like all the other women of the Thoreau family, she was an ardent antislavery activist and a member of the Concord Ladies' Antislavery Society. It is believed that she was the person who went to the house of Concord tax collector, Sam Staples, on the night of 23 or 24 July 1846, and paid Henry's poll tax to get him released from imprisonment for his refusal to pay. Aunt Maria was the longest-living member of the Thoreau family and the last one to die.

---

[*] *Maine Antique Digest*, 1999

1906 – *The Writings of Henry David Thoreau, Manuscript Edition, Set 174*

The Writings of Henry David Thoreau: Manuscript Edition was published by Houghton, Mifflin and Company, Boston and New York. Six hundred sets were published, each consisting of 20 volumes, numbered and signed by the publisher. Each set has one two-sided leaf of Thoreau's original manuscript enclosed in Volume 1. This Set 174 contains a leaf from the essay "Autumnal Tints".

There is an accompanying transcript of this leaf by Professor Elizabeth Witherell, editor-in-chief of *The Writings of Henry D. Thoreau* (Princeton University Press):

Transcribed by Elizabeth Witherell, March 2019

Roman text is in ink in the manuscript; italic text is in pencil. Notes in square brackets are supplied by the transcriber. Curly brackets indicate that the text is illegible or that a reading is uncertain.

[recto]

        {*61*}   61 covered by paper frame; see "Context", below

forming a considerable part of the

oak wood brought to our market,

and is thus conspicuous & distinct

in the autumn, is not commonly

distinguished from the black & red oaks

        except that it is called the "gray oak" by some woodchoppers.
We have no common name for it,

and when I write this, I do not know

        my   *accurately distinguishes this species*

a person in ~~the~~ town who ~~is acquainted~~   cancelled in pencil
                  is acquainted with it

cancelled in pencil
~~with it~~ beside myself. There are a

black and Scarlet oak standing near

together on our Agricultural Ground, our altered from the   A altered from a

*The Writings of Henry David Thoreau:
Manuscript Edition* (1906), Set 174: the
set, a single volume and Volume 1 with
tipped-in MS leaf and publisher's
signature

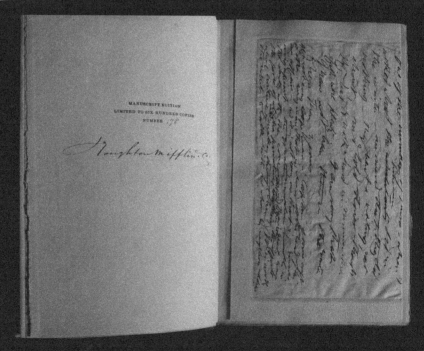

but of the thousands that are annu-

ally gathered there from various parts

of the county, I do not believe that

more than one or 2, can name them.

    The largest scarlet oak that
      hereabouts
I remember ^ stands by the small

pool at the west end of Sleepy Hollo[w]   w covered by paper frame

cemetery.

Bradford   Bradford is the printer's name

    The sap is now, (& even far into   (cancelled with multiple marks

November,) frequently ~~if not commonly,~~) cancelled with multiple marks

flowing fast in these trees, as in

             parently   parently add in another hand,
                           prob. the printer's

{ }Maples in the spring, and ap.^ their   illegible mark in margin
                           M altered from m

bright tints, now that most other

oaks are withered, are connected

with this phenomenon. They are full

of life. It has a pleasantly astringent

acorn-like taste–this strong oak

wine,–as I find on tapping them with   dash cancelled in ink

[verso]

62   my knife.

                this
0   Looking across a wooded valley,

a quarter of a mile wide, how rich

those Scarlet Oaks imbosomed in pines,

their bright red branches intimately

intermingled with them! They have

their full effect there. The Pine

boughs are the green calyx to their

red petals.

              we
Or, as ^I go along a road in the

woods, the sun striking endwise

through it, & lighting up the red

tints of the oaks, which on each

side are mingled with the liquid

green of the Pines,–makes a

very gorgeous scene. Indeed, With-

out the evergreens for contrast the

autumnal tints would lose much

of their effect.

                    a
The Scarlet Oak asks ~~the~~ clear

                late Oct. days
sky and the brightness of ~~the Indian~~

~~summer~~. These bring out its colors.

If the sun goes into a cloud, they

become comparatively indistinct.

    As I sit on a cliff in the S.outh W.est

S written over s O written over o

P written over p

P written over p

Indeed written over pencilled Indeed

S written over s

the Indian summer cancelled in pencil

colors] s added in pencil

our

part of ~~the~~^ town, the sun is now

getting low, and the woods in Lincoln

Context of the manuscript:

This leaf is part of the printer's copy for the essay 'Autumnal Tints,' which was published in the *Atlantic Monthly* for October 1862.

In the 'Table of Alterations' for this essay in Excursions (Princeton University Press, 2007), the editor, Joseph Moldenhauer, documented the alterations in the thirty surviving pages of the printer's copy that he had identified. Page 60 of the printer's copy ends with the sentence that precedes the first sentence following the cancelled material in this MS, which is the thirty-first surviving page of printer's copy. The number in the upper right corner of the recto of this leaf, which is mostly hidden under the paper frame, must be '61'; see Excursions, pp. 618 and 629.

Bradford, whose name appears in the left margin of the recto, next to the first two lines below the cancelled material, was a typesetter. Each typesetter indicated the material he was responsible for setting by writing his name in this way. 'Bradford' appears twice in the printer's copy for 'Walking,' which Thoreau sent to Ticknor and Fields on March 11, 1862, along with corrected proofs for 'Autumnal Tints.' (Excursions, p. 565)

Of the cancelled material, I have found a related passage in the Journal only for the final paragraph, in an entry for October 26, 1858:

The largest scarlet oak that I remember hereabouts stands by the penthorum pool in the Sleepy Hollow cemetery, and is now in its prime. I found the sap was flowing fast in it. White birches, elms, chestnuts, Salix alba (small willows), and white maple are a long time falling. The scarlet oak generally is not in prime till now, or even later. (Journal, 1906, 11: 251)

1906 – *The Writings of Henry David Thoreau: Manuscript Edition*, Set 10, Vol. 1

The T.G.M. Rare Book Museum has Volume 1 of *The Writings of Henry David Thoreau: Manuscript Edition*, Set 10 (See MS Edition, Set 174, p. 85). This volume contains a rare and important MS leaf. The recto of the tipped-in leaf is the first page of a letter dated 13 December 1860, that Henry D. Thoreau received from Horace Greeley about spontaneous generation of trees. This recto and its transcription by Elizabeth Witherell on 3 March 2021 are reproduced below.

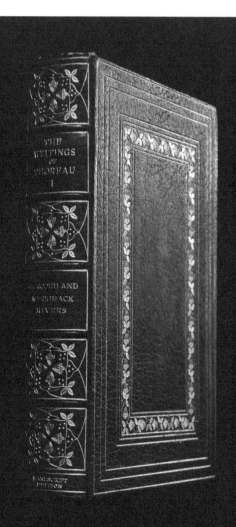

The Writings of Henry David Thoreau: Manuscript Edition (1906), Set 10, Vol. 1

Horace Greeley to Henry David Thoreau – Dec 13, 1860

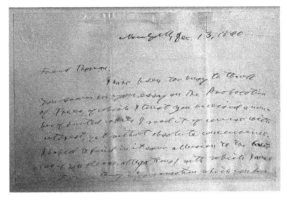

New York, Dec. 13, 1860.

Friend Thoreau:

I have been too busy to thank you sooner for your essay on The Propagation of Trees, of which I trust you received a number of printed copies. I read it of course with interest, yet without absolute concurrence. I hoped to find in it some allusion to the facts (or, if you please, allegations) with which I once combated your theory in a conversation which you have

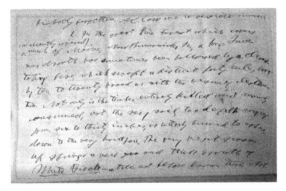

probably forgotten. Allow me to restate them:

1. In the great Pine Forest which covers (or recently covered) much of Maine, New Brunswick, &c., a long Summer drouth has sometimes been followed by a devastating fire, which swept a district forty miles long by ten to twenty broad as with the besom of destruction. Not only is the timber entirely killed and mainly consumed, but the very soil, to a depth varying from six to thirty inches, is utterly burned to ashes, down to the very hard pan. The very next season up springs a new ~~gro~~ and thick growth of <u>White Birch</u>–a tree not before known there. Not

****

The Writings of Henry David Thoreau: Manuscript Edition (1906), Set 10, Vol. 1, tipped-in MS leaf and its transcription by Elizabeth Witherell

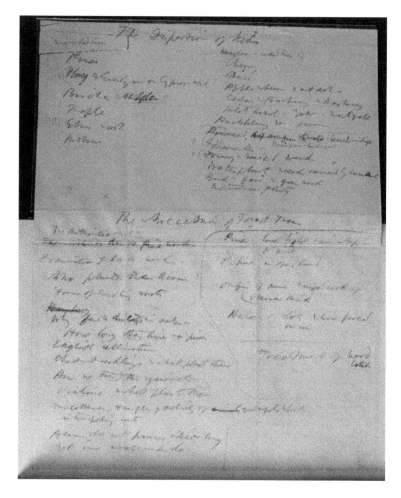

The Writings of Henry David Thoreau: Manuscript Edition (1906), Set 10, Vol. 1, verso of tipped-in MS leaf and its transcription (overleaf) by Elizabeth Witherell

The verso of the tipped-in leaf in this Set 10 of the MS edition is in Henry D. Thoreau's handwriting. He scribbled the topics and drew the outline for a major work on natural history entirely in pencil. This "work-sheet" gives extraordinary insight into how Henry D. Thoreau crafted his essays "Dispersion of Seeds" and "The Succession of Forest Trees". This verso and its transcription with marginal notes and correlation with passages in *Faith in a Seed* (page numbers in red) by Elizabeth Witherell on 3 March 2021 are reproduced here.[*]

---

[*] Henry D. Thoreau, *Faith in a Seed* (Washington, D.C.: Island Press, 1993)

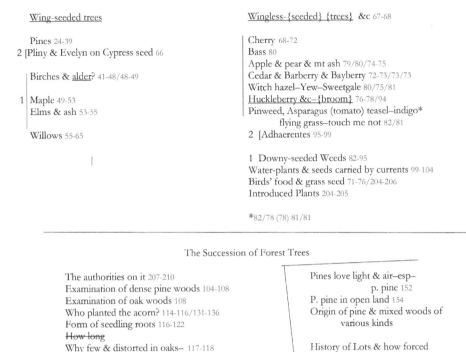
The T.G.M. Rare Book Museum also has MS Edition, Set 155 with a MS leaf containing portions of Thoreau's draft for "The Dispersion of Seeds", Set 198 with a MS leaf containing portions of *Cape Cod*, and Set 321 with a MS leaf containing portions of "Walking".

HENRY THOREAU

AS REMEMBERED BY
A YOUNG FRIEND

EDWARD WALDO EMERSON

BOSTON AND NEW YORK
HOUGHTON MIFFLIN COMPANY
The Riverside Press Cambridge
1917

The cover and title page of *Henry Thoreau as Remembered by a Young Friend* (1917)

1917 – *Henry Thoreau as Remembered by a Young Friend*

This first edition of *Henry Thoreau as Remembered by a Young Friend* by Edward Waldo Emerson (R.W. Emerson's son) was published by Houghton Mifflin Company, Boston, The Riverside Press. This copy is stamped "The Old Corner Book Store Inc. Boston, Mass". This book contains a portrait of Edward Waldo Emerson.

> I can remember Mr. Thoreau as early as I can remember anybody, excepting my parents, my sisters, and my nurse. He had the run of our house, and two occasions was man of the house during my father's absences. He was to us children the best kind of an older brother.
>
> ...
>
> I watched with him one of the last days of his life, when I was about seventeen years old.
>
> Twenty-seven years ago I was moved to write a lecture, now taking the form in this book, because I was troubled at the want of knowledge and understanding, both in Concord and among his readers at large, not only of his character, but of the events of his life, – which he did not tell to everybody, – and by the false impressions given by accredited writers who really knew him hardly at all. Mr. Lowell's essay on Thoreau is by no means worthy of the subject, and has unhappily prejudiced many persons against him.
>
> From the Preface

1931 – *The Transmigration of the Seven Brahmans,* Translation by Henry D. Thoreau

Henry D. Thoreau translated this book from *Harivansa*, which was translated by Alexandre Langlois (1788–1854) into French from the original Sanskrit. *Harivansa* (also written *Harivamsa*) literally means "the lineage of Hari". Thoreau's previously undiscovered manuscript was edited with an introduction and notes by Arthur Christy, and published by William Edwin Rudge, New York, in 1931. The book contains a facsimile of Thoreau's manuscript. The first edition consisted of 1,200 copies, of which 200 were printed on hand-made paper and numbered – this is copy number 154. The introduction in the book mentions that Thoreau borrowed Langlois' *Harivansa* from the Harvard College Library on 11

September 1849. S.A. Langlois' translation, published in Paris in 1834, was entitled *Harivansa; Ou, Histoire de la famille de Hari, ouvrage formant un appendice du Mahabbarata.*

The top line reads: "The world is founded upon the sraddha".[*]

The following excerpts give an idea of Thoreau's familiarity with ancient Indian literature. In September 1854, Thomas Cholmondeley stayed with the Thoreaus in Concord, MA.

> October 3, 1855
>
> My dear Thoreau
>
> I have been busily collecting a nest of Indian books for you, which, accompanied by this note, Mr. Chapman will send you-& you will find them at Boston carriage paid (mind that, & do'nt [*sic*] let them cheat you) at Crosby and Nicholls.
> …
>
> > Adieu dear Thoreau & immense affluence to you
> >
> > > > Ever yours,
> > > > Thos Cholmondeley.

On 9 December 1855, Thoreau wrote to H.G.O. Blake:

> I have arranged them in a case which I made in the meanwhile, partly of river boards. I have not dipped far into the new ones yet – One is splendidly bound & illuminated. They are in English-French Latin-Greek – & Sanscrit. I have not made out the significance of this godsend yet.
>
> > Farewell, & bright dreams to you!
> >
> > > > Henry D. Thoreau

By 25 December, Thoreau wrote to Daniel Ricketson that he got:

> a royal gift in the shape of twenty-one distinct works (one is in nine volumes – forty-four volumes in all) almost exclusively relating to Hindoo literature and scarcely one of them to be bought in America. I am familiar with many of them and know how to prize them. I send you this information as I might of the birth of a child.
>
> *The Writings of Henry D. Thoreau: The Correspondence, Vol. 2: 1849–1856,*
> > Robert N. Hudspeth, Elizabeth Witherell and Lihong Xie (eds)
> > (Princeton University Press, 2018), pp. 355–94

---

[*]   Rites honouring ancestors

The cover, title page and facsimile of page 1 of the MS of *The Transmigration of the Seven Brahmans* (1931)

Thoreau quotes extensively from *Harivansa* in his journal in 1851. On 6 May he wrote:

> The Harivansa describes a substance called 'Poroucha,' a spiritual substance known also under the name of Mahat, spirit united to the five elements, soul of being, now closing itself in a body like ours, now returning to the eternal body; it is mysterious wisdom, the perpetual sacrifice made by the virtue of the 'Yoga,' the fire which animates animals, shines in the sun, and is mingled with all bodies. …
>
> Free in this world, as birds in the air, disengaged from every kind of chain.
>
> Thus the Yogin, absorbed in contemplation, contributes for his part to creation: he breathes a divine perfume, he hears wonderful things. Divine forms traverse him without tearing him, and united to the nature which is proper to him, he goes, he acts, as animating original matter.
>
> *The Writings of Henry David Thoreau: Manuscript Edition: Journal, Vol. 2*
(Boston: Houghton Mifflin, 1906), pp. 190–1

Thoreau was not an ardent reader of fiction, but he had read Kālidāsa's drama:

> The sulphur-like pollen of the pitch-pine soon covered the pond and the stones and rotten wood along the shore, so that you could have collected a barrel-ful. This is the 'sulphur showers' we hear of. Even in Calidas' drama of Sacontala, we read of 'rills dyed yellow with the golden dust of the lotus.'
>
> "Spring" in *Walden*, Ticknor and Fields
(Boston, 1854), pp. 340–1

James Mathew was not able to find the above quote cited by Thoreau in the copy of the English translation of *Śacontalā* translated by William Jones (1790) in the T.G.M. Rare Book Museum. Which translation of *Śacontalā* did Henry read?

1968 – Indira Gandhi's Letter about Henry D. Thoreau

This letter from Indira Gandhi, written on 25 December 1968, contains comments on the influence of Thoreau in India. The Prime Minister writes to Professor John McAleer of Boston College – an Emerson and Thoreau scholar who met Mahatma Gandhi and Jawaharlal Nehru (Indira Gandhi's father) when he was in India during the Second World War – about a book McAleer was compiling on Thoreau.

PRIME MINISTER'S HOUSE
NEW DELHI

No.424-PMH/68   December 25, 1968

Dear Prof. McAleer,

        Thank you for your letter with its moving references to Mahatma Gandhi and to my father. It is good for our people to have friends like you.

        I hope the volume of Thoreau which you are editing will find many readers. Whoever reads Thoreau is struck by the ethical force of his ideas and the clarity of his writing. Thoreau's great influence on Mahatma Gandhi is well-known. His words ring long in the mind. Those who live in the storm of politics need the quiet pool within for sustenance. Thoreau lived by such a pool.

                        Yours sincerely,

                        (Indira Gandhi)

Prof. John J. McAleer,
Department of English,
Carney Faculty Center 435,
Boston College,
Chestnut Hill,
Massachusettes 02167. USA.

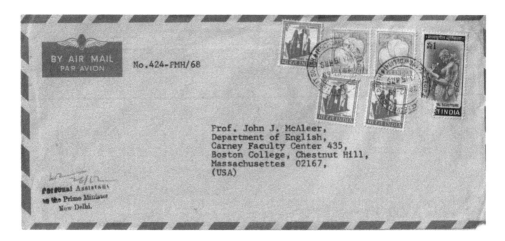

A letter (previous page) from Indira Gandhi, Prime Minister of India, with the envelop and wax
seal (1968)

Thank you for your letter with its moving references to Mahatma Gandhi and to
my father. It is good for our people to have friends like you.

I hope the volume of Thoreau which you are editing will find many readers.
Whoever reads Thoreau is struck by the ethical force of his ideas and the clarity
of his writing. Thoreau's great influence on Mahatma Gandhi is well-known. His
words ring long in the mind. Those who live in the storm of politics need the
quiet pool within for sustenance. Thoreau lived by such a pool.

The latter few sentences of this letter were included in a preface to
McAleer's book, *Artist and Citizen Thoreau* (1971).

2015 – *Life and Legacy of Henry David Thoreau*, DVD

DVD of the dramatic reading performance, *Life and Legacy of Henry David Thoreau* (2015)

This DVD (69 minutes), *Life and Legacy of Henry David Thoreau*, contains the audio-visual recording of a dramatic reading performance that took place on 9 May 2015 in Milwaukee, WI. This performance was written and directed by James Mathew.* A feature broadcast on the live performance can be seen on *Lake Effect*, a news magazine of WUWM, the Milwaukee Affiliate of National Public Radio.† A trailer can be seen on YouTube at Digital Thoreau.‡

---

* Copyright James Mathew, 2015, US Library of Congress Registration Number PAU 3-897-476

† Thoreau's life and legacy comes to life at Cardinal Stritch University, https://www.wuwm.com/podcast/lake-effect-segments, published 8 May 2015, accessed 13 May 2021

‡ Thoreau Society Annual Gathering 2016, Proceedings, http://commons.digitalthoreau.org, accessed 13 May 2021

RALPH WALDO EMERSON

1832 – *The Christian Minister's Affectionate Advice to a New Married Couple,* signed by R.W. Emerson

Ralph Waldo Emerson (1803–1882) signed this copy of Reverend James Bean's *The Christian Minister's Affectionate Advice to a New Married Couple* and presented it to Almira Heard. This early Emerson signature (1832) in a poignant context is symbolic of the trajectory of Emerson's life. Emerson officiated at the recipient's wedding in 1832 – right before he left being a minister and headed to Europe.

What makes this small artifact very compelling is that it represents one of Emerson's last acts as a minister.

Ellen Tucker Emerson (1811–1831), from a painting of 1829
(painter unknown), *The Journals of Ralph Waldo Emerson*
(Boston: Houghton Mifflin, 1909)

The cover and the page with R.W. Emerson's inscription of *The Christian Minister's Affectionate Advice to a New Married Couple* (1832)

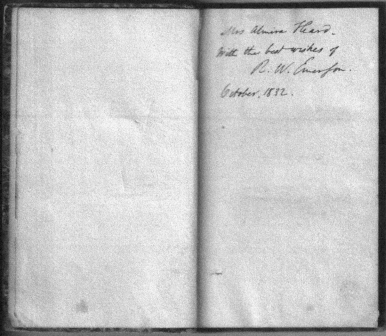

On 8 February 1831, his first wife, Ellen Tucker, died at the age of 20. He had met Ellen on Christmas Day 1827 and married her on 30 September 1829, when she turned 18.

In his journal, dated 29 March 1832, Emerson wrote, "I visited Ellen's tomb & opened the coffin."

While R.W. Emerson was educated as a minister (like his father before him), the more he thought about it, he was not comfortable with some of the tenets of the Church. He struggled with the ceremony of the Eucharist, and eventually asked his parishioners at the Second Church of Boston if he could skip that portion of the service. A committee of church elders debated the issue, but they decided against allowing him to do that. Emerson resigned.

Officiating at the wedding of Elmira Patterson, the daughter of Enoch Patterson, a church elder who had rejected his proposal, Emerson inscribed the book, "Mrs Almira Heard/With the best wishes of/R. W. Emerson/October, 1832."

On 25 December 1832, Emerson sailed off to Europe to recuperate from ill health, as well as from losses both in his private and public life.

On 13 July 1833, Emerson visited the Jardin des Plantes in Paris. The sight of the Linnaean arrangement of the plants at the garden lifted a mist that veiled a mystery, and revealed to him a rhythm and order in nature that he had not ere understood. Emerson got hooked on nature. On 5 November 1833, he lectured to the Boston Natural History Society at the Masonic Temple. "Nature" was published in 1836.

This artifact marks a critical point in the trajectory of Emerson's life, American literature and its psyche.

1840 – R.W. Emerson Solicits Contributions for *The Dial*

This is the letter which Ralph Waldo Emerson sent to Rev. Thomas T. Stone of East Machias, Maine. James Mathew transcribed it:

[To Rev. Thomas T. Stone, East Machais, ME]

Concord, 18 April, 1840.

My dear Sir, Many years have passed since we have seen each other, but it has given me pleasure always to hear of your welfare and advancing influence. Last summer my aunt, Miss Emerson, enclosed to me a letter which you had written to her apparently after seeing my address to the Divinity College at Cambridge. That letter I read with great content. I found nothing in it to contradict, and thought Plotinus could not have made the statement bolder or truer. As the letter in the nature of its contents soared out of all privacy or etiquette, I did not hesitate to show it to George Ripley, to whom I found you were already known, & to my friend Margaret Fuller, a lady who is related to all in it. Miss Fuller has lately written to me to request me to ask that letter of you for the first number of her Journal, which is to be published in July next, under the name of The Dial. And this

[2]

request has an ulterior view which is to introduce a request for your further aid to the same paper. The same appetite for expression that belongs to all circles apprised with new thoughts has driven a number of worthy persons in & around Boston to the project of a new quarterly journal. Mr Ripley proposed to Miss Fuller that if she would conduct it, he would undertake the whole pecuniary management of it and on that condition, she assented. Her own qualification for this trust, is, not only her wit, acquisitions, & various accomplishments, but mainly the force of her character, and the good relation she sustains to a large number of cultivated persons. Besides the aid of Mr Ripley, she has the help of J. S. Dwight, C. P. Cranch, Theodore Parker, A. B. Alcott, W. H. Channing, and others, and a few anonymous correspondents on whose writings I set a high value. Henry D. Thoreau, a youth teaching a school in this town, has given me for her a beautiful poem. I have promised her some contribution for

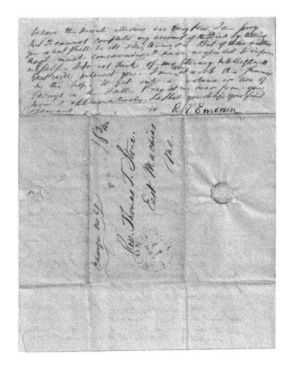

R.W. Emerson's four-page letter to Rev. Thomas T. Stone (1840)

[3]

each number for a year; and am really disposed to borrow & beg heartily for her. The contributions to this first number, & perhaps to a second, will be gratuitous, until it can be seen whether a journal of religion, philosophy & poetry can support itself. If it is not a better journal than any other in this country, I do not wish it to live.

Under these circumstances will you not give us your valuable aid. If you have any passage of autobiography, of philosophy, of faith, any [unclear word] in short, any piece of the heart, (& not of the understanding only, which has organs enough,) will you not send it to me that its light & heat may glow for many, and may indicate on this Dial a brighter Hour. And in the first place, will you not let me extract from this letter ^{above mentioned,} what suits a public purpose, & print it – with initials, or anonymously? If, possibly, you have any copy of it, you may choose to revise it. If not, and you consent so far, I will see to its correct printing & omit whatever is omissible. Mr R has it at this moment, but I

[4]

believe the private allusions are very few. I am sorry that I cannot complete my account of the Dial by telling you what shall be its size, terms & C. But of these matters though much concerning I have neglected to inform myself. I do not think of any literary intelligence that will interest you. I am ^{to be} at work this summer in the hope to get out a volume or two of Essays in the Fall. Pray let me hear from you soon & affirmatively. So shall you oblige your friend & servant,

R.W. Emerson [The original signature is missing]

The inaugural issue of *The Dial*, published in July 1840, carried the poem "Sympathy" by Henry D. Thoreau.

1845 – R.W. Emerson Returns Borrowed Books

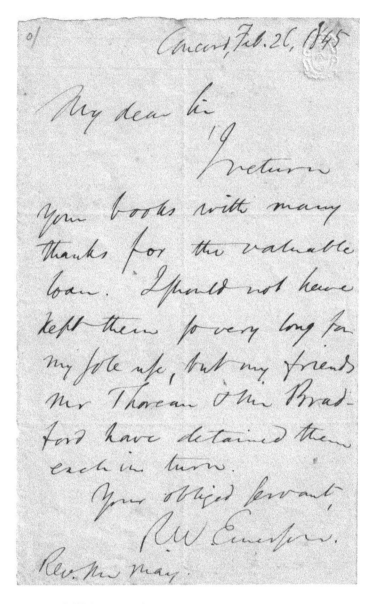

R.W. Emerson's letter to Rev. Samuel J. May (1845)

This is the letter which R.W. Emerson sent to Rev. Samuel Joseph May along with the books he had borrowed from Rev. May. This letter was transcribed by James Mathew:

Concord, Feb. 26, 1845

My dear Sir,

I return your books with many thanks for the valuable loan. I would not have kept them for so very long for my sole use, but my friends, Mr. Thoreau & Mr. Bradford have detained them each in turn.

Your obliged servant,
R.W. Emerson

Rev. Mr. May

It was usual practice to pass books around in R.W. Emerson's circle – the "New England Book Club"!

Rev. Samuel Joseph May (1797–1871) was Louisa May Alcott's maternal uncle. He led several reform movements for freedom and civil rights for minorities.

It is remarkable that in this letter R.W. Emerson justified both right and left margins!

POEMS.

BY

R. W. EMERSON.

BOSTON:
JAMES MUNROE AND COMPANY.
1847.

1847 – *Poems* by R.W. Emerson

This is a first edition of Ralph Waldo Emerson's *Poems*, with the ownership signature of George William Curtis. It is bound in a contemporary full Morocco binding. (See 1843 – *The Confessions of St. Augustine*, p. 160, for more about George W. Curtis.) This book was purchased while George and his brother, J. Burrill Curtis, were at the famous utopian experiment, Brook Farm. This volume has the later ownership signature of Richard Hartshorne.

Poems is Emerson's first volume of poetry and contains some of his best work including "The Sphinx", "Uriel", "Hamatreya", "The Rhodora", "The Humble Bee", "The Snow-Storm", "Wood Notes", "Monadnoc", "Saadi", "From the Persian of Hafiz" and "Threnody".

Poems also contains the "Concord Hymn", the hymn sung at the Concord Monument dedication on 19 April 1836, which opens, "By the rude bridge that arched the flood/Their flag to April's breeze unfurled/Here once the embattled farmers stood/And fired the shot heard round the world."

Emerson wrote "Threnody" at the loss of his first-born, Waldo Emerson (1836–1842). Lines from "Threnody" adorn little Wallie's gravestone: "The hyacinthine boy, for whom/Morn well might break and April bloom, – /The gracious boy, who did adorn/The world whereinto he was born". (The inscription is in capital letters without punctuation.)

George William Curtis was a close friend of a number of nineteenth-century authors, including Nathaniel Hawthorne and Ralph Waldo Emerson. He published a number of books, including *Nile Notes of a Howadji* (1851), *Lotus-Eating* (1852), *Potiphar Papers* (1853) and *Prue and I* (1856). He served as editor of *Harper's Weekly* for a number of years.

1856 – R.W. Emerson's Poem "Brahma", in His Own Handwriting

Emerson's poem, "Brahma", in his handwriting (1856)

This leaf is a fair copy of Ralph Waldo Emerson's seminal poem, "Brahma". Note that Emerson signed the poem. When the poem was published in the November 1857 issue of the *Atlantic Monthly*, it seemed to generate more parodies than praise. The poem has fared well over time and is now regarded as one of Emerson's finest.

Brahma

If the red slayer think he slays,
    Or if the slain think he is slain,
They know not well the subtle ways
    I keep, and pass, and turn again.

Far or forgot to me is near;
    Shadow and sunlight are the same;
The vanished gods to me appear;
    And one to me are shame and fame.

They reckon ill who leave me out;
    When me they fly, I am the wings;
I am the doubter and the doubt,
    And I the hymn the Brahmin sings.

The strong gods pine for my abode,
    And pine in vain the sacred Seven;
But thou, meek lover of the good!
    Find me, and turn thy back on heaven.

The poem echoes the dictums in the *Katha Upaniṣad* and the *Bhagavad Gita*:

Katha Upaniṣad, Section 2

Stanza 1

[Yama said]: Different is the good, and different, indeed, is the pleasant. These two, with different purposes, bind a man. Of these two, it is well for him who takes hold of the good; but he who chooses the pleasant, fails of his aim.

Commentary by the Editor – *The highest good of man is not pleasure but moral goodness.*

Stanza 19

[Yama said]: If the slayer thinks that he slays or if the slain think that he is slain, both of them do not understand. He neither slays nor is he slain.

Commentary by the Editor – *The self is eternal and death does not refer to it.*

The Principal Upaniṣads, S. Radhakrishnan (ed.)
(London: George Allen and Unwin, 1953), pp. 607–17

The *Bhagavad Gita*, Chapter II

Stanza 19

[The blessed Lord spoke]: He who knows it as the slayer, and he who knows it as the slain, they both know not rightly; it kills not, nor is killed.

Stanza 20

[The blessed Lord spoke]: Never is this [Self] born, nor does it die, nor having born does it ever cease to be; unborn, eternal, undecaying, ancient; this is not disintegrated by the disintegration of the body.

The Bhagavad Gîtâ, Mohini Chatterji (trans.)
(Boston: Ticknor and Fields, 1887), pp. 33–8

1857 – Autograph of Ralph Waldo Emerson

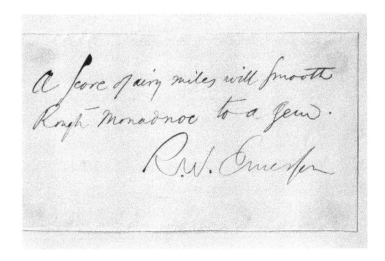

R.W. Emerson's autograph quoting himself (1857)

Emerson quoting himself, writes and signs R.W. Emerson. This holograph is accompanied by a postcard photo of Emerson. The verso of the card reads, "Ralph Waldo Emerson c. 1857/Photograph by Southworth and Hawes. International Museum of Photography/George Eastman House/Fotofolio/Box 661, Canal Sta., NY 10013." The holograph reads:

A score of airy miles will smooth
Rough Monadnoc to a gem.

These lines were from the following poem:

Day by day for her darlings to her much she added more;
In her hundred-gated Thebes every chamber was a door,
A door to something grander, – loftier walls, and vaster floor.

She paints with white and red the moors
To draw the nations out of doors.

A score of airy miles will smooth
Rough Monadnoc to a gem.

"Nature", in *The Complete Writings of Ralph Waldo Emerson: Vol. II*
(New York: Wm. H. Wise & Company, second edition, 1929), p. 928

1867 – Ralph Waldo Emerson's *May-Day*, Inscribed to Edward Rockwood Hoar

This presentation copy of the first edition of Ralph Waldo Emerson's *May-Day and Other Pieces* is inscribed to his long-time friend and neighbour, the judge, E. Rockwood Hoar (1816–1895). As described elsewhere in this book (see 1863 – E. Rockwood Hoar's copy of … *Excursions*, p. 43), Judge Hoar was a member of what has been called Concord's "royal family".

Emerson had approximately 100 of these copies especially bound for presentation, and his journal indicates that he signed at least that many,[*] dating them 1 May 1867, as seen in this copy.

May-Day and Other Pieces is the second book of poetry published by Emerson. According to some scholars, it was his last major volume prior to his decline in the 1870s.

The second poem in the book, "The Adirondacs", is dedicated to "My fellow-travelers in August 1858." E. Rockwood Hoar, James Russell Lowell, Louis Agassiz, Jeffries Wyman, Horatio Woodman and others accompanied Emerson on a journey to camp on the shores of Follensby Pond in the Adirondacks.[†]

That Emerson continued to think very highly of Hoar is captured in several comments recorded in his journals. He lists Hoar amongst a handful of "stout & sincere persons who"

> recommend the country and the planet to us. T's not a bad world this, as long as I know that John Murray Forbes & William Hathaway Forbes & Judge Hoar (& General Grant) & Agassiz, & my three children, & twenty other shining creatures whose faces I see looming through the mist, are walking in it. Is it the thirty millions of America, or is it your ten or twelve units that encourage your heart from day to day?[‡]

On 1 July 1869, Emerson wrote:

---

[*]   *The Journals and Miscellaneous Notebooks of Ralph Waldo Emerson*, Vol. XVI (1982), pp. 56–61

[†]   See James Schlett, *A Not Too Greatly Changed Eden: The Story of the Philosophers' Camp in the Adirondacks* (2015)

[‡]   *The Journals and Miscellaneous Notebooks of Ralph Waldo Emerson*, Vol. XVI (1982), p. 142

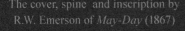

The cover, spine and inscription by
R.W. Emerson of *May-Day* (1867)

Judge Hoar in his speech at the Alumni dinner at Cambridge yesterday, was a perfect example of Coleridge's definition of Genius, 'the carrying of feelings of youth into the powers of manhood'; And the audience were impressed and delighted with the rare combination of the innocence of a boy with the faculty of a hero.[*]

In a list of nineteen persons R.W. Emerson recorded in 1871 under the title "My Men", E.R. Hoar stands beside the names of Henry David Thoreau, A. Bronson Alcott, Thomas Carlyle, Oliver Wendell Holmes, John Muir and others.[†]

May-Day and Other Pieces includes Emerson's enigmatic poem, "Brahma". (See 1856 – R.W. Emerson's Poem "Brahma" on p. 114.)

Included at the end of *May-Day* is a section entitled "Translations" – poems of Michel Angelo Buonarotti, Rumi, Hafiz and others. The last poem in "Translations" is the "Song of Seid Nimetollah of Kuhistan" with an introduction by Emerson:

[Among the religious customs of the dervishes is an astronomical dance, in which the dervish imitates the movements of the heavenly bodies, by spinning on his own axis, whilst at the same time he revolves round the Sheikh in the centre, representing the sun; and, as he spins, he sings the Song of Seid Nimetollah of Kuhistan.]

Spin the ball! I reel, I burn,/Nor head from foot can I discern,
Nor my heart from love of mine,/Nor the wine-cup from the wine.
All my doing, all my leaving,/Reaches not to my perceiving;
Lost in whirling spheres I rove,/And know only that I love.

I am seeker of the stone,/Living gem of Solomon;
From the shore of souls arrived,/In the sea of sense I dived;
But what is land, or what is wave,/To me who only jewels crave?
Love is the air-fed fire intense,/And my heart the frankincense;
As the rich aloes flames, I glow,/Yet the censer cannot know.
I'm all-knowing, yet unknowing;/Stand not, pause not, in my going.

---

[*] *The Journals and Miscellaneous Notebooks of Ralph Waldo Emerson*, Vol. XVI (1982), pp. 154–5

[†] *The Journals and Miscellaneous Notebooks of Ralph Waldo Emerson*, Vol. XVI (1982), p. 188

Ask not me, as Muftis can,/To recite the Alcoran;

Well I love the meaning sweet, – /I tread the book beneath my feet.

Lo! the God's love blazes higher,/Till all difference expire.

What are Moslems? what are Giaours?*/All are Love's, and all are ours.

I embrace the true believers,/But I reck not of deceivers.

Firm to Heaven my bosom clings,/Heedless of inferior things;

Down on earth there, underfoot,/What men chatter know I not.

pp. 203–5

Accompanying this copy of *May-Day* are two early studies of Emerson from the library of E. Rockwood Hoar which are perfect bookends for Hoar's copy of *May-Day*. Both volumes, *Emerson at Home and Abroad* (1882) by Moncure D. Conway, with Judge Hoar's annotation on page 372, and *Ralph Waldo Emerson: His Life, Writings and Philosophy* (1882) by George W. Cooke, are signed on the title page "E. R. Hoar". In the latter, on page 50, Hoar corrected a statement attributed to his writing, suggesting it came from something he said instead.

In *Ebenezer Rockwood Hoar: A Memoir* by Moorfield Storey and Edward W. Emerson (Houghton Mifflin and Company, 1911), a niece offers a humorous account of an exchange between Emerson and her uncle, which is also an illustration of the transcendentalists' penchant for puns:

> A niece of the Judge tells that one winter day, when the sleighing was fast going, he drove down with her to Mr. Emerson's and asked to speak with him at the door. When their talk was ended and the Judge was going, Mr. Emerson remarked on the gayly painted sleigh. "As you said in your poem 'Brahma,' this is a case where 'the red slayer thinks he slays,' replied the Judge."

1878 – Etching of R.W. Emerson, Signed by Emerson and the Engraver, Stephen A. Schoff

This portrait of R.W. Emerson was first captured in a crayon drawing by Samuel Rowse, well-known for his sketches of other luminaries such as Henry David Thoreau. According to the definitive study of Emerson's iconography, *Picturing Emerson: An Iconography* by Joel Myerson and Leslie P. Wilson,[†] this drawing of Emerson, commissioned by Charles

---

*   Giaours are unbelievers.

†   *Harvard Library Bulletin*, Spring/Summer 2016, Vol. 27, Nos. 1–2, pp. 32–6 (also published by Houghton Library of the Harvard College Library 2017 – ISBN 0674975979)

Eliot Norton, was received well, and was the basis for an engraving by Stephen A. Schoff that was reproduced in *The Correspondence of Thomas Carlyle and Ralph Waldo Emerson* by Thomas Carlyle. According to Myerson and Wilson, the engraving by Schoff was later used for the production of a larger image.

Etching of R.W. Emerson by Stephen A. Schoff (1878)

This copy of the etching by Stephen Schoff with original signatures of both Emerson and Schoff was apparently the only one to appear in the market in decades. The signatures are in pencil. This is a truly striking presentation of the serene, wise countenance of Ralph Waldo Emerson.

Signatures of Emerson and Schoff below the etching of Emerson

1842 and 1843 – *The Dial* for April 1842 and January 1843

These are rare single copies of the transcendentalist magazine, *The Dial*, for April 1842 and January 1843. *The Dial* was initially edited by Margaret Fuller, but Emerson took over after the first two years. These two issues included contributions from A. Bronson Alcott, William E. Channing, Christopher P. Cranch, Ralph Waldo Emerson, Margaret Fuller, Theodore Parker, Elizabeth Peabody and Henry D. Thoreau.

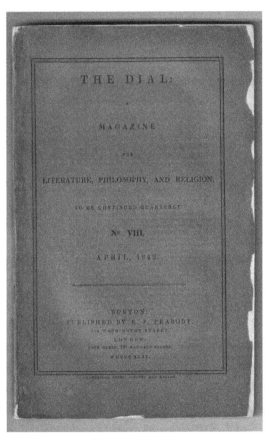

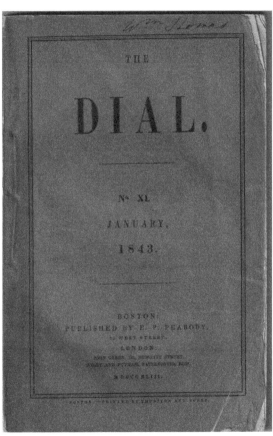

Cover of the April 1842 issue of *The Dial*   Cover of the January 1843 issue of *The Dial*

The January 1843 issue printed the "Laws of Menu", with an introduction by the editors:

THE LAWS OF MENU.

[In pursuance of the design intimated in our Number for July, to give a series of ethnical scriptures, we subjoin our extracts from the Laws of Menu. We learn, from the preface of the translator, that "Vyasa, the son of Parasara, has decided that the Veda, with its Angas, or the six compositions deduced from it, the revealed system of medicine, the Puranas, or sacred histories, and the code of Menu, were four works of supreme authority, which ought never to be shaken by arguments merely human." The last, which is in blank verse, and is one of the oldest compositions extant, has been translated by Sir William Jones. It is believed by the Hindoos "to have been promulged in the beginning of time, by Menu, son or grandson of Brahma," and "first of created beings." Brahma is said to have "taught his laws to Menu in a hundred thousand verses, which Menu explained to the primitive world in the very words of the book now translated." Others affirm that they have undergone successive abridgments for the convenience of mortals, "while the gods of the lower heaven, and the band of celestial musicians, are engaged in studying the primary code."

"A number of glosses or comments on Menu were composed by the Munis, or old philosophers, whose treatises, together with that before us, constitute the Dherma Sastra, in a collective sense, or Body of Law." Culluca Bhatta * was one of the more modern of these.]

CUSTOM.

"Immemorial custom is transcendent law."

"The roots of the law are the whole Veda, the ordinances and moral practices of such as perfectly understand it, the immemorial customs of good men, and self-satisfaction."

"Immemorial custom is a tradition among the four pure classes, in a country frequented by gods, — and at length is not to be distinguished from revelation."

TEMPERANCE.

"The resignation of all pleasures is far better than the attainment of them."

"The organs, being strongly attached to sensual delights, cannot so effectually be restrained by avoiding incentives to pleasure, as by a constant pursuit of divine knowledge."

"But, when one among all his [the Brahmin's] organs fails, by that single failure his knowledge of God passes away, as water flows through one hole in a leathern bottle."

---

* In the following selections his gloss is for the most part omitted, but when retained is printed in Italics.

Page 331 of the January 1843 issue of *The Dial* with the "Laws of Menu"

In pursuance of the design intimated in our Number for July, to give a series of ethnical scriptures, we subjoin our extracts from the Laws of Menu. We learn, from the preface of the translator, that 'Vyasa, the son of Parasara, has decided that the Veda, with its Angas, or the six compositions deduced from it, the revealed system of medicine, the Puranas, or sacred histories, and the code of Menu, were four works of supreme authority, which ought never to be shaken by arguments merely human.' The last, which is in blank verse, and is one of the oldest compositions extant, has been translated by Sir. William Jones. It is believed by the Hindoos 'to have been promulged in the beginning of time, by Menu, son or grandson of Brahma,' and 'first of created beings.' Brahma is said to have 'taught his laws to Menu in a hundred thousand verses, which Menu explained to the primitive world in the very words of the book now translated.'

…

pp. 331–40

The January 1843 issue also contains Henry D. Thoreau's English translation of *Prometheus Bound* with an introduction by the editors:

We present our readers with a new and careful translation of the tragedy of Aeschylus, in which fidelity to the text, and to the best text, is what is mainly attempted. We are the more readily drawn to this task, by the increasing value which this great old allegory is acquiring in universal literature, as a mystical picture of human life, and the most excellent work in that kind that exists in Greek poetry. Coleridge said of this play, that 'it was more properly tragedy itself, in plenitude of the idea, than a particular tragic poem.'

pp. 363–86

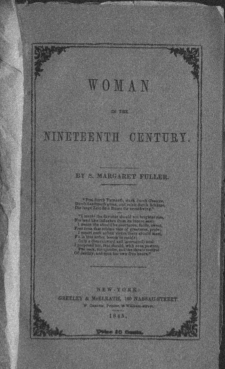

Woman in the Nineteenth Century (1845): brown-paper wrapping with writings on it by
Daniel Ricketson, the cover, signature of Maria Louisa Ricketson and the title page.

1845 – *Woman in the Nineteenth Century* by S. Margaret Fuller, Annotated by Daniel Ricketson

This is a first edition of S. Margaret Fuller's *Woman in the Nineteenth Century*, published by Greeley & McElrath, New York. The first edition included 1,500 copies. This copy has home-made brown-paper wrappers affixed to it, signed on the top-right corner "Danl. Ricketson" and hand-titled:

> Woman/in/The Nineteenth Century/By Margaret Fuller/1845. The author of this work with her/husband and child was/drowned in the spring of 1850/on the shore of Long Island/from the wreck of the brig/Elizabeth on which they came/from Italy.

The decorated front page is signed "Maria Louisa Ricketson/1845". The inside back wrapper has written on it "The Rights of Woman/by Mary Wolstoncraft" (twice) in Ricketson's hand.

Poet and historian Daniel Ricketson (1813–1898) and his wife Maria were Quakers. Ricketson was also a transcendentalist and a close friend of Henry D. Thoreau. (For more on Ricketson and his connection to Emerson and Thoreau, see 1835 – *The Phenix*, p. 153.) Ricketson was secretary of the Anti-Sabbath Convention which included Maria Chapman, Lucretia Mott, Theodore Parker and William Lloyd Garrison. They were for the most part the post-Civil War group that founded the Free Religious Association. Of course, they were the same people who were key figures in the anti-slavery movement and the women's rights movement.

Margaret Fuller edited the transcendental movement's journal, *The Dial*, publishing in its July 1843 issue her essay "Man vs. Men. Woman vs. Women."

THE DIAL.

VOL. IV.   JULY, 1843.   No. I.

THE GREAT LAWSUIT.

MAN *versus* MEN. WOMAN *versus* WOMEN.

THIS great suit has now been carried on through many ages, with various results. The decisions have been numerous, but always followed by appeals to still higher courts. How can it be otherwise, when the law itself is the subject of frequent elucidation, constant revision? Man has, now and then, enjoyed a clear, triumphant hour, when some irresistible conviction warmed and purified the atmosphere of his planet. But, presently, he sought repose after his labors, when the crowd of pigmy adversaries bound him in his sleep. Long years of inglorious imprisonment followed, while his enemies revelled in his spoils, and no counsel could be found to plead his cause, in the absence of that all-promising glance, which had, at times, kindled the poetic soul to revelation of his claims, of his rights.

Yet a foundation for the largest claim is now established. It is known that his inheritance consists in no partial sway, no exclusive possession, such as his adversaries desire. For they, not content that the universe is rich, would, each one for himself, appropriate treasure; but in vain! The many-colored garment, which clothed with honor an elected son, when rent asunder for the many, is a worthless spoil. A band of robbers cannot live princely in the prince's castle; nor would he, like them, be content with less than all, though he would not, like them, seek it as fuel for riotous enjoyment, but as his principality, to administer and guard for the use of all living things therein. He cannot be satisfied with any one gift of the earth, any one department of knowledge, or telescopic peep at the heavens. He feels

VOL. IV. — NO. I.   1

A page from *The Dial* for July 1843 with
"Man vs. Men. Woman vs. Women."

A year and a half later, the essay, considerably expanded, appeared as *Woman in the Nineteenth Century.* The first printing of 1,500 copies sold out. This is a seminal work that shows how strong and enduring the influence of women was in the transcendentalist movement. This important work belongs to both the transcendental and the feminist canons.

1874 – F.B. Sanborn's Set of *The Works of Margaret Fuller Ossoli*

This five-volume set of the writings of the extraordinary pioneering feminist Margaret Fuller Ossoli (1810–1850) was published by Roberts Brothers, Boston. This set was owned and annotated by Franklin B. Sanborn, friend and early biographer of the transcendentalists.

Each volume is signed on the front free endpaper "F. B. Sanborn/ Concord/1874".

Volumes in this set include *Woman in the Nineteenth Century, and Kindred Papers Relating to the Sphere, Condition, and Duties of Woman* (originally published in 1855), *At Home and Abroad; or, Things and Thoughts in America and Europe* (originally published in 1856), *Life Without and Life Within; or, Reviews, Narratives, Essays, and Poems* edited by her brother Arthur B. Fuller (originally published in 1859) and *Memoirs of Margaret Fuller Ossoli* by R.W. Emerson, W.H. Channing and J.F. Clarke in two volumes (originally published in 1859).

At the bottom of page 319 in Volume I of *Memoirs*, Sanborn adds a note to the effect that in 1839 Margaret Fuller was looking for a home in Concord for her mother and herself, and that on 15 February 1839, Emerson wrote to Thoreau asking him to "interest himself" in the search.

On page 275 of Volume II of *Memoirs*, there is a note about the child born to Margaret while in Italy with the man she later married, Count Ossoli. In her journal Margaret records, "Write the name of my child in your Bible, Angelo Ossoli, born September 5, 1848. God grant he may live to see you, and may prove worthy of your love!" Sanborn, having heard the child was born out of wedlock, draws a line from the passage and asks, "Dec 5, 1847 Where was Margaret?" – wondering where she was nine months earlier when Angelo was conceived.

Tragically, Margaret, her husband and their child all drowned in a shipwreck off Fire Island, NY, on 19 July 1850.

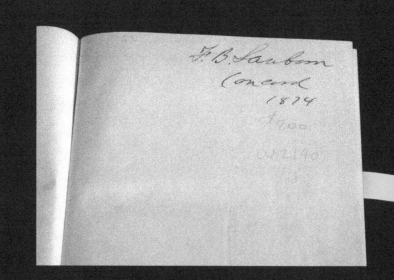

many ills and cares, we have had much joy together, in the sympathy with natural beauty, — with our child, — with all that is innocent and sweet.

I do not know whether he will always love me so well, for I am the elder, and the difference will become, in a few years, more perceptible than now. But life is so uncertain, and it is so necessary to take good things with their limitations, that I have not thought it worth while to calculate too curiously.

However my other friends may feel, I am sure that *you* will love him very much, and that he will love you no less. Could we all live together, on a moderate income, you would find peace with us. Heaven grant, that, on returning, I may gain means to effect this object. He, of course, can do nothing, while we are in the United States, but perhaps I can; and now that my health is better, I shall be able to exert myself, if sure that my child is watched by those who love him, and who are good and pure.

What shall I say of my child! All might seem hyperbole, even to my dearest mother. In him I find satisfaction, for the first time, to the deep wants of my heart. Yet, thinking of those other sweet ones fled, I must look upon him as a treasure only lent. He is a fair child, with blue eyes and light hair; very affectionate, graceful, and sportive. He was baptized, in the Roman Catholic Church, by the name of Angelo Eugene Philip, for his father, grandfather, and my brother. He inherits the title of marquis.

Write the name of my child in your Bible, ANGELO OSSOLI, *born September 5, 1848.* God grant he may live to see you, and may prove worthy of your love!

LIFE WITHOUT

AND

LIFE WITHIN;

OR,

REVIEWS, NARRATIVES, ESSAYS, AND POEMS.

BY

MARGARET FULLER OSSOLI,

AUTHOR OF "WOMAN IN THE NINETEENTH CENTURY," "AT HOME AND ABROAD," "ART, LITERATURE, AND THE DRAMA," ETC.

EDITED BY HER BROTHER,

ARTHUR B. FULLER.

BOSTON:
ROBERTS BROTHERS.
1874.

F.B. Sanborn's five-volume set of *The Works of Margaret Fuller Ossoli*: the set of volumes, a single volume, Sanborn's autograph, the title page of the volume, *Life Without and Life Within*, page 275 in *Memoirs Vol. II* with Sanborn's annotation and a portrait of Margaret Fuller in *Memoirs Vol. I* (1874)

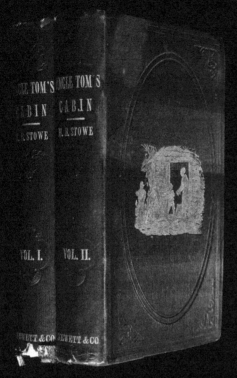

UNCLE TOM'S CABIN;

OR,

LIFE AMONG THE LOWLY.

BY

HARRIET BEECHER STOWE.

VOL. I.

FIFTEENTH THOUSAND.

BOSTON:
JOHN P. JEWETT & COMPANY.
CLEVELAND, OHIO:
JEWETT, PROCTOR & WORTHINGTON.
1852.

The two-volume set, the cover of
Volume 2 and the title page of Volume 1
of *Uncle Tom's Cabin* (1852)

1852 – *Uncle Tom's Cabin* by Harriet Beecher Stowe, Vols 1 and 2, One of the First Fifteen Thousand Sets

This set of two volumes is from the first 15,000 sets of Harriet Beecher Stowe's *Uncle Tom's Cabin.* This book was published by John P. Jewett Company, Boston.

President Abraham Lincoln greeted Harriet Beecher Stowe at the White House with the remark, "Is this the little woman who made the great war?"*

1856 – *My Bondage and My Freedom: Part I – Life as a Slave. Part II – Life as a Freeman* by Frederick Douglass

This first edition of the inspirational *My Bondage and My Freedom: Part I – Life as a Slave. Part II – Life as a Freeman* was signed and inscribed by the great social activist Frederick Douglass on the front free endpaper for Mary L. Depro. The book was published by Miller, Orton and Mulligan, New York and Auburn. While there is no doubt the inscription is in the hand of Douglass, the inscription suggests Depro giving the book back to Douglass in 1878. The reason for this paradox is debatable. Depro was a resident of Washington, D.C., and Douglass lived in D.C. during the last eighteen years of his life from 1877.

---

*   Annie Fields, *Atlantic Monthly*, 78 (August 1896), p. 148

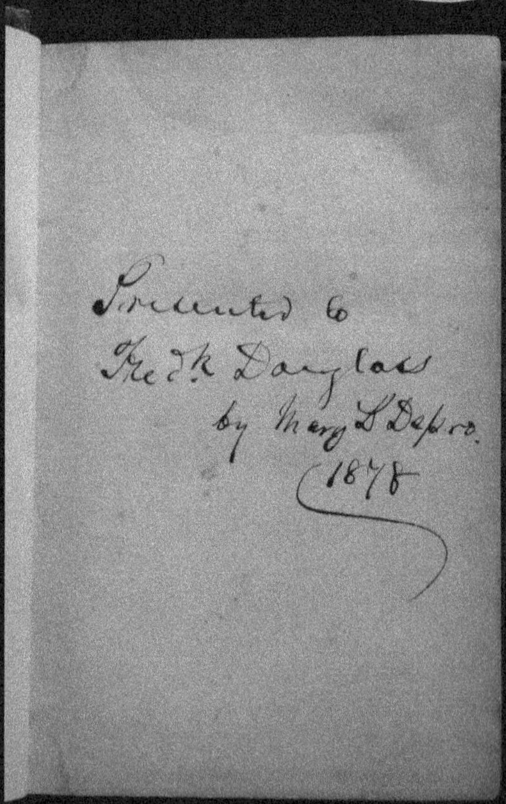

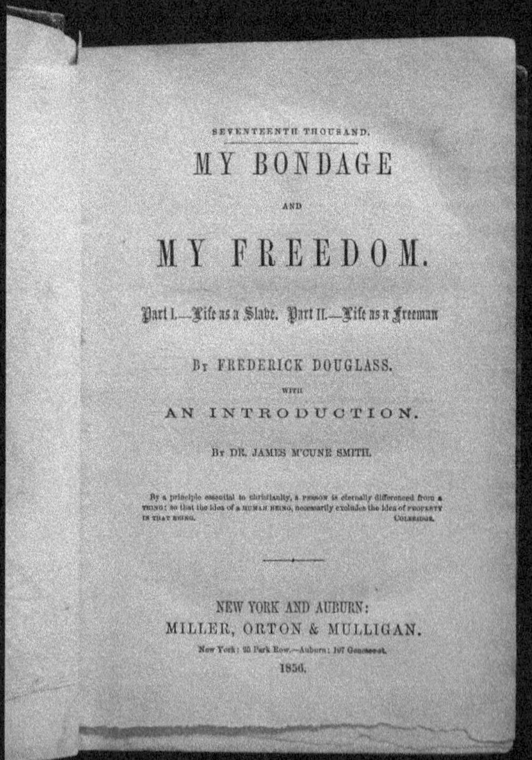

SEVENTEENTH THOUSAND.

MY BONDAGE

AND

MY FREEDOM.

Part I.—Life as a Slave. Part II.—Life as a Freeman

By FREDERICK DOUGLASS.

WITH

AN INTRODUCTION.

By DR. JAMES M'CUNE SMITH.

By a principle essential to christianity, a PERSON is eternally differenced from a
THING; so that the idea of a HUMAN BEING, necessarily excludes the idea of PROPERTY
IN THAT BEING.   COLERIDGE.

NEW YORK AND AUBURN:
MILLER, ORTON & MULLIGAN.
New York: 25 Park Row.—Auburn: 107 Genesee st.
1856.

*Presented to
Fred.k Douglass
by Mary L Depro.
1878*

The cover, the inscription by Frederick Douglass and the title page of
My Bondage and My Freedom (1856)

Frederick Douglass (1817–1895) met President Lincoln for the first time in August 1863:

> When I entered he was seated in a low chair, surrounded by a multitude of books and papers, his feet and legs were extended in front of his chair. On my approach he slowly drew his feet in from the different parts of the room into which they had strayed, and he began to rise, and continued to rise until he looked down upon me, and extended his hand and gave me a welcome. I began with some hesitation, to tell him who I was and what I had been doing, but he soon stopped me, saying in a sharp, cordial voice: 'You need not tell me who you are, Mr. Douglass, I know who you are. Mr. Sewell has told me all about you.' He then invited me to take a seat beside him.

Frederick Douglass went to the White House to greet President Lincoln at the reception following his inaugural address on 4 March 1865. Policemen seized him and prevented his entry. Douglass was eventually able to relay a message through a gentleman who was going in: "Just say to Mr. Lincoln that Fred. Douglass is at the door." In less than one minute, he was invited into the East Room of the White House:

> I could not have been more than ten feet from him when Mr. Lincoln saw me; his countenance lighted up, and he said in a voice which was heard all around: 'Here comes my friend Douglass.' As I approached him he reached out his hand, gave me a cordial shake, and said, 'I saw you in the crowd to-day listening to my inaugural address. There is no man's opinion that I value more than yours: what do you think of it?'

Douglass replied, "Mr. Lincoln, it was a sacred effort."[*]

This last meeting between Abraham Lincoln and Frederick Douglass took place in the East Room of the White House 152 years before its occupant in 2017 remarked, in the present tense, to a group of African American leaders in the same room: "Frederick Douglass is an example of somebody who's done an amazing job and is getting recognized more and more, I notice." (*The Atlantic*, 1 February 2017)

---

[*]   Allen Thorndike Rice, excerpt from "Reminiscences of Abraham Lincoln by distinguished men of his time", Digital Public Library of America, http://dp.la/item/a0019ca333238274892f 912728ba710d

1858 – Albumen Photo of Captain John Brown

This is an albumen print of the portrait of Captain John Brown (1800–1859). The footnote reads: "Original photograph presented to Allan Pinkerton by John Brown 1858." Albumen print was the most common process for making prints of photos, usually from the original daguerreotypes, in the latter half of the nineteenth century.

This print is from the photo taken in May 1858, in New York, by Martin M. Lawrence. An enhanced negative of this photo was attributed to James Wallace Black.[*]

Brown and Pinkerton met in Chicago in 1858, the year before John Brown's attack at Harpers Ferry. Allan Pinkerton was in charge of security for Abraham Lincoln when he journeyed from Springfield, IL, to Washington, D.C., for his first inauguration.

Albumen photo of Captain John Brown (1858)

---

[*]   Jean Libby, *John Brown Photo Chronology: Catalog of the Exhibition at Harper's Ferry 2009* (Allies for Freedom publishers)

1860 – Horatio N. Rust's Copy of *Echoes of Harper's Ferry* by James Redpath

This first edition of *Echoes of Harper's Ferry* by James Redpath was published by Thayer and Eldridge, Boston. It is signed "HN Rust, Springfield, September 1, 1865." The bracketed annotation on page 41 in pencil is presumably by Rust – "A counterfeiting law-factory, standing half in a slave land and half in a free! What kind of laws for free men can you expect from that?"

Horatio N. Rust (1828–1906) was a United States Indian Agent, a collector of Native Indian archaeological artifacts and a horticulturist. He was born in Amherst, MA. He received a gift of a prehistoric stone axe during his childhood. This gift, and a visit to the prisoners of the slave ship *Amistad* with his father, inspired his interest in archaeological artifacts and exposed him to the horror of slavery. In 1857, while working as a druggist in Collinsville, CT, he met Captain John Brown, who was visiting relatives nearby. He became a friend and supporter of Brown and helped him secure a contract for buying 1,000 pikes. Rust later helped salvage the memorial stone of John Brown's grandfather, a soldier in the Revolutionary War. The same stone now bears the names of John Brown, his grandfather, and three of his sons – one killed in Kansas and two at Harpers Ferry. Rust wrote to a friend, "I remember when Capt. Brown was near his execution. He said to our representative who visited him in prison, 'My only anxiety is for my family.' The reply (a proper one) was *we* (meaning those of us who had encouraged and helped him) will take care of the family. I have always felt that the promise rested upon me and I have not forgotten it." John Brown's daughter Ruth related to Rust, "You of all the friends and admirers of John Brown have stood by his children through all circumstances. You have been *true* and *truth* itself."

Horatio Rust moved to Pasadena, CA, in 1881. John Brown's children Ruth, Jason and Owen all moved to the Pasadena area after John Brown's execution. Rust helped establish Pasadena's first public library. He advocated for Indian rights and established an Indian school in Perris, CA. A collection of photographs compiled by him, mostly related to Native Americans and John Brown and his descendants living in the West, is at the Huntington Library, San Marino, CA.[*]

---

[*] Online Archive of California, oac.cdlib.org, accessed 26 April 2020; ch.ucpress.edu, accessed 26 April 2020

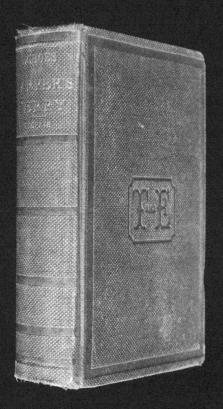

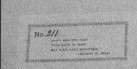

The cover, owner's signature and
the title page of Horatio Rust's
copy of *Echoes of Harper's Ferry*
(1860)

ECHOES

OF

HARPER'S FERRY.

"By the rude Bridge that arched the flood,
  Their flag to April's breeze unfurled;
Here once the embattled farmers stood,
  And fired the shot heard round the World."

R. W. EMERSON.

JAMES REDPATH.

BOSTON:
THAYER AND ELDRIDGE,
114 AND 116 WASHINGTON ST.
1860.

The book contains speeches and essays by Henry David Thoreau, Ralph Waldo Emerson, Victor Hugo, Louisa May Alcott and others upon the trial and execution of Captain John Brown in 1859:

> The murderer always knows that he is justly punished; but when a government takes the life of a man without the consent of his conscience, it is an audacious government, and is taking a step towards its own dissolution. Is it not possible that an individual may be right and a government wrong?
>
> H.D. Thoreau's speech, Concord, MA, 30 October 1859

> Nothing is more absurd than to complain of this sympathy, or to complain of a party of men united in opposition to Slavery. As well complain of gravity, or the ebb of the tide. Who makes the Abolitionist? The Slaveholder.
>
> R.W. Emerson's speech, Salem, MA, 8 January 1860

> For – yes, let America know it, and ponder it well – there is something more terrible than Cain slaying Abel – it is Washington slaying Spartacus.
>
> Victor Hugo's letter, Hauteville House, 2 December 1859

1860 – *The Public Life of Capt. John Brown* by James Redpath

This first edition of *The Public Life of Capt. John Brown* was published by Thayer and Eldridge, Boston.

James Redpath, the author, was a journalist who admired and made acquaintance with Brown shortly before his attack at Harpers Ferry, VA (now WV). Proceeds from Redpath's books about John Brown were to be donated to Brown's family.

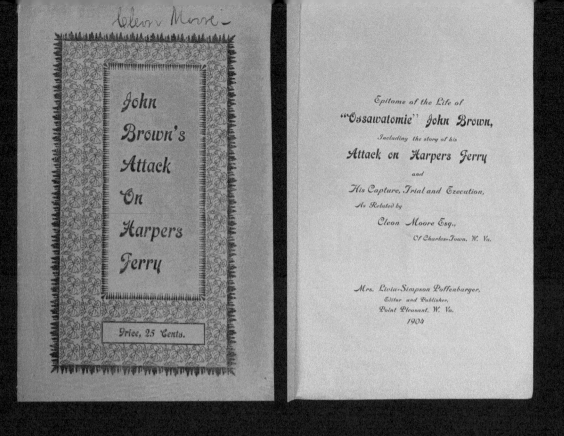

1904 – *John Brown's Attack on Harpers Ferry* by Cleon Moore

This is the first edition of the book, which was edited and published by Mrs. Livia Simpson-Poffenbarger, Point Pleasant, WV. It is signed on the cover "Cleon Moore", suggesting this was the author's personal copy.

This small book may be considered the epitome of the public life of John Brown: the story of his attack on Harpers Ferry, his capture, trial and execution. It was written by Cleon Moore of Charles Town, VA, (now WV) who was an eyewitness to these events.

The stories of the insurrection were as varied as the clouds in the heavens, and we doubt if as impartial a story of the raid was ever published as that which we have had the good fortune to procure from Mr. Cleon Moore, one of the prominent attorneys of Charles-Town, West Virginia.

Mr. Moore's father was the Clerk of the Court in which Brown was tried and received his sentence of execution. Mr. Cleon Moore afterward saw service through out the civil war [*sic*], enlisting in the Confederate army. At the solicitation of his friends some two years ago he wrote the story, but never consented to its publication until we learned of it through Judge Faulkner, of Martinsburg, who went with us to Mr. Moore's office and importuned him to consent to the publication of the article which is now given to the public for the first time.

From the Editor's Introduction

In this book, Cleon Moore states that "There were no negroes near the wagon, at the jail, nor at any time on the way to the place of execution." (p. 15) This statement by Moore is significant because it invalidated a contemporary legend that John Brown, on his way to the gallows, kissed a child held up by a slave woman. This legend had its origin in a report published in the *New York Tribune*, 5 December 1859. This report was later discredited, but it became the basis of a poem, "Brown of Osawatomie", written by John Greenleaf Whittier and published in the *New York Independent*, 22 December 1859. Subsequently, Louis Ransom painted that scene which Currier and Ives, New York, printed and sold.*

The story gained such wide currency at the time that even Henry D. Thoreau was sold on it:

"No theatrical manager could have arranged things so wisely to give effect to his behavior and words," Thoreau wrote. "And who, think you, was the manager? Who placed the slave-woman and her child, whom he stooped to kiss for a symbol, between his prison and the gallows?"

"The Last Days of John Brown",
Prepared for delivery by R.J. Hinton at John Brown's grave
in North Elba, NY, on 4 July 1860

---

* James C. Malin, *Kansas Historical Quarterly*, Vol. 8, No. 4 (1939), pp. 339–41

ABRAHAM LINCOLN

1861 – Abraham Lincoln's First Inauguration Photo

Press photo of Abraham Lincoln's
first inauguration in 1861

Note that Lincoln's image in the photo
is circled. No hat today!

Verso:

Lincoln Abraham Inauguration – I

THE SUN

WIDE WORLD PHOTOS

The earliest date stamped is April 22, 1922
There is a barcode: BJX-886-BS

1862 – Abraham Lincoln Arranges a Meeting Between Treasury Secretary Salmon Chase and Justice David Davis

Autograph note written and signed by President Lincoln at Washington, D.C., requesting Salmon Chase, his Secretary of Treasury, to see his "friend", Justice David Davis.

President Abraham Lincoln's note to Sec. Salmon Chase (1862)

Sec. of Treasury, please
see my friend, Judge
Davis.

    A. Lincoln

Dec. 3, 1862.

When Abraham Lincoln was practising law in Illinois, he argued several cases before the circuit court judge David Davis. They became friends. At the Republican Convention of 1860, Judge Davis led the effort to secure Lincoln the nomination. In February 1861, he accompanied the president-elect to Washington, D.C., and served as his advisor until late 1862.

Supreme Court Justice John A. Campbell from Alabama resigned in protest against Lincoln's intent to go to war with the seceding Southern states. On 17 October 1862, Lincoln filled the seat with David Davis in a recess appointment, as the Congress was not in session. Congress received Davis' formal nomination on 3 December 1862, the day after returning to session. Five days later, David Davis was confirmed on a voice vote.

On the very day Congress received Davis' nomination for Supreme Court Justice, Abraham Lincoln wrote this letter requesting his Secretary of Treasury to see "my friend, Judge Davis." To the best of knowledge, this letter has not been published in any of the papers of Lincoln.

The subject of the meeting may be conjectured. The first of the Prize cases was pending at the Supreme Court. At stake was the U.S. Navy's seizure of Southern ships in 1861 and the sale of their cargo, the proceeds of which went into the Treasury. The meeting might have been about this case. Justice Davis was soon on the slim five-member majority ruling of the Supreme Court upholding the seizure of the ships and blockade of Southern ports ordered by the President without congressional authorization. A loss in the court would have invalidated the grounds of the blockade and other executive actions taken as the Civil War got underway. Alternatively, the meeting might have been about the budget for the Supreme Court.

1863 – Abraham Lincoln Summons Senator Collamer to Strategize for the Thirteenth Amendment

On Thursday 1 January 1863, President Lincoln signed the Emancipation Proclamation into effect. The proclamation had been announced on 22 September 1862.

Senator Jacob Collamer was foremost among the legal scholars in Lincoln's circle. He had been elected to the House of Representatives in 1842, and to the Senate in 1855. He was a prominent Whig leader, the forerunner of the Republican party, and an ardent advocate for the abolition of slavery. He was a lawyer and a former judge of the Circuit Court.

On Sunday 11 January 1863, the President invited the Senator to the White House to strategize for the Thirteenth Amendment to the Constitution of the United States.

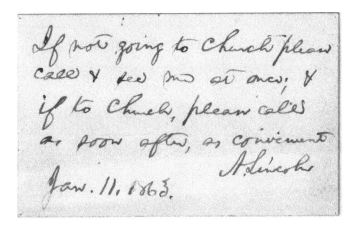

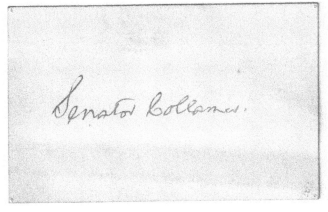

President Abraham Lincoln's note to Sen. Collamer (1863)

This is the autograph note written and signed by President Abraham
Lincoln addressed to Senator Jacob Collamer:

> If not going to church please
> call & see me at once; &
> if to church, please call
> as soon after, as convenient
> > A. Lincoln

Jan. 11, 1863.

Walter Crockett in his *History of Vermont* states that no sooner than he
returned from church, Collamer proceeded to the White House, and did
not emerge for twelve hours. Apparently, there are no records of the

content of their conversation. Lincoln had called upon Collamer's legal expertise and creativity on prior occasions to hatch his tough eggs.

On 14 December 1863, Rep. James Ashley of Ohio introduced a constitutional amendment abolishing slavery. Sen. John Henderson of Missouri – a former slave-owner – introduced a similar measure in the Senate. In April 1864, the 13th Amendment passed in the Senate. But two months later, the measure failed in the House. Following his re-election in November 1864, Lincoln forcefully pursued congressional passage of the Amendment. On 1 January 1865, Congress approved the 13th Amendment to the Constitution. The next day, without waiting to send it along to the states for ratification, Lincoln signed the Amendment, calling it a "King's cure" for the evils of slavery. On 6 December 1865, the 13th Amendment was finally ratified.

By the President of the United States of America

A proclamation

..., shall be then, thenceforward, and forever free; ...

And upon this act, sincerely believed to be an act of justice, warranted by the constitution, upon military necessity, I invoke the considerate judgement of mankind, and the gracious favor of Almighty God.

On Good Friday, 14 April 1865, President Abraham Lincoln was shot.

At 07:22 in the City of Washington, on the fifteenth day of April, in the year of our Lord one thousand eight hundred and sixty-five, and of the Independence of the United States of America the eighty-ninth, Abraham Lincoln gave up his physical form.

Lincoln's Proclamation remains as immortal as Lincoln.

1890 – *Abraham Lincoln: A History* by Nicolay and Hay

This is a first edition of *Abraham Lincoln: A History* by John G. Nicolay and John Hay. This ten-volume set was published by The Century Company, New York. Copyright 1886 and 1890 was by Nicolay and Hay. It had previously been serialized in the *Century Magazine.*

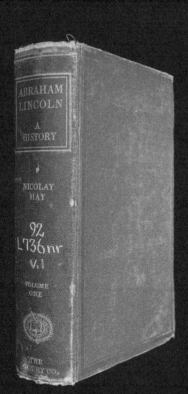

The ten-volume set of *Abraham Lincoln: A History*
(1890) and the cover, title page and portrait of Lincoln
from Volume 1

It is the almost unbroken testimony of his contemporaries that by virtue of certain high traits of character, in certain momentous lines of purpose and achievement, he was incomparably the greatest man of his time.

From the Preface

This work, the most authoritative and complete account of Abraham Lincoln's public life, was written by his personal secretaries. The authors "formed the design of writing this history and began to prepare for it during the war years. President Lincoln gave it his sanction and promised his cordial cooperation."

Gift from the East

This section includes ancient writings, especially Indian and Persian, which influenced the authors who are included in the previous section. The original works in Sanskrit and Persian were translated into European languages beginning in the late eighteenth century, and thus found their way into the hands of the transcendentalists – *The Phenix*, *The Sánkhya Kārikā*, St. Augustine, *Poetry of the East* by William Alger, Sheik Saadi of Shiraz, Omar Khayyām, the *Bhagavad Gita*, the *Upaniṣhads* with commentary by S. Radhakrishnan, Kālidāsa and  *Ancient Ballads and Legends of Hindustan* by Toru Dutt. This section also pertains to the works of visionaries from the West and the East who re-awakened interest in these writings from the late nineteenth to the mid-twentieth centuries – Leo Tolstoy, *The Buddhist Ray*, Annie Besant and Swami Vivekananda.

The entries in this section are not arranged according to the age of their origins. The *Upaniṣhads*, which are a part of the *Vedas*, have their origins in the period 1500–500 BC. The *Gita* has its origins in 500–200 BC. The *Vishnu Purana* is from 300 BC to 1000 AD. Kālidāsa lived in the fourth-fifth century AD. The first English translation of the *Gita* was published by Charles Wilkins in 1785. The first English translation of *Śacontalā* was published by William Jones in 1789.

The cover, the owner's signature, the title page and writings on back endpages by Daniel Ricketson of *The Phenix* (1835)

1835 – *The Phenix*

This is a copy of the first edition of the *Phenix; A collection of Old and Rare Fragments*. It was published by William Gowan, 121 Chatham Street, New York. This copy belonged to Daniel Ricketson, who signed and dated it in several places: 1836 and 22 October 1836. At the back, he has written the name of his home in New Bedford, MA, "Brooklawn" and then three dates: "June 29th, 1864/April 5th, 1866/July 31st, 1871." These may be dates that he read or re-read the book – or that he loaned it. Ricketson has also written a few notes in the rear endpapers such as, "The Sanscrit is the most ancient language of which we have any account. The Pancrit succeeded the Sanscrit as the Spanish and Italian languages succeeded the Latin."

Daniel Ricketson (1813–1896) was a friend of Alcott, Emerson and Thoreau. It was at Ricketson's house that Thoreau, according to A. Bronson Alcott, not only sang, but "danced a jig"! Was it "Tom Bowling" that he sang?

The Phenix was important to the transcendentalists as it was one of the earliest texts available with excerpts of the *Morals of Confucius* and *Oracles of Zoroaster.* Both Emerson and Alcott utilized several of the sayings of Zoroaster, copying them into their respective notebooks.

On page 104, Ricketson has placed an asterisk next to Confucian Moral #34: "Prefer poverty and banishment to the most eminent offices of state, when it is a wicked man that offers them, and would constrain thee to accept them," and written "Hawthorne" at the bottom of the page. This was a reference to the Concord crowd's anger at Nathaniel Hawthorne's life-long support of his old Bowdoin College classmate, Franklin Pierce, who – even as president (1853–1857) – opted for compromise with pro-slavery forces over and over again. Hawthorne's thin campaign biography of Pierce, *Franklin Pierce* (Ticknor and Fields, 1852), was referred to by some as the "best fiction" he ever wrote, as the author glossed over rumours of excessive alcohol consumption and ineptitude. The subsequent appointment by President Pierce of Hawthorne to the potentially lucrative position of American consul in Liverpool is, no doubt, what was on Ricketson's mind when he highlighted this moral of Confucius. Hawthorne had been reluctant to undertake the biography and even shared with another Bowdoin classmate, Horatio Bridge, that, "Though the story is true, yet it took a romancer to do it."

THE

SÁNKHYA KÁRIKÁ,

OR

MEMORIAL VERSES ON THE SÁNKHYA PHILOSOPHY.

BY

ÍSWARA KRISHNA;

TRANSLATED FROM THE SANSCRIT

BY

HENRY THOMAS COLEBROOKE, ESQ.

ALSO

THE BHÁSHYA OR COMMENTARY OF

GAURAPÁDA;

TRANSLATED, AND ILLUSTRATED BY AN ORIGINAL COMMENT.

BY

HORACE HAYMAN WILSON, M.A. F.R.S.

MEMBER OF THE ROYAL ASIATIC SOCIETY, AND OF THE ASIATIC SOCIETIES OF PARIS
AND CALCUTTA, &c. &c.;
AND BODEN PROFESSOR OF SANSCRIT IN THE UNIVERSITY OF OXFORD.

OXFORD,
PRINTED FOR THE ORIENTAL TRANSLATION FUND OF GREAT BRITAIN
AND IRELAND,
BY S. COLLINGWOOD, PRINTER TO THE UNIVERSITY.
PUBLISHED AND SOLD BY A. J. VALPY, A.M., LONDON.
1837.

The cover and title page of *The Sánkhya Káriká* (1837)

1837 – *The Sánkhya Kārikā, or Memorial Verses on the Sánkhya Philosophy,* by Iswara Krishna

This is the first edition of the English translation of *The Sánkhya Kārikā; or Memorial Verses on the Sánkhya Philosophy* by Iswara Krishna. The translator was the scholar Henry Thomas Colebrooke. This book combines with it the English translation of *The Bháshya or Commentary of Guarapáda.* The translator of the latter is Horace Hayman Wilson. This book was printed for the Oriental Translation Fund of Great Britain and Ireland, and published by A.J. Valpy, Oxford, in 1837. The etching in the title page depicts the sun rising over water with the maxim "Ex Oriente Lux" written underneath.

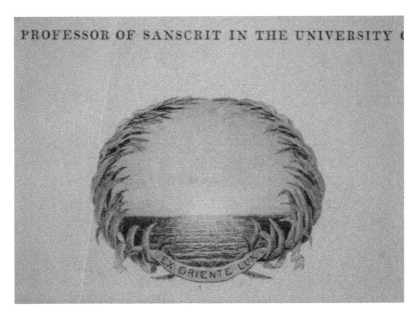

The insignia on the title page of *The Sánkhya Kārikā* (1837)

This text and its commentary were favourite readings for Thoreau, who copied passages into his journal. On 6 May 1851, Thoreau wrote:

A commentary on the Sankhya Karika says, 'By external knowledge worldly distinction is acquired; by internal knowledge, liberation.'

155

The Sankhya Karika says, 'By attainment of perfect knowledge, virtue and the rest become causeless; yet soul remains awhile invested with body, as the potter's wheel continues whirling from the effect of the impulse previously given to it.'

6 May 1851,
The Writings of Henry David Thoreau: Manuscript Edition: Journal, Vol. 2 (Boston, 1906), p. 192

28 January 1850, Cambridge, Mass.

Thoreau checks out 'The Vishnu Purana, A System of Hindu Mythology and Tradition, The Sankhya Karika; or, Memorial Verses on the Sankhya Philosophy by Isvarkrsna,' and 'The Works of Sir William Jones' from the Harvard College Library ('Companion to Thoreau's Correspondence,' p. 289).

The Thoreau Log. 1850, walden.org

Thoreau's journal for 1850* begins with comments on religions:

The Hindoos are more serenely and thoughtfully religious than the Hebrews. They have perhaps a purer, more independent and impersonal knowledge of God. Their religious books describe the first inquisitive and contemplative access to God; the Hebrew bible a conscientious return, a grosser and more personal repentance. Repentance is not a free and fair highway to God. A wise man will dispense with repentance. It is shocking and passionate. God prefers that you approach him thoughtful, not penitent, though you are the chief of sinners. It is only by forgetting yourself that you draw near to him.

The calmness and gentleness with which the Hindoo philosophers approach and discourse on forbidden themes is admirable.

What extracts from the Vedas I have read fall on me like the light of a higher and purer luminary, which describes a loftier course through a purer stratum, – free from particulars, simple, universal. It rises on me like the full moon after the stars have come out, wading through some far summer stratum of the sky.

The Vedant teaches how, 'by forsaking religious rites,' the votary may 'obtain purification of mind.'

One wise sentence is worth the state of Massachusetts many times over.

The Vedas contain a sensible account of God.

---

* The editors note that a new book is begun here, but the first entry date is 12 May 1850. Therefore, the first entries in this journal book may or may not belong to this year.

The religion and philosophy of the Hebrews are those of a wilder and ruder tribe, wanting the civility and intellectual refinements and subtlety of the Hindoos.

Man flows at once to God as soon as the channel of purity, physical, intellectual, and moral, is open.

With the Hindoos virtue is an intellectual exercise, not a social and practical one. It is a knowing, not doing.

I do not prefer one religion or philosophy to another. ... I like Brahma, Hari, Buddha, the Great Spirit, as well as God.

The Writings of Henry David Thoreau: Manuscript Edition: Journal, Vol. 2 (Boston, 1906), pp. 3–4

Thoreau wrote in *A Week*:

In comparison with the philosophers of the East, we may say that modern Europe has yet given birth to none. Beside the vast and cosmogonal philosophy of the Bhagvat-Geeta even our Shakspeare seems sometimes youthfully green and practical merely. Some of these sublime sentences, as Chaldæan oracles of Zoroaster, for instance, still surviving after a thousand revolutions and translations, alone make us doubt if the poetic form and dress are not transitory, and not essential to the most effective and enduring expression of thought. 'Ex oriente lux' may still be the motto of scholars, for the Western world has not yet derived from the East all the light which it is destined to receive thence.

"Monday" in *A Week on the Concord and Merrimack Rivers*, (Boston and Cambridge: James Munroe and Company, 1849), p. 149

Sutra VI on page 25 of this translation of *The Sánkhya Káriká* must have caught the transcendentalists' attention.

Curiously enough, this copy was discarded by the Andover-Harvard Theological Library. Perhaps its curator's view was akin to that of Lord Thomas Babington Macaulay, who wrote in 1832: "I have never found one among them [orientalists] who could deny that a single shelf of a good European library was worth the whole native literature of India and Arabia. The intrinsic superiority of the Western literature is indeed fully admitted by those members of the committee [the Committee of Public Instruction] who support the oriental plan of education."*

---

* Minute by the Hon. T.B. Macaulay, Member of the Council of India, dated 2 February 1835, http://www.columbia.edu/itc/mealac/pritchett/00generallinks/macaulay/txt_minute_ education_1835.html, accessed 20 April 2020

port of texts derived from holy writ; which knowledge is of itself proof, as obtained from the Védas, which are not of human origin, and fit to exempt from all fear of error*.' The first term, *vákya*, is explained to signify, 'the Véda is the teacher of religion †;' and the expression *vákyártha* is equivalent to *dherma*, 'religion or virtue.' 'Religion is heard by it; as, "Let one desirous of heaven perform the *jyotishíoma* sacrifice :" such is a text (of scripture) ‡.' The texts of the Védas and of other inspired works are authority, as having been handed down through successive births by the same teachers as JAIGÍSHAVYA says, 'By me living repeatedly in ten different great creations ‖.' So 'the Véda was remembered by KAPILA from a former state of being §.' The *Mimánsakas* distinguish between *ápta vákya* and *véda vákya:* the former is human, the latter inspired, authority.

VI.

SENSIBLE objects become known by perception; but it is by inference (or reasoning) that acquaintance with things transcending the senses is obtained: and a truth which is neither to be directly perceived, nor to be inferred from reasoning, is deduced from revelation.

BHÁSHYA.

By inference from analogy; of things beyond the senses—the ascertainment of existing things which transcend the senses. Nature and soul are

---

* श्रुतिवाक्यजनितं वाक्यार्थज्ञानं तच्च स्वतः प्रमाणमपौरुषेयवेदजनित त्वेन सकलदोषशंकाविनिमुक्तेर्युक्तं । † धर्मबोधकः श्रुतिः । ‡ श्रूयते धर्मोऽनेन यथा ज्योतिष्टोमेन स्वर्गकामी यजेतेति वाक्यं । ‖ दशम हासर्गेषु विपरिवर्त्तमानेन मया । § आदिविदुपश्चकपिलस्य कल्पादौ कल्पान्तराधीतश्रुतिस्मरणसम्भवः ।

H

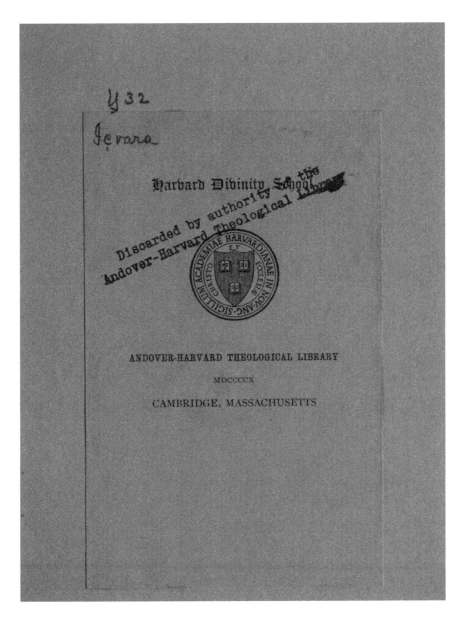

The discard stamp of *The Sánkhya Kāriká* by the Andover-Harvard Theological Library

N.B. When this copy was acquired, the text lay within a library binding that erroneously labelled it as "Bottler's Tamil Dictionary/Vol. I/Part I" – offering a benign explanation for discarding it. The label was subsequently replaced to match the content. To preserve the chain of provenance, the erroneous label has been tipped-in at the end of the book.

1843 – *The Confessions of St. Augustine*

This first American edition of *The Confessions of St. Augustine* was published by Elizabeth Palmer Peabody, Boston. The book was signed by Burrill Curtis (brother of George William Curtis) on 7 January 1843, when the Curtis brothers were at the utopian community, Brook Farm. On 20 January 1843, Burrill Curtis asked his father for $35 to acquire more books from Ms. Peabody's shop in Boston, explaining that he had already gone through his allowance for purchasing books. In a letter from New York City later that same year, George Curtis refers to reading the works of St. Augustine and others with Burrill Curtis.

On page 50 of this book, in the blank space at the top of the chapter titled "The Fourth Book: Augustine's Life from nineteen to eight and twenty", someone has artfully sketched three hearts in pencil. Two are in the sky and flaming; one floats in the sea, pierced by arrows. There are marginal markings of the text in a few places.

Ralph Waldo Emerson gave Peabody's edition of *The Confessions* a glowing review in the January 1843 issue of *The Dial*:

> Confessions of St. Augustine. Boston: E.P. Peabody.
>
> We heartily welcome this reprint from the recent London edition, which was a revision, by the Oxford divines, of an old English translation. It is a rare addition to our religious library. The great Augustine, – one of the truest, richest, subtlest, eloquentest of authors, comes now in this American dress, to stand on the same shelf with his far-famed disciples, with A-Kempis, Herbert, Taylor, Scougal, and Fenelon. The Confessions have also a high interest as one of the honestest autobiographies ever written. In this view it takes even rank with Montaigne's Essays, with Luther's Table Talk, the Life of John Bunyan, with Rousseau's Confessions, and the Life of Dr. Franklin. In opening the book at random, we have fallen on his reflections on the death of an early friend.
>
>> 'O madness, which knowest not how to love men like men! I fretted, sighed, wept, was distracted, had neither rest nor counsel. For I bore about a shattered and bleeding soul, impatient of being borne by me, yet where to repose it I found not. All things looked ghastly; yea the very light; whatsoever was not what he was, was revolting and hateful, except groaning and tears. In those alone found I a little refreshment. I fled out of my country; for so should mine eyes look less for him where they were not wont to see

The cover, the title page and a pencil drawing on page 50
of *The Confessions of St. Augustine* (1843)

him. And thus from Thagaste I came to Carthage. Times lose no time; nor do they roll idly by; through our senses they work strange operations on the mind. Behold, they went and came day by day, and by coming and going introduced into my mind other imaginations and other remembrances; and little by little patched me up again with my old kind of delights unto which that my sorrow gave way. And yet there succeeded not indeed other griefs, yet the causes of other griefs. For whence had that former grief so easily reached my inmost soul but that I had poured out my soul upon the dust in loving one, that must die, as if he would never die. For what restored and refreshed me chiefly, was the solaces of other friends with whom I did love what instead of thee I loved: and this was a great fable and protracted lie, by whose adulterous stimulus our soul, which lay itching in our ears, was defiled. But that fable would not die to me so oft as any of my friends died. There were other things which in them did more take my mind; to talk and jest together; to do kind offices by turns; to read together honied books; to play the fool or be earnest together; to dissent at times without discontent, as a man might with his own self; and even with the seldomness of those dissentings, to season our more frequent consentings; sometimes to teach, and sometimes learn; long for the absent with impatience, and welcome the coming with joy.'

The Dial, Vol. 3, No. 11, 1843, pp. 414–15

This copy has the bookplate of a subsequent owner, the twenty-first-century transcendentalist scholar Philip Gura.

1856 – *Poetry of the East* by William Alger, Inscribed to Samuel Osgood

This book is the first edition of William Alger's *Poetry of the East*. It was published by Whittmore, Niles and Hall, Boston, in 1856. The book contains a selection of early Sanskrit, Chinese, Arabic and Hebrew poetry.

> With small pretensions, with fervid interest in the subject, this humble offering, brought from the altar of the Oriental Muses, and laid on the shrine of American Literature, is commended to the kind notice of all whose curiosity or sympathy responds to the strange fascination of Eastern gorgeousness, reverie, and passion.
>
> From the Preface

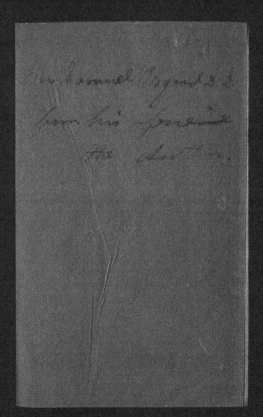

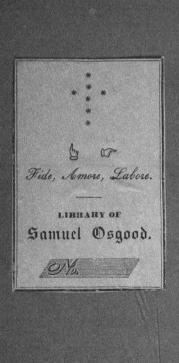

The cover, the title page, inscription by William Alger and the book plate of Samuel Osgood of *Poetry of the East* (1856)

   …

   Hadst thou, degenerate prince! but shown
   One single virtue as thy own,
   Then thou hadst gloried in my fame,
   And built thyself a deathless name.
   O Mahmoud! though thou fear me not,
   Heaven's vengeance will not be forgot;
   Shrink, tyrant! from my words of fire,
   And wither in a poet's ire!

Quoted from *Fraser's Magazine*, Vols XVIII–XXI, pp. 56–7

In this poem, Firdousi couldn't be admonishing a present "prince" – or could he?

William Rounseville Alger (1822–1905) was an American poet and a Unitarian minister. He was an early figure in the study of comparative theology. It was William Alger who purchased the first copy of *Walden* (see 1854 – *Walden*, p. 41). Alger inscribed this copy of the *Poetry of the East* to Samuel Osgood, another Unitarian minister who belonged to the Transcendental Club and the Town and Country Club. While living in Louisville, Kentucky, (1836–1837) Samuel Osgood edited four issues of *The Western Messenger.* The latter was established in Cincinnati in 1835 "to set forth and defend Unitarian views of Christianity."* Of the over 70 articles Osgood wrote, perhaps the most notable is his review of Ralph Waldo Emerson's first published work, "Nature", in which he praises Emerson for being "not such a dreamer on the beauties of the universe, as to forget its material uses."

1865 – *The Gulistan or Rose Garden* by Sheik Saadi of Shiraz

This volume is the first edition of *The Gulistan or Rose Garden* by Musle-Huddeen Sheik Saadi of Shiraz, translated into English by Francis Gladwin. It was published by Ticknor and Fields, Boston, with a prefatory essay by Ralph Waldo Emerson, dated February 1864. This copy belonged to Frederic Ives Carpenter, and it carries his extensive annotations

---

* Clarence Gohdes, "The Western Messenger" and "The Dial", *Studies in Philology*, 26, No. 1 (1929), pp. 67–84, accessed 6 June 2020

THE

GULISTAN

OR ROSE GARDEN.

BY

MUSLE-HUDDEEN SHEIK SAADI,

OF SHIRAZ.

TRANSLATED FROM THE ORIGINAL BY

FRANCIS GLADWIN.

WITH AN ESSAY ON SAADI'S LIFE AND GENIUS,

By JAMES ROSS,

AND A PREFACE,

By R. W. EMERSON.

BOSTON:
TICKNOR AND FIELDS
1865.

The cover, the title page and the book plate of the owner of *The Gulistan* (1865)

– particularly in Emerson's preface – as he quoted from it in his study, *Emerson and Asia*, published by Harvard University Press (1930). Carpenter taught at the University of Chicago, Harvard University, and the University of California, Berkeley, resigning from the latter in 1953 rather than signing a loyalty oath.

> One day, through the ignorance of youth, I spoke sharply to my mother, which vexing her to the heart, she sat down in a corner and wept, saying: 'Have you forgotten all the trouble that you gave me in your infancy, that you thus treat me with unkindness? What a good saying was that of an old woman to her son, when she saw him able to subdue a tiger, having the strength of an elephant. If you had but recollected your time of childhood, when you lay helpless in my arms, you would not treat me with violence, now that you have the strength of a lion, whilst I am an old woman.'
>
> Chapter VI, Tale VI, pp. 303–4

1879 – Lafcadio Hearn's Copy of *The Rubāiyāt of Omar Khayyām*

This is Lafcadio Hearn's copy of *The Rubāiyāt of Omar Khayyām; and the Salāmān and Ābsāl of Jāmī,* translated by Edward Fitzgerald. This fourth edition of *The Rubāiyāt* and the first edition of the *Salāmān and Ābsāl of Jāmī* was published by Bernard Quaritch, London, in 1879. It has Hearn's ownership stamp on both the half-title and the title pages. Hearn (1850–1904) was a key figure in helping East and West meet in the late nineteenth century. His father was a British naval surgeon who met his mother and married her on the Greek island of Lefkas, where Hearn was born. Back in England, his parents divorced when he was six, and his father sent him to be raised by a great-aunt in Dublin. He came to America as a young man, becoming a journalist in Cincinnati. He was fired when he married a mulatto street-walker he tried to save, and moved to New Orleans where he continued to write and began to make a serious study of the weird, the bizarre and the occult. He was a prodigious student of Hinduism and Buddhism. In 1890 he sailed to Japan on assignment for *Harper's Magazine* and never came back to the States. He married a Japanese woman, took a Japanese name, taught English and American literature at various universities, and continued to write eloquent pieces on a variety of literary, spiritual, artistic and cultural topics.

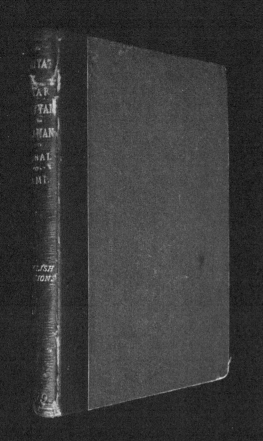
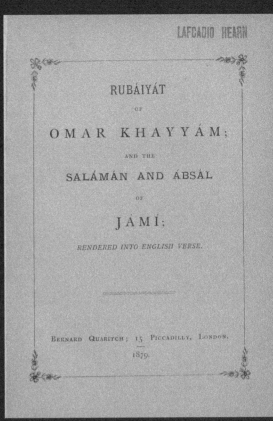

A Book of Verses underneath the Bough,
A Jug of Wine, a Loaf of Bread – and Thou
Beside me singing in the Wilderness –
Oh, Wilderness were paradise enow!

XII, p. 4

The Worldly Hope men set their Hearts upon
Turns Ashes – or it prospers; and anon,
Like Snow upon the Desert's dusty Face,
Lighting a little hour or two – was gone.

XVI, p. 5

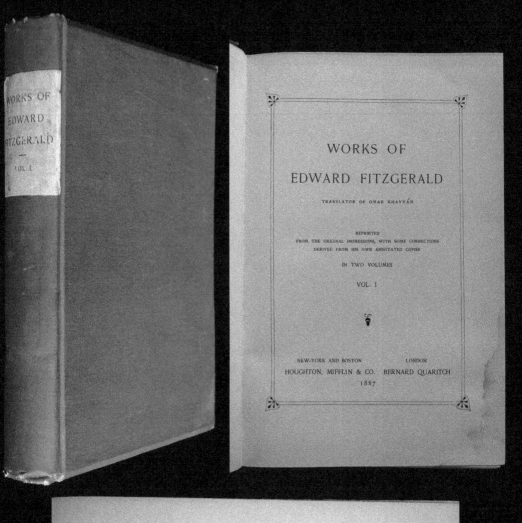

The cover, the title page and the inscription by Sarah Orne Jewett to Annie Fields
of *The Rubáiyát of Omar Khayyám* (1887)

1887 – Sarah O. Jewett's Copy of *The Rubāiyāt of Omar Khayyām*

This is Sarah Orne Jewett's copy of *The Rubāiyāt of Omar Khayyām*, Volume 1 of the *Works of Edward Fitzgerald* in two volumes published by Houghton, Mifflin Company, Boston, and Bernard Quaritch, London, in 1887. Pasted on the inside of the front cover of the book is a note that states, "Deposited in the Jewett Homestead by Harvard College Library, 1933."

The story behind this book's journey was that Jewett had no children. Her nephew, who inherited her books, bequeathed them to Harvard College, his alma mater. Harvard College retained some of the books and returned the rest to the Sarah Orne Jewett Homestead in South Berwick, Maine. From there they found their way into the hands of wheelers and dealers.

Mind ye, who donate and bequeath!

Sarah Orne Jewett (1849–1909) from South Berwick, Maine, was an enormously popular writer of "realistic" sketches that were published widely in various magazines of the late nineteenth and early twentieth centuries. She was seen as the most gifted of what became known as the "local colorists". While her work has never been forgotten, the last forty years have seen a resurgence of interest, with three biographies published in the last two decades. As a child, Sarah grew up in a large house in the centre of town, where she often skipped school to accompany her father on his medical rounds. She was a keen observer of people and places, and she tried to practise her father's maxim to "not write about things, but tell them just as they are." While she always considered South Berwick her home, as an adult she wintered in Boston and summered in Manchester, Massachusetts, with her friend, Annie Fields.

Annie Fields was the widow of the renowned publisher James T. Fields and, along with her husband, had been a friend and associate of Longfellow, Emerson, Hawthorne and Dickens. From the early 1880s to Sarah's death in 1909, she and Annie lived together at 148 Charles Street in perhaps the most famous of what writer Henry James (another friend) called a "Boston Marriage". Each provided the other with companionship and support for their individual work (Sarah's writing and Annie's social service program) and their joint projects, such as trips to Europe and literary salons. In the twilight of her life, Jewett served as literary mentor to the young Willa Cather (1873–1947), so much so that Cather dedicated her *O Pioneers* to Jewett.

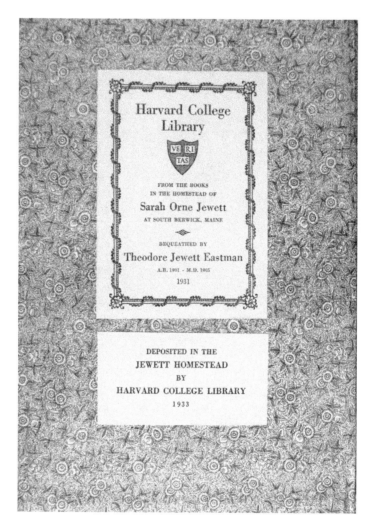

Plate from Harvard College Library in Sarah Orne Jewett's copy of
The Rubāiyāt of Omar Khayyām (1933)

1887 – *The Bhagavad Gitâ*, Translated by Mohini M. Chatterji, Inscribed by the Translator

This first edition of Mohini M. Chatterji's translation of the *Bhagavad Gita* is inscribed by the translator, dated 21 September 1887. The book was titled *The Bhagavad Gitâ or the Lord's Lay, with Commentary and Notes, as well as References to the Christian Scriptures.* It was published by Ticknor and Company, Boston, in its waning days before it transmuted into Houghton Mifflin and Company.

The *Gita* (short for the *Bhagavad Gita*, which in English can be written in various ways) constitutes eighteen chapters in the middle of the epic *Mahabharata.* It is the wisdom imparted to Arjuna, the archer, by Sri Krishna, his charioteer, when the five Pandava brothers assembled for battle with their one hundred strong cousins, the Kouravas, in the field of the Kurus. It was Charles Wilkins (1749–1836) who first translated the *Gita* into English from the original Sanskrit, and published under the title *Bhagvat-Geeta, or Dialogues of Kreeshna and Arjoon* (1785).

> The right performer of action, abandoning fruit of action, attains to rest through devotion; the wrong performer of action, attached to fruit thereof on account of desire, remains bound.
>
> V:12, p. 97

Henry D. Thoreau said of the *Bhagavad Gita*:

> I would say to the readers of the Scriptures, if they wish for a good book to read, Read the Bhagvat-Geeta, an episode to the Mahabharat, said to have been written by Kreeshna Dwypayen Veias, – known to have been written by –––––, more than four thousand years ago, – it matters not whether three or four, or when, – translated by Charles Wilkins. It deserves to be read with reverance even by Yankees, as a part of the sacred writings of a devout people; and the intelligent Hebrew will rejoice to find in it a moral grandeur and sublimity akin to those of his own Scriptures.
>
> "Monday" in *A Week on the Concord and Merrimack Rivers*
(Boston and Cambridge: James Monroe and Company, 1849), p. 147

As a Theosophist in England, Mohini Chatterji (1858–1936) had impressed W.B. Yeats, who in later years wrote a poem about him.

The cover and the title page with inscription by the translator on the opposite page of *The Bhagavad Gîtâ* translated by Mohini Chatterji (1887)

Chatterji was received well during his tour in the United States. Louisa May Alcott recorded in her journal, on 7 April 1887, that she saw Chatterji "With Miss Mary to hear the Baboo Mohini at Mr Hale's church. Very good on brotherhood."[*] Chatterji adopted a popular point of view that drew similarities between the teachings of Sri Krishna and Jesus Christ. Chatterji returned to India and became a successful lawyer in Bombay. He also ran a home for fallen women.

---

[*]   J. Myerson and D. Shealy (eds), *The Journals of Louisa May Alcott* (Boston: Little, Brown and Company, 1989), p. 296

THE PHILOSOPHY
OF THE UPANIṢADS

BY

S. RADHAKRISHNAN

WITH A FOREWORD BY

RABINDRANATH TAGORE

AND AN INTRODUCTION BY

EDMOND HOLMES
AUTHOR OF " THE CREED OF BUDDHA," ETC.

LONDON : GEORGE ALLEN & UNWIN LTD.
RUSKIN HOUSE, 40 MUSEUM STREET, W.C. 1
NEW YORK: THE MACMILLAN COMPANY

1924 – *The Philosophy of the Upaniṣads* by S. Radhakrishnan

This volume is the first edition of *The Philosophy of the Upaniṣads* by S. Radhakrishnan. It was published by George Allen & Unwin, London, in 1924, with a foreword by Rabindranath Tagore and an introduction by Edmond Holmes.

> I feel strongly that this, for us, is the teaching of the Upaniṣads, and that this teaching is very much needed in the present age for those who boast of the freedom enjoyed by their nations, using that freedom for building up a dark world of spiritual blindness, where the passions of greed and hatred are allowed to roam unchecked, having for their allies deceitful diplomacy and a wide-spread propaganda of falsehood, where the soul remains caged and the self battens upon the decaying flesh of its victims.
>
> From the foreword by Rabindranath Tagore

Sarvepally Radhakrishnan (1888–1975) was an academic, philosopher and statesman. He taught at universities in India, the United States and the United Kingdom. In India, he held the King George V Chair of Mental and Moral Science at the University of Calcutta (appointed 1921). In the US, he was Haskell Lecturer in Comparative Religion at the University of Chicago (appointed 1930). In the UK, he was Spalding Professor of Eastern Religion and Ethics at Oxford University (appointed 1936). He was Vice President (1952–1962) and President (1962–1967) of India.

1953 – *The Principal Upaniṣads*, Translated by S. Radhakrishnan

This is the first edition of *The Principal Upaniṣads, Edited with Introduction, Text, Translation and Notes by S. Radhakrishnan.* It was published by George Allen & Unwin, London.

> The word 'upaniṣad' is derived from upa (near), ni (down) and sad (to sit), i.e. sitting down near. ... It is a living stream of spiritual life.
>
> From the Introduction by S. Radhakrishnan, p. 19

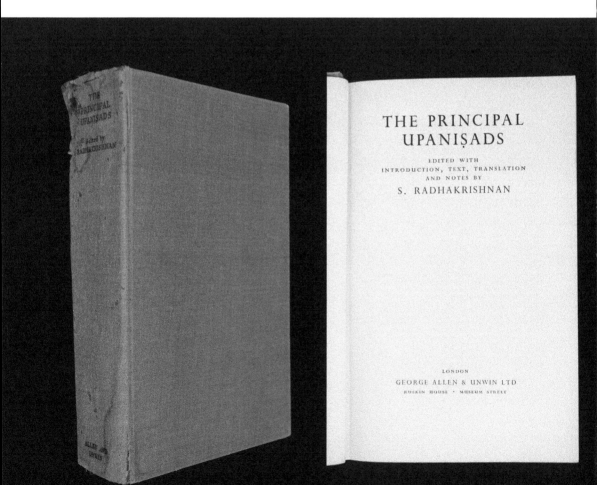

KĀLIDĀSA

SACONTALÁ;

OR,

THE FATAL RING:

AN

INDIAN DRAMA.

BY

CÁLIDÁS.

Sir W. Jones

TRANSLATED FROM THE ORIGINAL SANSCRIT AND PRÁCRIT.

LONDON:

Printed for EDWARDS, PALL MALL;

By J. COOPER, No. 31, Bow Street, Covent Garden,

WITH HIS NEW-INVENTED INK.

M.DCC.XC.

---

their manes, erected their ears, and rather glided than gallopped over the smooth plain.

DUSHM. They soon out ran the swift antelope. Objects which, from their distance, appeared minute, presently became larger: what was really divided, seemed united, as we passed; and what was in truth bent, seemed straight. So swift was the motion of the wheels, that nothing, for many moments, was either distant or near.

[*He fixes an arrow in his bowstring.*

[*Behind the scenes.*] He must not be slain. This antelope, O king, has an asylum in our forest: he must not be slain.

CHAR. [*Listening and looking.*] Just as the animal presents a fair mark for your arrow, two hermits are advancing to interrupt your aim.

DUSHM. Then stop the car.

CHAR. The king is obeyed.   [*He draws in the reins.*

Enter a HERMIT *and his* PUPIL.

HERM. [*Raising his hands.*] Slay not, O mighty sovereign, slay not a poor fawn, who has found a place of refuge. No, surely, no; he must not be hurt. An arrow in the delicate body of a deer would be like fire in a bale of cotton. Compared with thy keen shafts, how weak must be the tender hide of a young antelope! Replace quickly, oh! replace the arrow which thou hast aimed. The weapons of you kings and warriors are destined for the relief of the oppressed, not for the destruction of the guiltless.

DUSHM. [*Saluting them.*] It is replaced.

[*He places the arrow in his quiver.*

HERM. [*With joy.*] Worthy is that act of thee, most illustrious of monarchs; worthy, indeed, of a prince descended from Puru. Mayst thou have a son adorned with virtues, a sovereign of the world!

PUP. [*Elevating both his hands.*] Oh! by all means, may thy son be adorned with every virtue, a sovereign of the world!

DUSHM. [*Bowing to them.*] My head bears with reverence the order of a Bráhmen.

The cover, the title page and page 4 of *Sacontalá* (1790)

1790 – *Sacontalá; or, The Fatal Ring*

This is the first European edition of the first English translation of *Śacontalā* by Kālidāsa. It was "Printed for Edwards, Pall Mall; By J. Cooper, No. 31, Bow Street, Covent Garden (London), M.DCC.XC. with His New-Invented Ink".

Kālidāsa lived in the fourth and fifth centuries AD. He was the court poet of King Chandragupta II (380–415 AD). *Śacontalā* was first translated into English from the original Sanskrit and Pracrit by Sir William Jones. It was first published in Calcutta in 1789. The first European publication followed in 1790. As Max Muller wrote in the Introduction to his *A History of Ancient Sanskrit Literature* published by Williams and Norgate, London, in 1860,* this translation was a major event in the intellectual and literary world:

> Full seventy years have passed since Sir William Jones published his translation of Śakuntala, a work which may fairly be considered as the starting-point of Sanskrit philology. The first appearance of this beautiful specimen of dramatic art created at the time a sensation throughout Europe, and the most rapturous praise was bestowed upon it by men of high authority in matters of taste.

As Max Muller points out in the following footnote,

> Goethe was one of the greatest admirers of Śakuntala, as may be seen from the lines written in his Italian Travels at Naples, and from his well-known [1791] Epigram:
>
> > 'Wilt thou the blossoms of spring and the fruits that are later in seen,
> > Wilt thou have charms and delights, wilt thou have strength and support,
> > Wilt thou with one short word encompass the earth and the heaven,
> > All is said if I name only Sacontala, thee.'

Here follow excerpts from two scenes from *Śacontalā* as translated by Monier Williams and published by Stephen Austin in 1855 (pp. 9–79).

King Dushyanta is on a hunting expedition with his retinue. As the king takes aim to kill a game animal, a hermit springs from the bushes.

Hermit [Raising his hand]

---

* https://archive.org/stream/in.ernet.dli.2015.279340/2015.279340.A-History#page/n19/mode/2up, accessed 2 June 2020

This deer, O King, belongs to our hermitage. Kill it not! Kill it not!
Now heaven forbid this barbĕd shaft descend
Upon the fragile body of a fawn,
Like fire upon a heap of tender flowers!
Can thy steel bolts no meeter quarry find
Than the warm life-blood of a harmless deer?
Restore, great prince, thy weapon to its quiver
More it becomes thy arms to shield the weak,
Than to bring anguish on the innocent.

p. 9

In another scene, the king makes advances, in subtle ways and suggestive language, on the damsel Śacontalā, who is alone in the hermitage, her female attendants having politely withdrawn themselves.

King: Distress not thyself, sweet maiden. Thy adorer is at hand to wait upon thee.
Oh, let me tend thee, fair one, in the place of thy friends;
and with broad lotus fans,
Raise cooling breezes to refresh thy frame,
Or shall I rather, with caressing touch,
Allay the fever of thy limbs, and soothe
Thy aching feet, beauteous as blushing lilies?

Sakoontala: Nay, touch me not. I will not incur the censure of those whom I am bound to respect. [Rises and attempts to go] ...

The king implies that she is old enough to consent without consulting her parents.

Sakoontala: Infringe not the rules of decorum, mighty descendant of Puru.
Remember, though I love you, I have no power to dispose of myself. ...

Sakoontala: Leave me, leave me; I must take counsel with my female friends.

King: I will leave thee when –

Sakoontala: When?

King: When I have gently stolen from thy lips
Their yet untasted nectar, to allay
The raging of my thirst, e'en as the bee
Sips the fresh honey from the opening bud.
[Attempts to raise her face. Sakoontala tries to prevent him.]

pp. 78–80

1902 – *The Raghuvança*, Translated by P. De Lacy Johnstone

This is the first edition of *Raghuvança* (trans. *The Story of Raghu's Line*) by Kālidāsa, which was translated by P. De Lacy Johnstone and published by J.M. Dent and Company, London. In this book, Kālidāsa traces the lineage of Sri Rama, the hero of the Hindu epic *Rāmāyaṇa*.

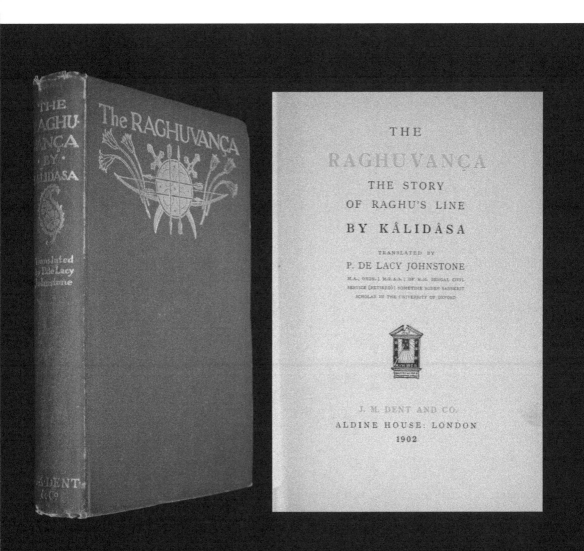

The cover and the title page of *The Raghuvança* (1902)

1911 – *Meghaduta* in Sanskrit

This is Kālidāsa's *Mēghadūta* (trans. *Cloud Messenger*) edited with commentary by A. Vallabhadev and published under the patronage of the Royal Asiatic Society of Great Britain and Ireland, London. The latter was "founded by the generosity of H.H. Maharaja of Cochin, the Maharaja Gajapati Rao, the Raja of Parlakimedi and other Chiefs and Gentlemen of Southern India." It has a Sanskrit–English vocabulary by E. Hultzsch. Horace Hayman Wilson had published an English paraphrase of *Mēghadūta* in Calcutta in 1813 in his *editio princeps*. In 1814, Wilson's translation was reprinted in London. Goethe read this translation and sent his copy to his friend Karl Ludwig von Knebel in 1817.

PRIZE PUBLICATIONS FUND
VOL. III

KALIDASA'S
MEGHADUTA

EDITED FROM MANUSCRIPTS

WITH THE

COMMENTARY OF VALLABHADEVA

AND PROVIDED WITH A COMPLETE

SANSKRIT-ENGLISH VOCABULARY

BY

E. HULTZSCH

PRINTED AND PUBLISHED UNDER THE PATRONAGE OF
THE ROYAL ASIATIC SOCIETY
AND SOLD AT
22 ALBEMARLE STREET, LONDON
1911

The cover and the title page of *Meghaduta* (1911)

1930 – *The Cloud-Messenger* by Kālidāsa, Translated by Charles King

This is the first edition of the English translation of Kālidāsa's *Mēghadūta* from the original Sanskrit by Charles King. Its full title is *The Cloud-Messenger, An Indian Love Lyric*. It was published by John Murray, London. Horace Hayman Wilson had published an English paraphrase of *Mēghadūta* in Calcutta in 1813 in his *editio princeps*. (For more on this translation by Wilson see 1911 – *Meghaduta*, above.)

XXVI

Out of repose, Sir, onward fare. Sprinkle with fresh rainy drops
the jasmine-stars of many a copse, the stars that spring along the side where
the woodland waters glide. Casting shade thou shalt be made for a moment
intimate with the faces of the flower-gathering girls; faded in their ear the blue
lotus doth appear, stricken in wiping the sweat from off their cheeks.

pp. 32–3

XXVIII

The serried birds that chatter at the rippling of the waves Nirvindhya hath for
girdling string. Sweetly she stealeth where she stumbleth; her naval is of eddies
manifest. In thy going learn her love and mingle with her; for women's first word
of love to lovers is a gesture amorous.

p. 33

THE
CLOUD-MESSENGER

WISDOM OF THE EAST

THE
CLOUD-MESSENGER
AN INDIAN LOVE LYRIC

TRANSLATED FROM THE ORIGINAL
SANSKRIT OF KALIDASA

BY CHARLES KING, B.A.
SOMETIME DOMUS EXHIBITIONER OF BALLIOL AND
RODEN SANSKRIT SCHOLAR IN THE UNIVERSITY OF OXFORD

LONDON
JOHN MURRAY, ALBEMARLE STREET, W.

1929 – *A Circle of the Seasons*, Translated by E. Powys Mathers

A Circle of the Seasons is a translation of *Ritu-Samhāra* of Kālidāsa made
from various European sources by Edward Powys Mathers, with
engravings by Robert Gibbings. On the back endpage, it is stated that this
book was "Printed by Robert Gibbings at the Golden Cockerel Press,
Waltham Saint Lawrence, Berkshire, and completed on the 8ᵗʰ day of
December 1928. *Compositors: A. H. Gibbs and F. Young. Pressman: A. C.
Cooper.* This edition is limited to 500 numbered copies, of which this is
No.140." Writing in pencil on the front endpage states: "Gibbings' only
work in copper."

> The clouds advance like rutting elephants,
> enormous and full of rain; they come forward
> as kings among tumultuous armies; their flags are
> the lightning; their thunder is their drum.
>
> The clouds come forward and mass together, like
> the dark blue petals of the lotus, like the full breasts
> of nursing women, like sombre fard upon the face
> of the sky.
>
> "Season of the Rains", p. 9
>
> May this season be favourable to you, my beloved,
> for it gives rain to the living, and is the mother of
> the buds and grasses, and tenderly ravishes the hearts
> of women.
>
> "Season of the Rains", p. 13

A
Circle of the Seasons

*A Translation of the Ritu-Samhāra of
Kālidāsa made from various European
sources by*
E. POWYS MATHERS

*With Engravings by
Robert Gibbings*

The Golden Cockerel Press
1929

The cover, the title page and the illustration for the poem about the clouds on page 9 of
A Circle of the Seasons (1929)

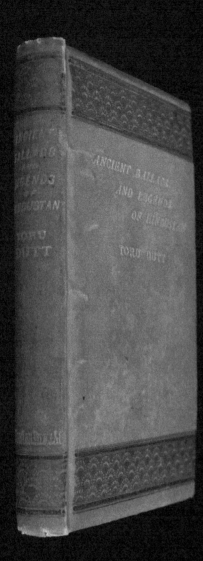

ANCIENT BALLADS
AND LEGENDS
OF HINDUSTAN

BY

TORU DUTT

AUTHOR OF "A SHEAF GLEANED IN FRENCH FIELDS," AND
"LE JOURNAL DE MADEMOISELLE D'ANVERS,"

WITH AN INTRODUCTORY MEMOIR

BY EDMUND W. GOSSE.

LONDON
KEGAN PAUL, TRENCH & CO.
MDCCCLXXXII

R. W. Gilder
from his friend
Edmund Gosse

24. 3. 82.

The cover, the title page and the
inscription by Edmund W. Gosse of
*Ancient Ballads and Legends of
Hindustan* (1882)

1882 – *Ancient Ballads and Legends of Hindustan* by Toru Dutt

This rare book was published by Kegan Paul, Trench, & Company, London. This is the first edition, with a 27-page introductory memoir by the noted English critic Sir Edmund W. Gosse. Gosse has inscribed this copy to his good friend, the American editor and author Richard W. Gilder, on the free front endpaper: "R. W. Gilder from his friend Edmund Gosse, 24.3.82." Richard Watson Gilder, an accomplished poet, was the long-time editor of the *Century Magazine*. Gilder published an essay entitled "Toru Dutt" in his magazine (January 1884) in which he wrote that Dutt's poetry "appeals to the highest and tenderest emotions in our nature and is permeated throughout with the influence of divine love." According to Edmund Gosse:

> No modern Oriental has given us so strange an insight into the conscience of the Asiatic [as Toru Dutt]. … The poetess seems in these verses to be chanting to herself those songs of her mother's race to which she always turned with tears of pleasure. They breathe a Vedic solemnity and simplicity of temper, and are singularly devoid of that littleness and frivolity which seem, if we may judge by a slight experience, to be the bane of modern India.

Toru Dutt (1856–1877) was an Indian poet who wrote in English and French. She was the youngest of the three children of father Govind Chandra Dutt and mother Kshetramoni of the Rambagan Dutt family. As a family, they converted to Christianity in 1862.

Dutt published *A Sheaf Gleaned in French Fields*, a volume of French poems she had translated into English. It was published by Saptahiksambad Press of Bhowanipore, India, in 1876. Eight of these poems had been translated by her elder sister Aru. Edmund Gosse reviewed it in the *Examiner* in 1877. *Sheaf* had a second Indian edition in 1878 and a third edition by Kegan Paul of London in 1880. Her other poems include "Sîta", "Lotus" and "Our Casuarina Tree". The latter poem, in which she reminisces about her happy childhood days through her memories of the tree, is popular even in modern times, and is taught in English classes at colleges in India.

But not because of its magnificence
Dear is the Casuarina to my soul:

Beneath it we have played; though years may roll,

O sweet companions, loved with love intense,

For your sakes, shall the tree be ever dear!

Blent with your images, it shall arise

In memory, till the hot tears blind mine eyes!

p. 138

Toru Dutt's novel *Bianca, or the Young Spanish Maiden* is the first known novel in English by an Indian woman. It was serialized in the *Bengal Magazine* in 1878. Another novel, *Le Journal de Mademoiselle d'Arvers*, published by Didier et Cie, Libraires-Editeurs, 35, Quai Des Augustins, Paris, in 1879, is the first known novel in French by an Indian. These two novels and an unfinished volume of original poems in English, *Ancient Ballads and Legends of Hindustan*, were discovered by her father after her death. In *Ancient Ballads*, she gives poetic expression to stories from Sanskrit scriptures, revealing her emotional attachment to her ancestry.

LEO TOLSTOY

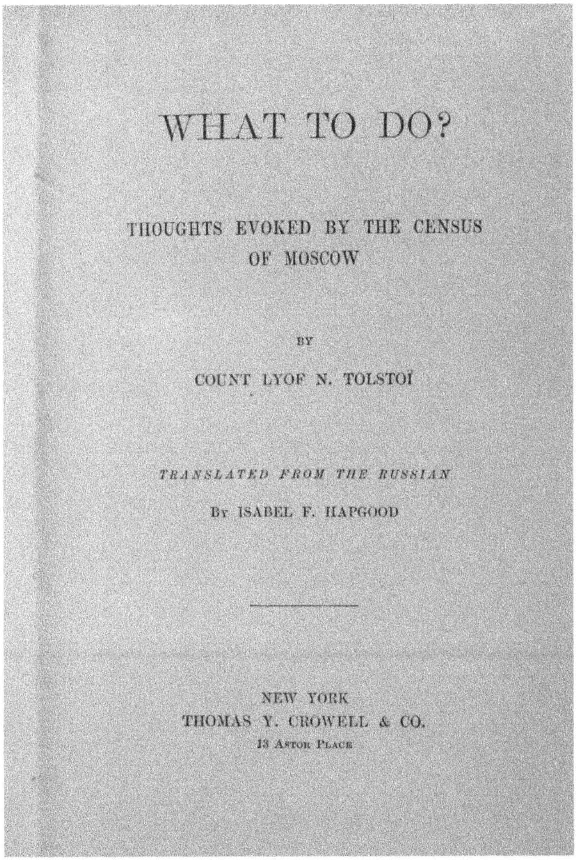

WHAT TO DO?

THOUGHTS EVOKED BY THE CENSUS
OF MOSCOW

BY

COUNT LYOF N. TOLSTOÏ

TRANSLATED FROM THE RUSSIAN

By ISABEL F. HAPGOOD

NEW YORK
THOMAS Y. CROWELL & CO.
13 ASTOR PLACE

The title page of *What to Do?* (1887)

The cover of *What to Do?* (1887)

1887 – *What To Do? Thoughts Evoked by the Census of Moscow*

This is the first edition of the English translation of the book written by Count Leo N. Tolstoy. It was translated by Isabel F. Hapgood and published by Thomas Y. Crowell and Company, New York. Tolstoy pours out his heart at the plight of the slum-dwellers of Moscow, where he volunteered to do census work, and ponders what can be done. He concludes:

> Such are the women, who, having fulfilled their destiny, reign over powerful men; such are the women who prepare the new generations of people, and fix public opinion: and, therefore, in the hands of these women lies the highest power of saving men from the prevailing and threatening evils of our times.
>
> Yes, ye women and mothers, in your hands, more than in those of all others, lies the salvation of the world!

Last two paragraphs of the book, p. 273

Graf Lev Nikolayevich Tolstoi (Count Leo Tolstoy) was born in Yasnayá Polyána, Zsarist Russia, in 1828. Tolstoy may be better known for his novels, but his non-fiction writings carry the fragrance of his life. His essay "The Root of the Evil" was published in the *North American Review* in 1901:

> Some can read four languages, and daily amuse themselves with the most varied pastimes; others do not even know their letters and have no pleasure but drink. Some know all and believe nothing; others know nothing and believe all the absurdities they are told. Some, when they fall ill, besides all manner of watering places, all possible care, cleanliness, and medicines, go about from place to place seeking for the most healing climate; others lie down on the stove in a chimneyless hut, and with unwashed wounds, without any food except dry bread, or any air besides an atmosphere tainted by the members of the family, by calves and sheep, rot alive and die before their time.
>
> Is this as it should be? …
>
> I remember the wise words of a Russian peasant, a religious and therefore a truly free-thinking man. Like Thoreau, he thought it wrong to pay taxes for purposes his conscience disapproved of, and, when the tax gatherers required him to pay his share, he asked for what purposes the taxes would be used, saying:

'If they are to be employed for righteous uses, I will immediately give not only what you require, but even much more; but if the taxes are destined for evil purposes, then I cannot and will not give a penny, and I refuse to do so of my own free will.'

Of course, none stopped to listen to him; instead, they burst open the doors he had closed, took away his cow and sold it for the taxes.

At the end of this essay in the *North American Review*, there was an extract from a letter from Count Tolstoy to Mr. Edward Garnett:

A Message to the American People

Yasnayá Polyána

When I read your letter it seemed to me impossible that I could send any message to the American people. But thinking over it at night, it came to me that, if I had to address the American people, I should like to thank them for the great help I have received from their writers who flourished about the fifties. I would mention Garrison, Parker, Emerson, Ballou and Thoreau, not as the greatest, but as those who, I think, specially influenced me. Other names are Channing, Whittier, Lowell, Walt Whitman – a bright constellation, such as is rarely to be found in the literatures of the world.

And I should like to ask the American people why they do not pay more attention to these voices (hardly to be replaced by those of financial and industrial millionaires, or successful generals and admirals), and continue the good work in which they made such hopeful progress.

Leo Tolstoy

"The Root of the Evil", *North American Review*,
Vol. 172, No. 533 (April 1901), pp. 481–503

Leo Tolstoy died in 1910. He is buried at Yasnayá Polyána. His "Message to the American People" rings equally relevant today as it did in 1901.

1894 – *'The Kingdom of God is Within You'*

This is the first edition of an English translation published by the Cassell Publishing Company, New York. Constance Garnett translated it from Tolstoy's original Russian. It was copyrighted by Cassell Publishing Company (1894). The preface by the translator was dated January 1894.

Tolstoy dated his preface to *'The Kingdom of God is Within You;' or, Christianity Not as a Mystical Teaching But as a New Concept of Life*, 14/26 May 1893. The book was first published in Germany in 1894 because its publication was banned in Russia. The British publisher, William Heinemann, commissioned Constance Garnett to translate the

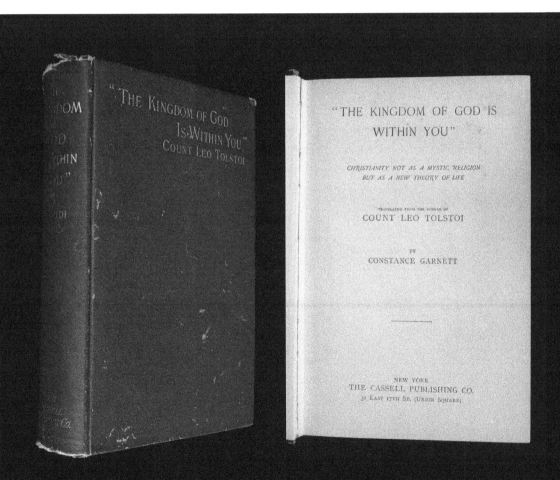

The cover and the title page of *'The Kingdom of God is Within You'* (1894)

book. It is known that her first English translation was published in 1894.* The curator of the T.G.M. Rare Book Museum, however, was unable to confirm if there was another publication of this translation by William Heinemann in England the same year.

In this book, Tolstoy affirms that the kingdom of God preached by Jesus is indeed within the reach of everyone, and that at its core is the principle of non-resistance to evil.

> Christianity in its true sense puts an end to government. So it was understood at its very commencement; it was for that cause that Christ was crucified. So it has always been understood by people who were not under the necessity of justifying a Christian government. Only from the time that the heads of government assumed an external and nominal Christianity, men began to invent all the impossible, cunningly devised theories by means of which Christianity can be reconciled with government. But no honest and serious-minded man of our day can help seeing the incompatibility of true Christianity – the doctrine of meekness, forgiveness of injuries, and love – with government, with its pomp, acts of violence, executions, and wars. The profession of true Christianity not only excludes the possibility of recognizing government, but even destroys its very foundations.
>
> pp. 236–7

> 'The kingdom of God cometh not with outward show: neither shall they say, Lo here! or, Lo there! for behold, the kingdom of God is within you.'
> (Luke xvii. 20, 21.)
>
> p. 368

1899 – *Resurrection*

This first edition of the English translation of Leo Tolstoy's *Resurrection* was translated by Louise Maude from the original Russian. The publisher was Grosset & Dunlap, New York. The original was "Copyright, 1899, by Dodd, Mead & COMPANY, and 1899, (as the 'Awakening,' BY JOHN BRISBEN WALKER."

---

* Rebecca Beasley, *Russomania* (New York: Oxford University Press, 2020), p. 63

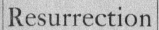

Resurrection

A NOVEL

By
LEO TOLSTOY

Author of
"Anna Karénina," "War and Peace," etc.

Translated by
MRS. LOUISE MAUDE

New York
GROSSET & DUNLAP
PUBLISHERS

This English version of "Resurrection" is published by Dodd Mead and Company by my authority

Leo Tolstoy

The cover, the title page and the authorization of publication by Leo Tolstoy
of *Resurrection* (1899)

In this novel, considered autobiographical, Tolstoy wrote of an aristocratic man who sits on a jury for the trial of a sex worker accused of murder. He recognizes the defendant as the girl he seduced when she was young. He underwent a transformation and attempted to make up for his sin by proposing to marry her, only to be spurned.

The front free endpaper reproduces a signed statement by Tolstoy: "This English version of *Resurrection* is published by Dodd, Mead and Company by my authority."

> Now he saw clearly what all the terrors he had seen came from, and what ought to be done to put a stop to them. The answer he could not find was the same that Christ gave to Peter. It was that we should forgive always an infinite number of times because there are no men who have not sinned themselves, and therefore none can punish or correct others. ...
>
> For many centuries people who were considered criminals have been tortured. Well, and have they ceased to exist? No; their numbers have been increased not alone by the criminals corrupted by punishment but also by those lawful criminals, the judges, procureurs, magistrates and jailors, who judge and punish men. Nekhlúdoff now understood that society and order in general exists not because of these lawful criminals who judge and punish others, but because in spite of men being thus deprived, they still pity and love one another.
>
> pp. 516–17

1890 – *The Buddhist Ray*

The Buddhist Ray was the first American journal on Buddhism. It was a monthly magazine devoted to Buddhism in general, and to the Buddhism in Swedenborg in particular. The publisher was Herman Vetterling. This issue in the T.G.M. Rare Book Museum is Volume 3, Number 5. The following passage is adapted from the Center for Swedenborgian Studies website.*

> Herman Vetterling was a lifelong scholar whose spiritual development and accompanying publications were in the vanguard of non-traditional American religious evolution from the 1870s to the 1920s. Born in Sweden in 1849,

---

*   Paul Tutwiler, "Herman Vetterling, The Philosopher of San Jose; Philangi Dasa, The Buddhist of Santa Cruz", Center for Swedenborgian Studies, occasional article, accessed 17 July 2021

Vetterling emigrated to Minnesota in 1871, turned away from his native Lutheranism, and in 1877 was ordained a Swedenborgian minister in Pennsylvania. Leaving the ministry in 1881, he graduated from the homeopathic medical school of Hahnemann Hospital in Chicago in 1883. Moving to a secluded home outside Santa Cruz, California, he published his first book, *Swedenborg the Buddhist*, in 1887, under the pseudonym of Philangi Dàsa. From there he also wrote (again as Philangi Dàsa) and published from 1888 to 1894 the monthly periodical *The Buddhist Ray*. Vetterling then moved to San Jose, California, where he practiced medicine, and where, in 1923, after 25 years of preparation, he published *The Illuminate of Goerlitz*, a detailed study of the Protestant mystic Jacob Boehme. In 1931 he died in San Jose, CA.

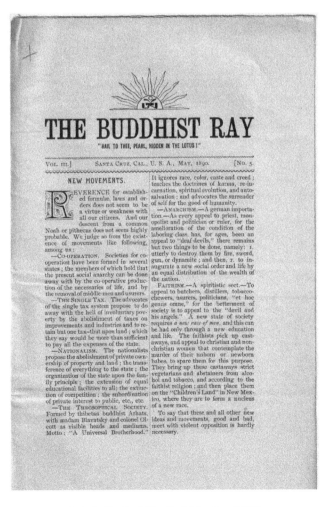

Vol. 3, No. 5 of *The Buddhist Ray* (1890)

1892 – Autograph Quote and Letter from Annie Besant

British reformer Annie Besant (1847–1933) was a Theosophist and a tireless campaigner for women's rights, including birth control and education. Later in life, she was a champion for India's independence. In 1917 she was elected President of the Indian National Congress.

> Think nobly & you will grow noble. Think basely & you will become base. For thought creates character.
>
> Annie Besant

This autographed letter (opposite, below), dated 14 June 1892, is from Annie Besant to another primary mover in the Theosophical Movement, Ms. Katharine Hillard. This is a detailed letter, composed on the provocative letterhead of Madame Blavatsky's Theosophical Monthly, *Lucifer*, arranging dates for Ms. Hillard to present to the London Theosophical Lodge.

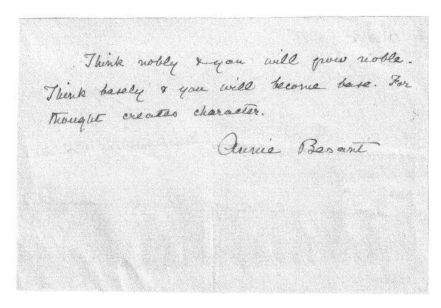

Autograph (undated) by Annie Besant, stamp from India (undated) honouring Annie Besant and autograph letter from Annie Besant to Katherine Hillard (1892)

❖ LUCIFER ❖

A THEOSOPHICAL MONTHLY.   FOUNDED BY H. P. BLAVATSKY.

EDITOR, ANNIE BESANT.   SUB-EDITOR, G. R. S. MEAD.

Editorial Department: 17 and 19, Avenue Road, Regent's Park, London, N.W. Terms of Subscription,
17/6 per annum, post-free; single numbers, 1/6 each. Telegraphic Address, "Blavatsky, London."

London. ——— *June 14 1892*

Dear Sister Stillard,

    I am glad we are to have the pleasure of seeing you so soon. Our Blavatsky Lodge open meetings are on Thursdays at 8.30 p.m. As you are only in London for two meetings, in one of these is Convention. I will put you down to lecture on July 7th; please send me title at once. Then we shall want you to make a quarter of an hour speech on the evening of the 14th, when all the speeches will be short. The Blavatsky Lodge meetings for members only are on Saturdays at 8.30 p.m. We shall be very glad to welcome you & Miss Hascall to them.

    Will you both come to dinner on the 7th at 6.45 prompt? W. Judge will

arrive on the 6th, I think. I will speak to Mead about Edinburgh; & I should think they would be pleased to have a lecture.

    It will be very pleasant to see you again, & to introduce you to our head quarters.

    Yours affectionately

    Annie Besant

All the meetings are here.

1904 – *A Study in Consciousness: A Contribution to the Science of Psychology* by **Annie Besant**

This volume of Annie Besant's *A Study in Consciousness* was sent as a review copy to Horace Traubel (1858–1919) for his paper, *The Conservator*. It is stamped "REVIEW COPY", signed "Horace Traubel/1904" and inscribed "For Mildred Bain/July 23d 1909". Traubel has marked the book in many places. Horace Traubel was very close to Walt Whitman in the latter's twilight years, becoming his literary executor and an early biographer. Traubel published nine volumes of recollections of Walt Whitman under the title, *With Walt Whitman in Camden*.

Traubel went on to be an influential figure in various progressive movements of the time, developing connections with socialists, bohemians, artists, and the Arts and Crafts movement of the early 1900s. From 1890 until his death in 1919, he published a monthly literary magazine, *The Conservator*. In 1905, he began a long relationship with a Canadian couple, Frank and Mildred Bain, during which he apparently had intimate relations with both of them and fathered two children with Mildred.[*] Horace Traubel sent books to the Bains. Each was inscribed to Frank or Mildred or both. During the course of eleven years from 1908, Traubel would send the Bains hundreds of books, most of which he received for review in *The Conservator*.[†]

---

[*] See Marylin J. McKay, "Walt Whitman in Canada: The Sexual Trinity of Horace Traubel and Frank and Mildred Bain", *Walt Whitman Quarterly Review*, Vol. 30, No. 1 (2012), pp. 1–30, http://ir.uiowa.edu/wwqr/vol30/iss1/2

[†] Ibid., p. 8

The cover, title page and page with inscription by Horace Traubel of *A Study in Consciousness: A Contribution to the Science of Psychology* (1904)

1896 – *Yoga Philosophy*, Lectures by Swami Vivekananda

This is the first edition of the book whose full title is *Yoga Philosophy: Lectures Delivered in New York, Winter of 1895–6 by the Swami Vivekananda on Rāja Yoga or Conquering the Internal Nature. Also Patanjali's Yoga Aphorisms, with Commentaries*. It was published by Longmans, Green and Company, London.

Swami Vivekananda (1863–1902) introduced Indian spirituality to the West in the late nineteenth and the early twentieth centuries. His first speech at the Parliament of World's Religions in Chicago in 1893, which began with the electrifying salutation "Sisters and brothers of America", sparked the beginning of his public life, which took a meteor-like course. He established the Vedanta Society of New York in 1894 and the Ramakrishna Mission in Calcutta in 1897.

This book was originally scheduled to have an introduction by the American philosopher William James, but Vivekananda decided to publish this book without the introduction as it was not forthcoming from James.

This copy has an inscription from Swami Saradananda, a student of the swami who also came to the West to teach:

'That intense love which the worldly & indiscriminating friend has for sense enjoyments, may I always feel that same intense love for thee, Oh! my Beloved.'

Pralhada (a great lover of God)

Sincerely yrs

Saradananda

YOGA PHILOSOPHY

LECTURES

DELIVERED IN NEW YORK, WINTER OF 1895-6

BY THE

SWÂMI VIVEKÂNANDA

ON

RÂJA YOGA

OR CONQUERING THE INTERNAL NATURE

ALSO PATANJALI'S YOGA APHORISMS, WITH COMMENTARIES.

LONGMANS, GREEN, AND CO.
LONDON, NEW YORK, AND BOMBAY.
1896
All rights reserved.

"That intense love which the worldly & indiscriminate mind has for sense enjoyments, may I always feel that same intense love for Thee Oh! my Beloved"

Prahlada
(A great lover of God)

Sincerely yrs
Saradânanda

RÂJA YOGA

The cover, the title page and page with
inscription by Swami Saradananda of
Yoga Philosophy (1896)

Inserted in this volume is a loose sheet with a parable written out (and signed) by Swami Saradananda:

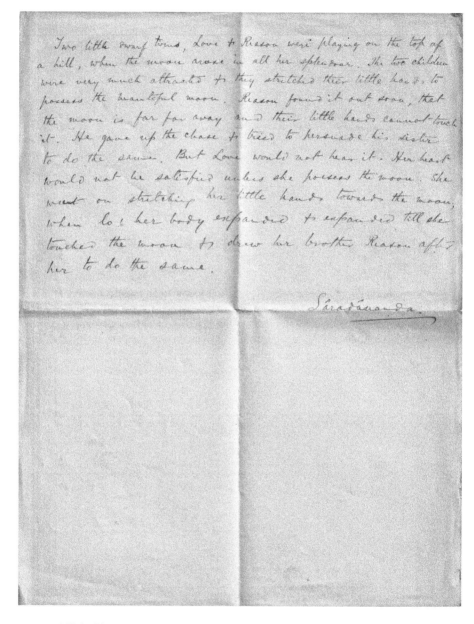

MS leaf by Swami Saradananda (undated) found in *Yoga Philosophy* (1896)

Two little dwarf twins, Love & Reason, were playing on the top of a hill, when the moon arose in all her splendor. The two children were very much attracted & they stretched their little hands to possess the beautiful moon. Reason found it out soon, that the moon is far far away and their little hands cannot touch it. He gave up the chase and tried to persuade his sister to do the same. But Love would not hear it. Her heart would not be satisfied unless she possess the moon. She went on stretching her little hands toward the moon when lo! her body expanded & expanded till she touched the moon & drew her brother Reason after her to do the same.

Saradananda

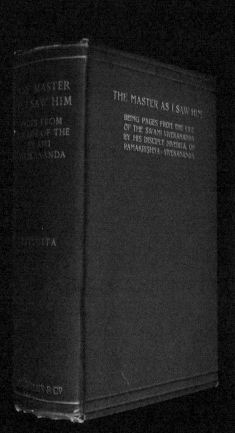

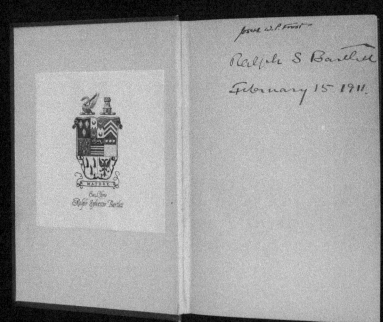

The cover, page with ownership inscription by Ralph S. Bartlett and the title page of
The Master as I saw Him (1910)

1910 – *The Master as I Saw Him* by Nivedita

This volume is the first edition of *The Master as I Saw Him: Being Pages from the Life of Swami Vivekananda by His Disciple – Nivedita*, with the ownership inscription of Ralph S. Bartlett. It was published by Longmans, Green and Company, London and New York, and printed by S.C. Ghose at the Lakshmi Printing Works, Calcutta.

Sister Nivedita (1867–1911) was born in Ireland as Margaret Noble. She became a devoted follower of Swami Vivekananda and moved to India to start a school at his request. Ralph S. Bartlett had a complex relationship with an American disciple of Swami Vivekananda, Sarah Chapman Bull (whom Vivekananda referred to as his "Mother"). Bartlett, an attorney and a photographer, had an affair and then a child with Sarah Bull's daughter, Olea. Upon her mother's death, Olea and Bartlett brought suit against the Sarah Chapman Bull estate to be sure that the Vedanta Society did not get any money – Sarah had left the bulk of her considerable estate to further Swami Vivekananda's work in India. This "scandalous trial" was front-page news in 1911. Olea and Bartlett were successful in their suit. Regardless of the interesting (and perhaps not so savoury) provenance, the book is an excellent and inspiring chronicle of what it was like for a Western female disciple to spend considerable time with her spiritual teacher, Swami Vivekananda.

1912 – *My Master* by Swami Vivekananda

This is the fourth edition of *My Master* by Swami Vivekananda with an appended extract from the *Theistic Quarterly Review*, October 1879. It was published by The Baker & Taylor Company, New York. The first edition was published in 1901, by the same publisher. The swami originally delivered this as a lecture in New York under the auspices of the Vedanta Society. The subject of the book is the message of Vivekananda's Master, Sri Ramakrishna Paramahamsa (1836–1886).

> Therefore, my Master's message to mankind is, 'Be spiritual and realize truth for yourself.' … To proclaim and make clear the fundamental unity underlying all religions was the mission of my Master.

p. 68

Swami Vivekananda's signature was a visual statement! This is a photo of his autograph in a copy of his book *Raja Yoga* (1896). Note that he abbreviated "yours affectionately" and signed "Vivekananda."

MY MASTER

BY THE
SWÂMI VIVEKÂNANDA

WITH AN APPENDED EXTRACT
FROM THE
THEISTIC QUARTERLY REVIEW

FOURTH EDITION.

NEW YORK
THE BAKER & TAYLOR COMPANY
1912

The cover and title page
of *My Master* (1912)

Signature of Swami
Vivekananda (courtesy of Kent
Bicknell)

Modern India's Gift

My poetry is for my countrymen, my paintings are my gift to the West.

Rabindranath Tagore

My life is my message.

Mahatma Gandhi

Rabindranath Tagore and Mahatma Gandhi were the two luminaries who rose in the East and ushered the dawn of a new era. Tagore the *jnanayogi* and Gandhi the *karmayogi* differed considerably in more ways than their physical appearances. But both fought on the same battlefield, the conscience of mankind, and for the same goals, the freedom and dignity of man. The Mahatma fasted his body almost to death and freed his soul. The poet sang his heart out and let the spirit soar. Together, they resurrected the phoenix.

RABINDRANATH TAGORE

The cover, autograph signature of Rabindranath Tagore
and title page of *Gitanjali* (1912)

GITANJALI

(SONG OFFERINGS)

BY

RABINDRA NATH TAGORE

18   GITANJALI

35

WHERE the mind is without fear and the
head is held high;

Where knowledge is free;

Where the world has not been broken up into
fragments by narrow domestic walls;

Where words come out from the depth of truth;

Where tireless striving stretches its arms towards perfection;

Where the clear stream of reason has not lost its
way into the dreary desert sand of dead habit;

Where the mind is led forward by thee into
ever-widening thought and action—

Into that heaven of freedom, my Father, let my
country awake.

Page 18 (poem number 35) in *Gitanjali* (1912)

1912 – *Gitanjali*, First Appearance in Book Format

Gitanjali (Song Offerings) is a collection of prose poems by Rabindranath Tagore that he translated into English from their original Bengali. This is a copy of the limited edition of *Gitanjali*, its very first appearance in book format. This was published for the India Society, London, by the Chiswick Press. The book contains an engraving of the poet by William Rothenstein and a glowing introduction by William Butler Yeats. 750 copies were printed, of which only 250 were for sale. This copy comes with an autograph card signed by Tagore.

The Nobel Prize for Literature in 1913 brought instantaneous fame to *Gitanjali* and its author. The first non-European to win a Nobel Prize in Literature, Tagore became a household name at the age of 54. In his "God-the-Father" image, with his message of brotherhood among men and peace among nations, Tagore would tirelessly trek the globe for the next twenty-nine years.

> Thou hast made me endless, such is thy pleasure.
> This frail vessel thou emptiest again and again, and fillest it ever with fresh life.
> This little flute of a reed thou has carried over hills and dales,
> and hast breathed through it melodies eternally new.
> At the immortal touch of thy hands my little heart loses its limits in a joy and gives birth to utterance ineffable.
> Thy infinite gifts come to me only on these very small hands of mine.
> Ages pass, and still thou pourest, and still there is room to fill.
>
> p. 1

> Leave this chanting and singing and telling of beads! Whom dost thou worship in this lonely dark corner of a temple with doors all shut? Open thine eyes and see thy God is not before thee!
>
> He is where the tiller is tilling the hard ground and where the path-maker is breaking stones. He is with them in sun and in shower and his garment is covered with dust. Put off thy holy mantle and even like him come down on the dusty soil!
>
> pp. 5–6

Gitanjali's songs and Tagore's voice reverberate through the ages.

1913 – *Gitanjali,* First Trade Edition

Gitanjali is a collection of prose poems by Tagore which he translated from their original Bengali, and presented to William Rothenstein, his host in England in 1912. A limited edition was published for the India Society, London, with an introduction by W.B. Yeats by Chiswick Press in 1912. This is the first trade edition, published by Macmillan, London, and printed by R. & R. Clark, Edinburgh. Most pages of this book are still uncut.

> These translations are of poems contained in three books – Naivedya, Kheya, and Gitanjali – to be had at the Indian Publishing House, 22 Cornwallis Street, Calcutta; and of a few poems which have appeared only in periodicals.
>
> Publisher's Note

The book contains an etching of the author's portrait by William Rothenstein and an introduction by W.B. Yeats.

There are "Some Press Opinions" in the back pages:

> Only the classics of mystical literature provide a standard by which this handful of 'Song Offerings' can be appraised or understood. … They are 'offerings,' from finite to infinite – oblations, as their creator holds that all art should be, laid upon the altar of the world.
>
> *The Nation*

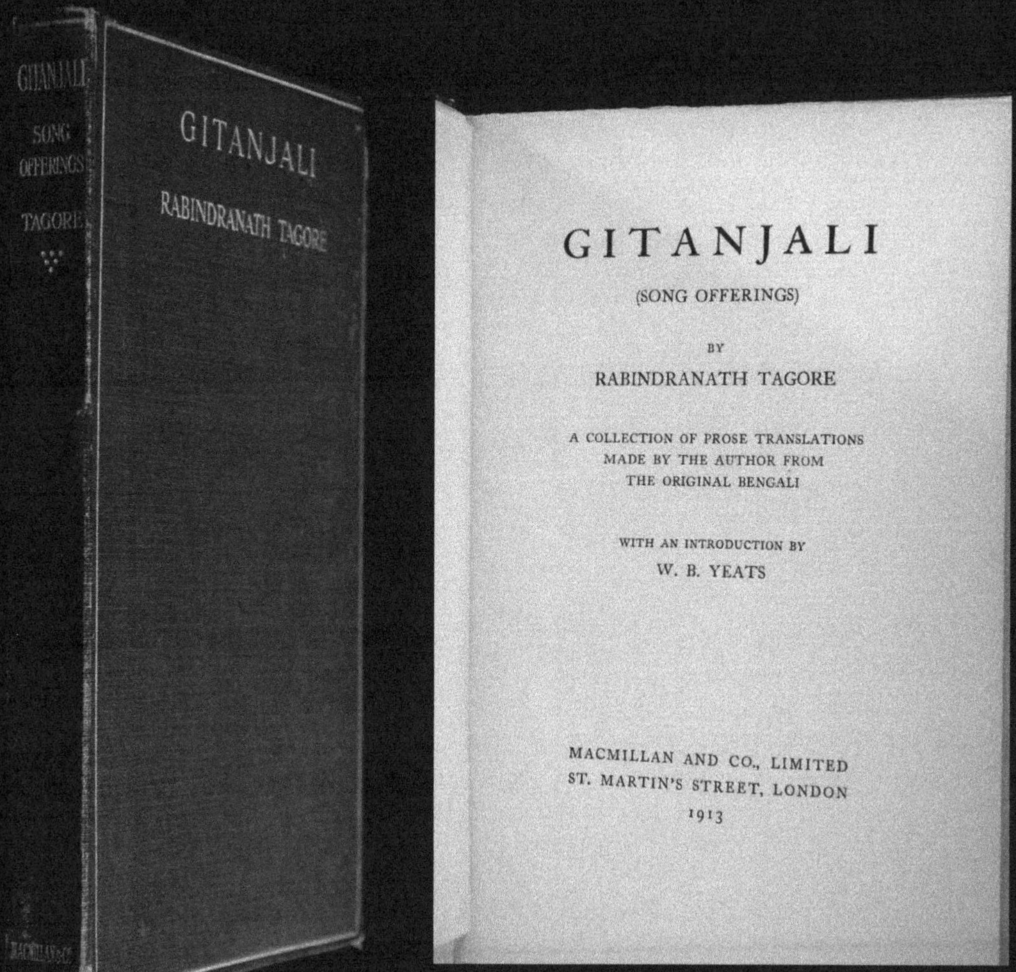

GITANJALI
SONG
OFFERINGS
TAGORE
GITANJALI
RABINDRANATH TAGORE
GITANJALI
(SONG OFFERINGS)
BY
RABINDRANATH TAGORE
A COLLECTION OF PROSE TRANSLATIONS
MADE BY THE AUTHOR FROM
THE ORIGINAL BENGALI
WITH AN INTRODUCTION BY
W. B. YEATS
MACMILLAN AND CO., LIMITED
ST. MARTIN'S STREET, LONDON
1913

The cover and title page of *Gitanjali* (1913)

1913 – *Chitra*

This first English translation of *Chitra, A Play in One Act* by
Rabindranath Tagore was published by the India Society, London, in 1913.
Five hundred copies of this edition were printed at the Chiswick Press,
Charles Whittingham Company, London, of which only two hundred and
fifty copies were for sale.

In this dramatic rendition of the love story between Chitrāngadā, the
daughter of the king of Manipur, and Arjuna, one of the five Pandava
brothers, in the Hindu epic the *Mahabharata*, Tagore throws light on the
transience of physical beauty and the endurance of spiritual beauty.

1913 – *Sādhanā*

Sādhanā: The Realization of Life is a collection of essays. This is the first edition of the book. It was published by the Macmillan Company, New York.

Perhaps it is well for me to explain that the subject-matter of the papers published in this book has not been philosophically treated, nor has it been approached from a scholar's point of view. The writer has been brought up in a family where texts of the Upanishads are used for daily worship; and he had before him the example of his father, who lived his long life in the closest communion with God, while not neglecting his duties to the world, or allowing his keen interest in all human affairs to suffer any abatement. So in these papers,

219

it may be hoped, western readers will have an opportunity of coming into touch with the ancient spirit of India as revealed in our sacred texts and manifested in the life of to-day.

From the Preface

The civilization of ancient Greece was nurtured within city walls. In fact, all the modern civilizations have their cradles of brick and mortar. These walls leave their mark deep in the minds of men. They set up a principle of 'divide and rule' in our mental outlook, which begets in us a habit of securing all our conquests by fortifying them and separating them from one another. We divide nation and nation, knowledge and knowledge, man and nature. It breeds in us a strong suspicion of whatever is beyond the barriers we have built, and everything has to fight hard for its entrance into our recognition.

"The Relation of the Individual to the Universe", p. 3

One day I was in a boat on the Ganges. It was a beautiful evening in autumn. The sun had just set; the silence of the sky was full to the brim with ineffable peace and beauty. The vast expanse of water was without a ripple, mirroring all the changing shades of the sunset glow. Miles and miles of a desolate sandbank lay like a huge amphibious reptile of some antediluvian age, with its scales glistening in shining colors. As our boat was silently gliding by the precipitous river-bank, riddled with the nest holes of a colony of birds, suddenly a big fish leapt up to the surface of the water and then disappeared, displaying on its vanishing figure all the colors of the evening sky. It drew aside for a moment the many-coloured screen behind which there was a silent world full of the joy of life. It came up from the depth of its mysterious dwelling with a beautiful dancing motion and added its own music to the silent symphony of the dying day. I felt as if I had a friendly greeting from an alien world in its own language, and it touched my heart with a flash of gladness. Then suddenly the man at the helm exclaimed with a distinct note of regret, 'Ah, what a big fish!' It at once brought before his vision the picture of the fish caught and made ready for his supper. He could only look at the fish through his desire, and thus missed the whole truth of its existence.

"Realization of Love", pp. 110–11

1913 – *The Crescent Moon*

The Crescent Moon contains child-poems translated from the original Bengali by the author. Macmillan and Company, London, published this first edition. It was printed at the University Press by Robert Maclehose and Company (Glasgow). Tagore dedicated this book to T. Sturge Moore. There are eight illustrations in colour, including from drawings by Nandalal Bose.

> When I bring you coloured toys, my child, I understand why there is such a play of colours on clouds, on water, and why flowers are painted in tints – when I give coloured toys to you, my child.
>
> When I sing to make you dance, I truly know why there is music in leaves, and why waves send their chorus of voices to the heart of the listening earth – when I sing to make you dance.
>
> When I bring sweet things to your greedy hands, I know why there is honey in the cup of the flower, and why fruits are secretly filled with sweet juice – when I bring sweet things to your greedy hands.
>
> …
>
> "When and Why", p. 18

THE
CRESCENT MOON

BY

RABINDRANATH TAGORE

TRANSLATED FROM THE ORIGINAL BENGALI
BY THE AUTHOR

WITH EIGHT ILLUSTRATIONS
IN COLOUR

MACMILLAN AND CO., LIMITED
ST. MARTIN'S STREET, LONDON
1913

To Shanti (Mukles)
on her 21st Birth-Day
with love and admiration
DAD.

The cover, the title page, Illustration by Nandalal Bose and page with inscription
by James Mathew of *The Crescent Moon* (1913)

Supposing I became a 'champa' flower, just for fun, and grew on a branch
high up that tree, and shook in the wind with laughter
and danced upon the newly budded leaves,
would you know me, mother?

You would call, 'Baby, where are you?' and I should laugh
to myself and keep quite quiet.

I should slyly open my petals and watch you
at your work.

When after your bath, with wet hair spread on your shoulders,
you walked through the shadow of the 'champa' tree
to the little court where you say your prayers,
you would notice the scent of the flower,
but not know that it came from me.

"The Champa Flower", p. 29

...

You have stained your fingers and face with ink while writing – is that why they
call you dirty?

O, fie! Would they dare to call the full moon dirty because it has smudged its
face with ink?

...

They make a long list of your misdeeds. Everybody knows how you love sweet
things – is that why they call you greedy?

O, fie! What then would they call us who love you?

"Defamation", p. 20–1

The T.G.M. Rare Book Museum has another copy of *The Crescent Moon,
Child-Poems*, published by Macmillan and Company, New York, in 1914.
This copy has an inscription on the front page: "To Shanti/on her 21st
Birth Day/with love and admiration/Dad."

2012 – *Gitanjali*, First Draft Manuscript Facsimile

This is a special-edition facsimile of the original manuscript of *Gitanjali*
brought by Rabindranath Tagore on his initial visit to William Rothenstein
in Oak Hill Park, UK. It was published by the Ministry of Culture,
Government of India, and it was printed by Shishu Sahitya Samsad,
Kolkata, India. This edition was brought out as part of the poet's 150th
birth anniversary celebration in 2012. It was for distribution only.

The original manuscript is part of the Rothenstein Collection preserved in
the Houghton Library of Harvard University in Cambridge, MA.

The inscription in ink by William Rothenstein reads:

> Original manuscript of Gitanjali
> which the poet brought me from India
> on his initial visit to us in Oak Hill
> Park.

Tagore's scheduled voyage to England on 19 March 1912 was cancelled
because of his ill health. He retired to Silaidaha on 24 March, for recuper-
ation. There he began translating some of his work in his "exercise
books." Tagore sailed to England from Bombay on 27 May and reached
London on 16 June. Swapan Majumdar, in an accompanying essay in this
book, writes that Tagore's son Rathindranath, who accompanied him to

GITANJALI
first draft manuscript

Rabindranath Tagore

Ministry of Culture
Government of India

original manuscript of Gitanjali which The poet brought me from India on his initial visit to us at Oak Hill Park.

I have got my leave. Bid me farewell, my brothers! I bow to you all and take my departure.
Here I give back the keys of my door—and I give up all claims to my house. I only ask for last kind words from you.
We were neighbours for long, but I received more than I could give. Now the day has dawned and the lamp that lit my dark corner is out. The summons have come and I am ready for my journey.

The cover, title page, page with inscription by William Rothenstein and a page of facsimile of *Gitanjali* First Draft Manuscript Facsimile (2012)

England, lost his father's briefcase containing the two "exercise books" at the rail station in Charing Cross. Fortunately, it was retrieved from the Left Luggage Office. Tagore presented the "notebooks" to Rothenstein, who made three sets of typescripts and sent them to William Butler Yeats, at Bradley and Stopford Brooke.

The path of *Gitanjali* and its author from that point has hardly a parallel in the history of literature. The very next year, 1913, Rabindranath Tagore became the first non-European Nobel Prize Laureate in Literature.

H.M. George Frederick Ernest Albert, King of the United Kingdom, and Emperor of India, bestowed a Knighthood upon Tagore in 1915, only to be renounced by Tagore following the Jallianwala Bagh massacre. On 30 May 1919, Tagore wrote to H.E. Lord Chelmsford, the Viceroy of India:

> The time has come when badges of honor make our shame glaring in their incongruous context of humiliation, and I for my part wish to stand, shorn of all special distinctions, by the side of my country men.

1914 – *The Post Office*

This volume is a special edition of *The Post Office: A Play by Rabindranath Tagore Translated by Devabrata Mukerjea.* Four hundred numbered copies were printed on hand-made paper, and its pages are still uncut – this is number 126. It was published by Elizabeth C. Yeats (Dublin, Ireland). W.B. Yeats wrote a preface to this edition:

> When this little play was performed in London a year ago by the Irish players, some friends of mine discovered much detailed allegory, the Headman being one principle of social life, the Curdseller or the Gaffer another; but the meaning is less intellectual, more emotional and simple. The deliverance sought and won by the dying child is the same deliverance which rose before his imagination, Mr. Tagore said, when once in the early dawn he heard amid the noise of a crowd returning from some festival, this line out of an old village song, 'Ferryman, take me to the other shore of the river.' It may come at any moment of life, though the child discovers it in death, for it always comes at the moment when the 'I,' seeking no longer for gains that cannot be 'assimilated with its spirit,' is able to say, 'All my work is thine' ('Sādhanā', pp. 162, 163). On the stage the little play shows that it is very perfectly constructed, and conveys to the right audience an emotion of gentleness and peace.

The last page of this special edition is reproduced here:

Sudha: Amal!

Physician: He's asleep.

Sudha: I have some flowers for him. Mayn't I give them into his own hands?

Physician: Yes, you may.

Sudha: When will he be awake?

Physician: Directly the king comes and calls him.

Sudha: Will you whisper a word for me in his ear?

Physician: What shall I say?

Sudha: Tell him Sudha has not forgotten him.

Here ends 'The Post Office' a play by Rabindranath Tagore, translated by Devabrath Mukerjea with a preface by William Butler Yeats. Printed and published by Elizabeth C. Yeats at the Cuala Press, Churchtown, Dundrum, in the County of Dublin, Ireland. Finished on Saint John's Eve in the year nineteen hundred and fourteen.

Elizabeth Corbet Yeats (1868–1940) was W.B. Yeats' sister.

The *Post Office* is about anticipation of "deliverance". The night Paris fell to the Axis forces in June 1940, Radio France broadcast *The Post Office*.

The T.G.M. Rare Book Museum has another copy of *The Post Office*, the first edition published by the Macmillan Company, New York, in 1914. This edition does not mention the translator's name, and it does not have a preface by W.B. Yeats. This copy is stamped:

Advance copy for editorial use
Review released for publication
APR 2, 1914.

THE GARDENER

BY

RABINDRANATH TAGORE

TRANSLATED BY THE AUTHOR FROM
THE ORIGINAL BENGALI

New York
THE MACMILLAN COMPANY
1915

THE GARDENER

Rabindranath Tagore

The title page and page with the signature of Rabindranath Tagore of *The Gardener* (1915)

1915 – *The Gardener*, Signed by Tagore

This is an early edition of *The Gardener* signed by the author. *The Gardener* was a spillover from *Gitanjali* of Rabindranath Tagore's translations from his original Bengali verses. This book was dedicated to W.B. Yeats. First published by the Macmillan Company in October 1913, it was reprinted in December 1913, January, February, March, April, July and October 1914, and March 1915.

> Most of the lyrics of love and life, the translations of which from Bengali are published in this book, were written much earlier than the series of religious poems contained in the book named 'Gitanjali.' The translations are not always literal – the originals being sometimes abridged and sometimes paraphrased.
>
> From the Preface

> The tame bird was in a cage, the free bird was in the forest.
> They met when the time came, it was a decree of fate.
>
> The free bird cries, 'O my love, let us fly to wood.'
> The cage bird whispers, 'come hither, let us both live in the cage.'
>
> Says the free bird, 'Among bars, where is there room to spread one's wings?'
>
> 'Alas,' cries the cage bird, 'I should not know where to sit perched in the sky.'
>
> From poem 6, pp. 14–15

> Who are you, reader, reading my poems an hundred years hence?
> I cannot send you one single flower from this wealth of the spring, one single streak of gold from yonder clouds.
>
> From the last poem, p. 146

1915 – *Six Portraits of Sir Rabindranath Tagore*

This is the first edition of *Six Portraits of Sir Rabindranath Tagore* by William Rothenstein. It was published by Macmillan and Company, London. It includes a prefatory note by Max Beerbohm (1872–1956):

> With all deference to photographers, and to such artists as hopefully vie with them on their own ground, one may take it to be rather through the eyes of Mr. William Rothenstein that posterity will regard the sages of our day.

Selected portraits from the *Six Portraits of Rabindranath Tagore* (1915)

RABINDRANATH TAGORE
FROM THE PORTRAIT IN COLOURS BY SASI KUMAR HESH

MY REMINISCENCES

BY
SIR RABINDRANATH TAGORE

WITH FRONTISPIECE FROM THE PORTRAIT
IN COLORS BY SASI KUMAR HESH

New York
THE MACMILLAN COMPANY
1917

The title page of *My Reminiscences* (1917) with a painting of Rabindranath Tagore
by Sasi Kumar Hesh on the frontispiece

1917 – *My Reminiscences*

The first edition of this English translation of *My Reminiscences* contains a portrait of Tagore in colour by Sasi Kumar Hesh on the frontispiece. It was published by the Macmillan Company in April 1917. This volume is marked "Advertisement copy not for sale".

> I know not who paints the pictures on memory's canvass; but whoever he may be, what he is painting are pictures; by which I mean that he is not there with his brush simply to make a faithful copy of all that is happening. … In short he is painting pictures, not writing history.
>
> p. 1

> The end of Sudder Street, and the trees on the Free School grounds opposite, were visible from our Sudder Street house. One morning I happened to be standing on the verandah looking that way. The sun was just rising through the leafy tops of those trees. As I continued to gaze, all of a sudden a covering seemed to fall away from my eyes, and I found the world bathed in a wonderful radiance, with waves of beauty and joy swelling on every side. This radiance pierced in a moment through the folds of sadness and despondency which had accumulated over my heart, and flooded it with this universal light.

> That very day the poem, 'The Awakening of the Waterfall,' gushed forth and coursed on like a veritable cascade. The poem came to an end, but the curtain did not fall upon the joy aspect of the Universe. And it came to be so that no portion or thing in the world seemed to me trivial or unpleasing.
>
> "Morning Songs", p. 216

1917 – *Nationalism*, Limited Edition

This special edition of *Nationalism* by Rabindranath Tagore is a collection of four essays published by Macmillan and Company for the Book Club of California, San Francisco, CA. The book is "COPYRIGHT, 1917, BY THE ATLANTIC MONTHLY COMPANY/COPYRIGHT, 1916 AND 1917, BY THE MACMILLAN COMPANY". Two hundred and fifty copies of this special edition were printed on Tuscany hand-made paper, of which this copy is No. 157. Its pages are still uncut. Tagore dedicated the book to C.F. Andrews. (For more on C.F. Andrews, see 1930 – *Mahatma Gandhi's Ideas*, p. 265.)

'Nationalism in the West' is one of a series of lectures delivered throughout the United States during the winter of 1916–17. 'Nationalism in Japan' is based upon two lectures delivered in Japan before the Imperial University and the Keio Gijuku University in June and July, 1916. 'Nationalism in India' written in the United States late in 1916, is the poet's reflection upon the state of his own country, and gives world-wide completeness to the discussion of Nationalism. The poem at the conclusion of the book 'The Sunset of the Century,' was written on the last day of the last century.

From the Preface

The last lines of "The Sunset of the Century" are:

> Be not ashamed, my brothers, to stand before the
> proud and the powerful
> > With your white robe of simpleness.
> Let your crown be of humility, your freedom the
> > freedom of the soul.
> Build God's throne daily upon the ample bareness
> > of your poverty
> And know that what is huge is not great and pride
> > is not everlasting.

p. 159

1919 – *The Home and the World*

Tagore wrote *The Home and the World* in Bengali in 1916. Surendranath Tagore translated the novel into English and the author revised it. This first English edition was published by Macmillan and Company, New York. Set in the context of India's struggle for independence, Tagore depicts the three principal characters of the story caught in tumultuous and conflicting internal and external forces.

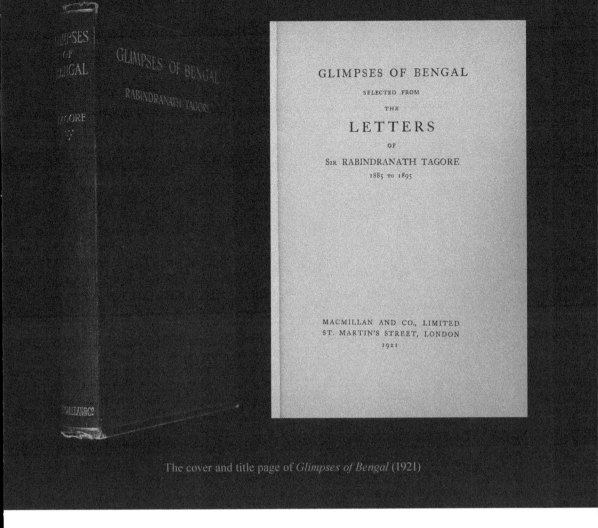

GLIMPSES OF BENGAL

SELECTED FROM

THE

LETTERS

OF

Sir RABINDRANATH TAGORE

1885 to 1895

MACMILLAN AND CO., LIMITED
ST. MARTIN'S STREET, LONDON

1921

The cover and title page of *Glimpses of Bengal* (1921)

1921 – *Glimpses of Bengal*

This is the first edition of *Glimpses of Bengal, Selected from The Letters of Sir. Rabindranath Tagore 1885 to 1895*, published by Macmillan and Company, London.

> The letters translated in this book span the most productive period of my literary life, when, owing to great good fortune, I was young and less known. …

> Hoping that the descriptions of village scenes in Bengal contained in these letters would also be of interest to English readers, the translation of a selection of that selection has been entrusted to one who, among all those whom I know, was best fitted to carry it out.

> 20th June 1920

> From the Introduction by Tagore

I am reminded of an incident at Shazadpur. My servant was late one morning, and I was greatly annoyed at his delay. He came up and stood before me with his usual 'salaam,' and with a slight catch in his voice explained that his eight-year-old daughter had died last night. Then, with his duster, he set to tidying up my room.

Shelidah, 14 August 1895, pp. 160–1

The night was far advanced. I closed the book with a bang and flung it on the table. Then I blew out the lamp with the idea of turning into bed. No sooner had I done so than, through the open windows, the moonlight burst into the room, with a shock of surprise. … What, for sooth, had I been looking for in the empty wordiness of the book? There was the very thing itself, filling the skies, silently waiting for me outside, all these hours!

If I had gone off to bed leaving the shutters closed, and thus missed this vision, it would have stayed there all the same without any protest against the mocking lamp inside. Even if I had remained blind to it all my life, – letting the lamp triumph to the end, – till for the last time I went darkling to bed, – even then the moon would have still been there, sweetly smiling, unperturbed and unobtrusive, waiting for me as she has throughout the ages.

Shelidah, 12 December 1895, pp. 165–6

1931 – *The Religion of Man*

This is the first edition of *The Religion of Man, Being the Hibbert Lectures for 1930*, published by Macmillan Company, New York.

The chapters included in this book, which comprises the Hibbert Lectures delivered in Oxford, at Manchester College, during the month of May 1930, contain also the gleanings of my thoughts on the same subject from the harvest of many lectures and addresses delivered in different countries of the world over a considerable period of my life.

September 1930

From the Introduction by Tagore

I felt that I had found my religion at last, the religion of Man, in which the infinite became defined in humanity and came close to me so as to need my love and co-operation.

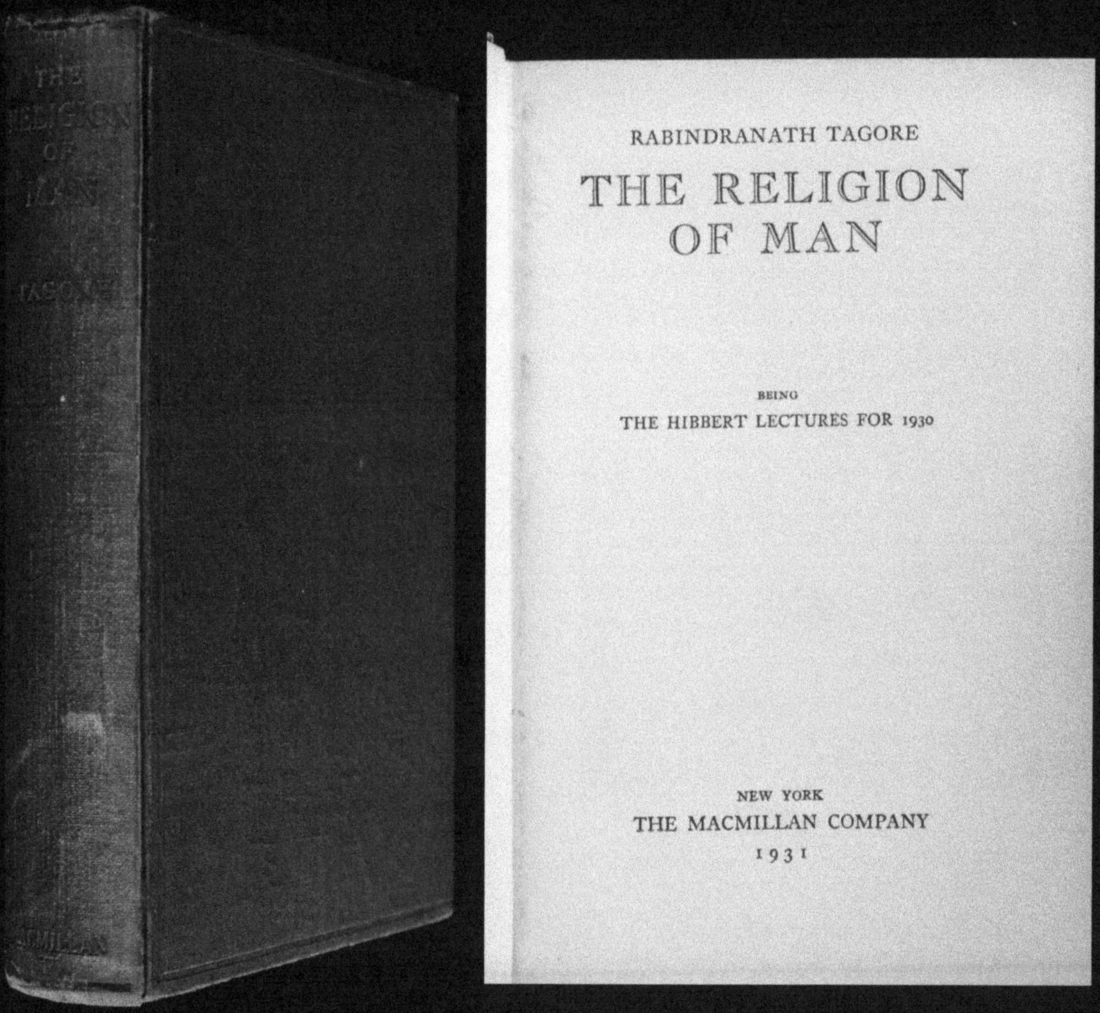

RABINDRANATH TAGORE

THE RELIGION
OF MAN

BEING
THE HIBBERT LECTURES FOR 1930

NEW YORK
THE MACMILLAN COMPANY
1931

The cover and title page of *The Religion of Man* (1931)

This idea of mine found at a later date its expression in some of my poems addressed to what I called 'Jivan devata,' the Lord of my life. Fully aware of my awkwardness in dealing with a foreign language, with some hesitation I give a translation, being sure that any evidence revealed through the self-recording instrument of poetry is more authentic than answers extorted through conscious questionings:

Thou who art the innermost Spirit of my being,
art thou pleased,
  Lord of my life?
For I gave to thee my cup
filled with all the pain and delight
that the crushed grapes of my heart had surrendered,
I wove with the rhythm of colors and songs the cover
  for thy bed,
and with the molten gold of my desires
I fashioned playthings for thy passing hours.

I know not why thou chosest me for thy partner,
  Lord of my life!

p. 95

1930 – *The Golden Book of Tagore*

This volume is number 674 of only 1,500 copies published by The Golden Book of Tagore Committee and printed at the Art Press, Calcutta, in December 1931. A tribute presented to Rabindranath Tagore on his 70th birthday by luminaries from home and abroad, it was sponsored by Mohandas Karamchand Gandhi, Romain Rolland, Albert Einstein, Kostes Palmas and Jagdis Chandra Bose. This volume contains a portrait of the poet based on a photograph by Martin Vos, and a facsimile of Tagore's reply on Viswa Bharati letterhead which reads:

It is hard for me to say in a few faltering words how I feel when voices greet me from my own country and from across the seas carrying to me the assurance that I have pleased many and have helped some and thus offering me the best reward of my life.

Dec. 27, 1931

THE GOLDEN BOOK OF TAGORE

A HOMAGE TO RABINDRANATH TAGORE
□ FROM INDIA AND THE WORLD □
IN CELEBRATION OF HIS SEVENTIETH BIRTHDAY

EDITED BY RAMANANDA CHATTERJEE
PUBLISHED BY THE GOLDEN BOOK COMMITTEE
CALCUTTA 1931

It is hard for me to say in a few
faltering words how I feel when voices
greet me from my own country and from
across the seas carrying to me the
assurance that I have pleased many
and have helped some and thus offering
me the best reward of my life

Rabindranath Tagore

Dec. 27, 1931

The cover, title page, a portrait of Rabindranath
Tagore on the frontispiece and inserted letter
from Tagore of *The Golden Book of Tagore*
(1930)

1961 – *Rabindranath Tagore: A Centenary Volume 1861–1961*

This book is "an offering to the memory of Rabindranath Tagore on the occasion of the Centenary of his birth." This is the first edition published by the Sahitya Akademi, New Delhi. The book has an introduction by Jawaharlal Nehru (1889–1964), the then Prime Minister of India:

> I have seldom been so hesitant about writing on any subject as I have felt about the writing of this Introduction to a book about Rabindranath Tagore. … Why have I been so reluctant?
>
> p. xiii

The book was planned and edited under the guidance of Dr. Sarvepally Radhakrishnan (1888–1975) who also wrote the tribute "Most Dear to All the Muses":

> What the world needs to-day is universal charity. In Hungary, near the Balaton Lake where he recouped from his illness, he planted a tree on 8 November 1926, and wrote in the Guest Book the following lines:
>
> > When I am no longer on this earth, my tree
> > Let the ever renewed leaves of thy spring
> > murmur to the wayfarers,
> > 'The poet did love while he lived.'
>
> In all his writings of great diversity and depth, he expressed the quality of the individual spirit, the spirit that is indestructible. In his best poems there are things which move the heart and fill the mind and which will live for long.
>
> p. xxv

This volume contains a copy of a pastel drawing of Rabindranath Tagore by Abanindranath Tagore (1871–1951), the poet's nephew.

RABINDRANATH TAGORE

A Centenary Volume 1861-1961

A Centenary
Volume

RABINDRANATH
TAGORE

1861-1961

SAHITYA AKADEMI
NEW DELHI

1961 – *Drawings and Paintings of Rabindranath Tagore, Centenary 1861–1961*

This is the first edition of the book published by Lalit Kala Academy as part of the centenary celebration of Rabindranath Tagore's birth. Its sole distributors were the Publication Division, Ministry of Information and Broadcasting, Delhi. The book consists of plates of selected drawings and paintings by Tagore produced under the supervision of Satyajit Ray, the eminent Indian filmmaker. It was printed at the Eagle Lithographing Company, Calcutta, on special paper made for the occasion by India Paper Pulp Company.

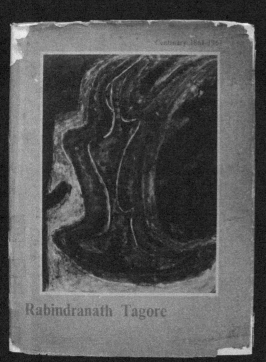
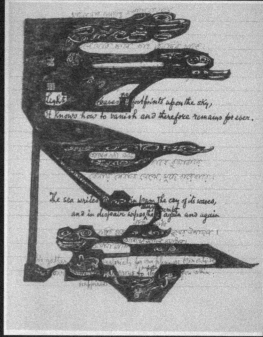

Selections from the *Drawings and Paintings of Rabindranath Tagore* (1961)

1961 – *Towards Universal Man*

This is the first edition of *Towards Universal Man*, a compilation of Tagore's essays. It was published by Asia Publishing House, Bombay, on behalf of the Tagore Commemorative Volume Society, New Delhi, in collaboration with the Ford Foundation, New York, and printed at Sree Saraswathy Press, Calcutta. It was published on 7 May 1961 to mark the centenary of the birth of the poet.

On 7 May 1941, on his 80th birthday, too weak to speak, the poet had his essay "Crisis in Civilization" read at Shantiniketan. Excerpts from an English translation from the original Bengali are given below:

> Today I complete eighty years of my life. As I turn back to the long stretch of years behind me and view them in clearer perspective, I am struck by the change that has taken place in my attitude and in the psychology of my countrymen, a change that is tragic. …
>
> There was a time when I used to believe that the springs of a true civilization would issue out of the heart of Europe. Today as I am about to quit the world, that faith has gone bankrupt. …
>
> I look back on the stretch of past years and see the crumbling ruins of a proud civilization lying heaped as garbage out of history! And yet I shall not commit the grievous sin of losing faith in Man, accepting his present defeat as final. I shall look forward to a turning in history after the cataclysm is over and the sky is again unburdened and passionless.
>
> Perhaps the new dawn will come from this horizon, from the East where the sun rises; and then, unvanquished Man will retrace his path of conquest, despite all barriers, to win back his lost heritage.
>
> The hour is near when it will be revealed that the insolence of might is fraught with great peril; that hour will bear out in full the truth of what the ancient sages have proclaimed:
>
>> 'By unrighteousness man prospers, gains what seems desirable, defeats enemies, but perishes at the root.'
>
> pp. 353–9

Rabindranath Tagore died in his ancestral home in Calcutta on 7 August 1941.

The cover and title page
with portrait of
Rabindranath Tagore on
the frontispiece of
Towards Universal Man
(1961)

TOWARDS
UNIVERSAL MAN

RABINDRANATH TAGORE

ASIA PUBLISHING HOUSE

BOMBAY · CALCUTTA · NEW DELHI
MADRAS · LONDON · NEW YORK

1909 – *The Auto-Biography of Maharshi Devendranath Tagore*

Maharshi Devendranath Tagore (1817–1905) was Rabindranath's father. Satyendranath Tagore (Rabindranath's brother) along with Indira Devi (Satyendranath's daughter) translated the autobiography of Devendranath into English. This volume is the first edition of the English translation. It was published by S.K. Lahiri & Company, Calcutta, and printed at Cotton Press, Calcutta.

This copy belonged to Alice Corbin Henderson who signed and wrote on the front page, "Translated, 5 years/before the UK ed." Alice C. Henderson (1881–1949) was an American poet who was assistant editor to Harriet Monroe, the editor of *Poetry* magazine. As she alluded to, Macmillan and Company, London, published an English translation of the autobiography in 1916.

THE
AUTO-BIOGRAPHY
OF
MAHARSHI DEVENDRANATH TAGORE

(WITH PORTRAITS)

TRANSLATED FROM THE ORIGINAL BENGALI
BY
SATYENDRANATH TAGORE
AND
INDIRA DEVI

Calcutta
S. K. LAHIRI & CO.
54, College Street
1909

Maharshi as Acharya.

The cover, title page, frontispiece with portrait of Devendranath Tagore and ownership inscription of the *Auto-Biography of Maharshi Devendranath Tagore* (1909)

1929–1930 – Rabindranath Tagore, an Autograph Letter

This third and last page of a type-written letter on Shantiniketan letterhead was signed in blue ink by Tagore. The letter was addressed to [probably Vachel] Lindsay. It reads, "I take this occasion to send to Mrs. Lindsay and yourself my kindest regards."

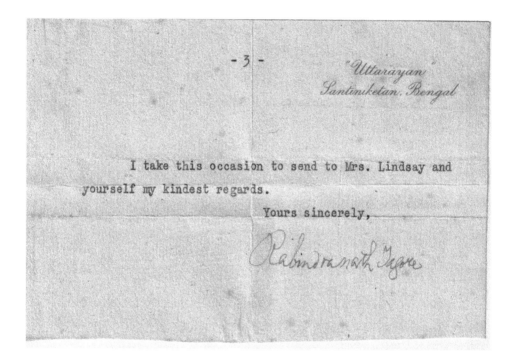

The last page of a letter signed in ink by Rabindranath Tagore (1929–1930)

There is no date on this page of the letter. Tagore visited America in 1912–13, 1916–17, 1920–1, 1929 and 1930. Vachel Lindsay (1879–1931) was an American poet. It is very likely that Vachel Lindsay met Tagore during the latter's visit to the US in 1929 or 1930, because Lindsay only married in 1925, and Tagore sends his regards to "Mrs. Lindsay and yourself."

A Portrait Collage of Rabindranath Tagore

A wire photo of Rabindranath Tagore as he arrives in New York City, NY (1930)

Verso: Famous Hindu mystic poet brings paintings to the U. S.
New York ... Sir Rabindranath Tagore, noted Hindu mystic and poet, arriving today on the S. S. Bremen for a three months visit to the United States following visits to Russia and Germany. The distinguished visitor is shown in a close-up photo just as he was about to land. He is bringing a collection of his own paintings with him, and they will be exhibited at the Boston Art Museum. Tagore won the Nobel Prize for Literature in 1913, and has previously made lecture tours in this country. PS 10-9-30

[Written all in capital letters in the original]

Autographed studio portrait of Rabindranath Tagore by Jindrich
Vanek

Photo autographed by Tagore

Verso:

Archltêkt Vanek, M. R. P. S. Praha
Bolerle vynlkajici asabnostich

Tagore visited Prague in 1921 and 1928. This photo was most probably taken during the second and longer visit to Czechoslovakia (now the Czech Republic and Slovakia). Tagore was highly regarded in Czechoslovakia. Thákurova Street in Prague 6, home to the city's Technical University, is named after Rabindranath Tagore.

Jindrich Vanek (1888–1965) was a Czech photographer better known for his photos of models clad less modestly than the mystic from India!

Studio portrait of Rabindranath Tagore by Norman Taylor (UK)

Verso:

Norman Taylor, 107 High St. Oxford,
Photographs taken by Day & Electric Light

Studio portrait of Rabindranath Tagore by Lizzie Caswall Smith (UK)

Stamped verso:

Copyright Lizzie Caswall Smith
90 Gt. Russell St. WC 1

Lizzie Caswall Smith (1870–1958) was a British photographer who
specialized in celebrity studio portraits. She was at Gainsborough Studio
at 309 Oxford Street from 1907 through 1920. After 1920, her studio was
at 90 Great Russell Street until she retired in 1930.

Wire photo of Rabindranath Tagore in Hindenburg, Germany (1926)

Verso:

International Newsreel ... L 354207
SLUG (Tagore)

Famed Indian philosopher visits Von Hindenburg

Berlin. – Photo shows the famous Indian philosopher, Rabindranath Tagore, leaving the palace of Pres. Von Hindenburg, after visiting the German President. F 9-27-26 A

Wire photo of Rabindranath Tagore with his daughter in Romania (1926)

Verso:

International Newsreel Photo SLUG (Tagore)
Romania. – First photo to arrive here of Rabindranath Tagore, famed Indian poet, with his daughter, who has never before been photographed. The famous poet got a rousing reception from the crowds at the station, later he attended a conference at the national theater where he spoke in the presence of the leading intellectuals and nobles of the country.
F 12-8-26

MOHANDAS K. GANDHI

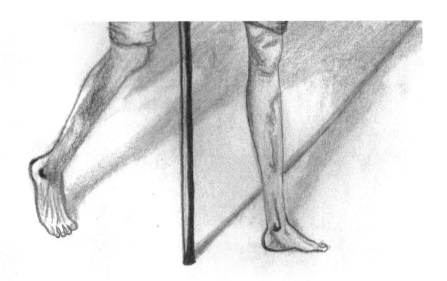

1927 – *Autobiography or The Story of My Experiments with Truth*, Vol. 1 of the First English Edition

This is the first of the two-volume set of the first edition of Mahatma Gandhi's autobiography in English. This was published by Navajivan Publishing House, Ahmedabad, India. Volume 1 covers his life from early childhood through 1921.

Gandhi's autobiography was initially serialized in weekly instalments from 1925 through 1928 in *Navjivan*, the weekly magazine in the Gujarati language that Gandhi edited and published from Ahmedabad. The English translations from the original Gujarati by Mahadave Desai were published in *Young India*, Gandhi's magazine in English. A major part of it was written during Gandhi's imprisonment at the Yerwada Central Jail near Pune.

Mohandas Karamchand Gandhi was born in Porbandar near Ahmedabad in Gujarat State, India, on 2 October 1869. He graduated in Law from the University College, London, England (1891) and went to South Africa (1893) where he led a successful struggle for civil rights for Indians in South Africa, which was then under British rule. Returning to India (1915), Gandhi led India's struggle for freedom from British rule. India won independence on 15 August 1947, but not without Pakistan being carved out of India, to Gandhi's agony. Gandhi was assassinated in New Delhi on 30 January 1948, by Hindu extremists.

While the honour "Mahatma" ("great-soul") is known to have been attributed to Gandhi earlier in the year, it was Rabindranath Tagore who cemented it as synonymous with his first name in 1915.

Mahatma Gandhi's admiration for Henry D. Thoreau's life and writings is well known. However, it is worth pointing out that Gandhi was practising non-violent resistance to state tyranny before he ever heard of Thoreau. In 1907, in the 26 October issue of *Indian Opinion* in South Africa, Gandhi wrote:

> Thoreau was a great writer, philosopher, poet, and withal a most practical man; he taught nothing he was not prepared to practice in himself. He was one of the greatest and most moral men America has produced. At the time of the abolition of slavery movement, he wrote his famous essay, 'On the Duty of Civil Disobedience.' He went to jail for the sake of his principles and suffering

The Story
OR
My Experiments with Truth

By
M. K. GANDHI

Translated from the original in Gujarati
BY
MAHADEV DESAI

NAVAJIVAN PRESS, AHMEDABAD
1927

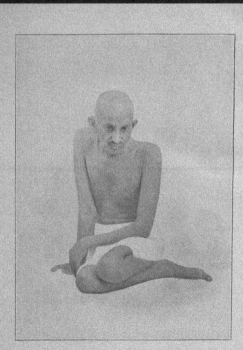

MAHATMA GANDHI

The cover, title page and frontispiece with portrait of Mahatma Gandhi of Volume 1 of the *Autobiography* of Gandhi (1927)

humanity. His essay has, therefore, been sanctified by suffering. Moreover, it is written for all time. Its incisive logic is unanswerable.

Gandhi's letter of 12 October 1929, in response to a request from the Thoreau's biographer, Henry S. Salt, also attests to the fact that Gandhi was already in the midst of his campaign when he first read Thoreau's "Civil Disobedience".

> My first introduction to Thoreau's writings, I think, was in 1907, or later, when I was in the thick of the passive resistance struggle. A friend sent me the essay on 'Civil Disobedience.' It left a deep impression on me. I translated a portion for the readers of 'Indian Opinion' in South Africa, which I was then editing, and I made copious extracts for the English part of the paper. The essay seemed to be so convincing and truthful that I felt the need for knowing more of Thoreau, and I came across your Life of him, his Walden, and other shorter essays, all of which I read with great pleasure and equal profit.

1922 – *Young India, 1919–1922*

This compilation volume of *Young India*, Mahatma Gandhi's magazine in English, was published by Tagore & Company, Madras, India.

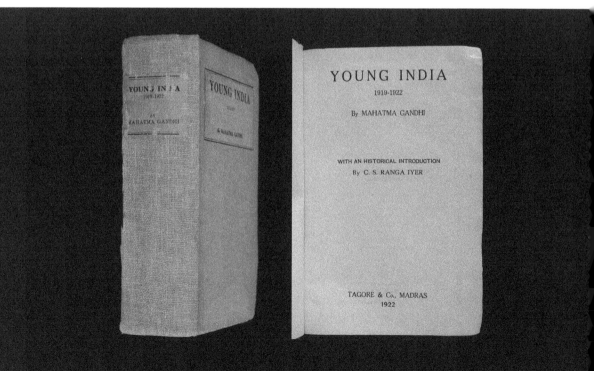

The cover and title page of *Young India, 1919–1922*

The cover and title page of *Young India, 1924–1926*

1926 – *Young India, 1924–1926*

This compilation volume of *Young India, 1924–1926*, Mahatma Gandhi's magazine in English, was published by the Viking Press, New York.

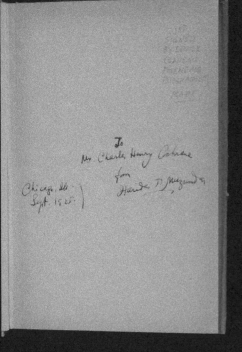

SERMON ON THE SEA

BY

MAHATMA GANDHI

WITH AN

INTRODUCTION

BY

JOHN HAYNES HOLMES
Minister, Community Church, New York City

EDITED BY

HARIDAS T. MUZUMDAR
Author of "Gandhi The Apostle"

"This book is a severe condemnation of modern civilisation."—*Gandhi.*

CHICAGO
UNIVERSAL PUBLISHING CO.
1924

The cover, title page and inscription by the editor, Haridas T. Mazumdar, of *Sermon on the Sea* (1924)

HIND SWARAJ
OR
INDIAN HOME RULE

M. K. GANDHI

NAVAJIVAN PUBLISHING HOUSE
AHMEDABAD

The cover of *Hind Swaraj or Indian Home Rule* (1939)

1924 – *Sermon on the Sea*

This edition of Gandhi's book *Indian Home Rule*, under the title *Sermon on the Sea*, was published by the Universal Publishing Company, Chicago, with an introduction by John Haynes Holmes. The book contains a foreword by Gandhi which was condensed from articles he published in *Young India* in 1921. The editor of the book, Haridas T. Mazumdar, inscribed this copy to Charles Henry Cochrane.

Gandhi wrote a pamphlet titled *Hind Swaraj* (trans. *Indian Home Rule*) in Gujarati during his return voyage from England to South Africa in November 1909. It was written in the style of a Socratic dialogue. It was initially published in Gujarati in the 11 and 18 December issues of the weekly periodical *Indian Opinion* in South Africa in 1909. "It was so much appreciated that it was published as a booklet. It attracted some attention in India. The Bombay Government prohibited its circulation. I replied by publishing its translation", Gandhi wrote. The translation was published by the International Printing Press, Phoenix, Natal, in 1910. The T.G.M. Rare Book Museum has a copy of the revised new edition of *Hind Swaraj or Indian Home Rule* published by Navajivan Publishing House, Ahmedabad, in 1939.

This pamphlet that M.K. Gandhi wrote at sea mentions salt – 21 years before the Mahatma marched to the sea and made salt to challenge the British Empire!

1924 – *Mahatma Gandhi* by Romain Rolland, Inscribed by the Author

Mahatma Gandhi: The Man who Became One with the Universal Being was written by Romain Rolland. This first edition in French was published by Librairie Stock, Paris, in 1924. Romain Rolland (1866–1944) was a French philosopher who won the Nobel Prize in Literature in 1915. Gandhi met him in Switzerland near Villeneuve at the eastern end of Lake Leman on 6 December 1931, on his way back from the Round Table Conference in London.

This volume is a presentation copy in the original French and inscribed by Romain Rolland to James H. Powers.

The last two paragraphs of the book, as translated by Catherine D. Groth (The Century Company, 1924), are reproduced below:

> This is Gandhi's message. The only thing lacking is the cross. Every one knows that had it not been for the Jews, Rome would not have given it to Christ. The British Empire is no better than ancient Rome. The impetus has been given. The soul of Oriental peoples has been moved in its deepest fibers, and its vibrations are felt the whole world over.
>
> The great religious apparitions of the Orient are ruled by a rhythm. One thing is certain; either Gandhi's spirit will triumph, or it will manifest itself again, as were manifested, centuries before, the Messiah and Buddha, till there finally is manifested, in a mortal half-god, the perfect incarnation of the principle of life which will lead a new humanity on to a new path.

ROMAIN ROLLAND

MAHATMA GANDHI

1924
LIBRAIRIE STOCK
Delamain, Boutelleau & Cⁱᵉ
7, rue du Vieux-Colombier
PARIS

MAHATMA GANDHI

The cover, title page and page
with inscription by the author of
Mahatma Gandhi (1924)

MAHATMA GANDHI'S IDEAS

INCLUDING SELECTIONS
FROM HIS WRITINGS

By
C. F. Andrews

NEW YORK
THE MACMILLAN COMPANY
1930

To Miss Anna T. Bogue
with gratitude and
affection
from
C. F. Andrews.

April 2. 1930

The cover, title page and
page with inscription by
the author of *Mahatma
Gandhi's Ideas* (1930)

1930 – *Mahatma Gandhi's Ideas* by C.F. Andrews, Inscribed by the Author

Mahatma Gandhi's Ideas, Including Selections from His Own Writings written by C.F. Andrews was first published by George Allen & Unwin, London, in 1929. This volume is the first American edition, published by the Macmillan Company, New York.

Charles Freer Andrews (1871–1940), a priest of the Church of England, was born in England. He was a friend of Mahatma Gandhi from the time they met in South Africa in 1914 until Andrews' death in Calcutta, India. Andrews was also a friend of Rabindranath Tagore.

This book is inscribed, "To Miss Anna T. Bogue/with gratitude and/ affection/from C. F. Andrews/April 2, 1930".

1947 – Original Prayer Speech Fragments of Mahatma Gandhi

These are nine fragments of hand-written notes of a prayer speech by Mahatma Gandhi. It appears that another person took notes which Gandhi extensively corrected in his own handwriting before giving it for publication. Speaking on 23 September 1947 at his prayer meeting in New Delhi, Gandhi urged Muslims not to flee Hindu India and likewise Hindus not to flee Pakistan. This is the text of the speech as published in the *Delhi Diary*:

> The Gita, the Quran, the Bible, the Granth Sahib, contain gems of wisdom, although the followers might belie their teachings.

> Speaking after prayers Gandhiji referred to the apology which Shrimati Manu Gandhi and Abha Gandhi had read out on the previous day. While they were singing the bhajan during the prayers on Sunday evening, they went out of tune and as a result could not suppress their laughter. It hurt him deeply. It showed that the girls did not realize the importance of prayer. They apologized to Gandhiji afterwards. Apology was unnecessary for he had no anger against them. He was angry with himself that though the girls were brought up under him, he had not impressed them with the necessity of losing themselves in God whilst they were at prayer. He was somewhat relieved when the girls repented. He advised public confession. They gladly accepted the advice, for, he believed

3

Gita, Quran,

Bible, Granth Saheb,

Zandavasta contains all

gems of wisdom of

~~the religious books~~

though the ~~followers~~

taught ~~the law~~

might belie their

eternal of truth

teachings

~~the~~

4

He was angry with himself

objected to the recitation

that though the girls were brought

up under him he had not impressed

~~on the Quran~~ he ~~had~~

them with the necessity of losing

themselves in God whilst they

~~always believed that~~

were at prayer. He was somewhat

relieved when the girls

~~public confession~~

repented. He advised public con-

fession. They gladly accepted

~~the advice followed~~

the advice. For he believed that

public confession made in

~~honour a ptapology would~~

sincerity purified the con

~~a repetition of the~~

~~floor & protects~~ him or her

against repetition of the

~~mistake supposed~~

errors

~~Himself the God~~

14

God was the protector

he would cheerfully die at

~~of all~~ He ~~hope with~~

the hands of any one be

who choose to take ~~this life~~

~~Camp was safe~~

then he would have done

as he advised all to do

~~under military protection~~

But ~~even if it was~~

not and they were

all annihilated, he

would not shed a

Fragments of
hand-written notes
of Mahatma
Gandhi's prayer
speech (1947)

266

that public confession made in sincerity purified the confessor and protected him or her against repetition of the wrong.

Turning to the day's work, Gandhiji said that he had seen a deputation of Hindus and Sikhs from Rawalpindi as also from Dera Gazi Khan. The Hindus and Sikhs had made Rawalpindi what it was. They were all well off there. Today they were refugees without shelter. It hurt him deeply. Who made modern Lahore as it was if not the Hindus and Sikhs? They were exiles from their own lands. Similarly, the Muslims had not a little to do with the making of Delhi. Thus all communities had worked together to make India what it was on the 15th of August last.

The Pakistan authorities should assure full protection to the remaining Hindus and Sikhs, in every part of Pakistan. It was equally the duty of both the governments to demand such protection for their minorities. He was told that there were still left over 18,000 Hindus and Sikhs in Rawalpindi and 30,000 in the Wah Camp. He would repeat his advice that they should all be prepared to die to a man rather than leave their homes … Then there would be no abductions and no forcible conversions. He knew that they were anxious that he should go to the Punjab at the earliest moment. He wanted to do so. But if he failed in Delhi, it was impossible for him to succeed in Pakistan. He wanted to go to all the parts and provinces of Pakistan under the protection of no escort save God. He would go as a friend of the Muslims as of others. His life would be at their disposal. He hoped that he would cheerfully die at the hands of anyone who chose to take his life. Then he would have done as he advised all to do. …

Gandhi often used the blank sides of letters, telegrams and even envelopes he received to write his notes. These nine fragments are no exceptions. One of these fragments was a letter he received from H.C. Dasappa (1894–1964), who later became a union minister in the Nehru government.

2016 – *Unto This Last: A Paraphrase* by M.K. Gandhi

John Ruskin's *Unto This Last: A Paraphrase* by M.K. Gandhi was originally published in Gujarati in South Africa under the title *Sarvodaya*, meaning "enlightenment of all". The English translation by Valji Govindji Desai was published by Navajivan Trust in 1956. This copy is a reprint published by Navajivan Publishing House, Ahmedabad (ISBN 978-81-7229-076-4).

Mahatma Gandhi in his *Autobiography* describes how his reading of *Unto This Last* on a train from Johannesburg to Durban in 1904 was a turning point in his life (Part IV, Chapter XVIII, "The Magic Spell of a Book").

> The train reached there in the evening. I could not get any sleep that night. I determined to change my life in accordance with the ideals of the book. ... I arose with the dawn, ready to reduce these principles to practice.

Gandhi summarized his take on the book as follows:

> 1. The good of the individual is contained in the good of all.
>
> 2. A lawyer's work has the same value as the barber's, as all have the same right of earning their livelihood from their work.
>
> 3. A life of labor, i.e., the life of the tiller of the soil and the handicraftsman is the life worth living.

In the last paragraph, Gandhi gives his vision of a free India:

> India must indeed have Swaraj but she must have it by righteous methods. Our Swaraj must be real Swaraj, which cannot be attained by either violence or industrialization. India was a golden land, because Indians then had hearts of gold. The land is still the same but it is a desert because we are corrupt. It can become a land of gold again only if the base metal of our present national character is transmuted into gold. The philosopher's stone which can effect this transformation is a little word of two syllables – satya ('Truth'). If every Indian sticks to truth, Swaraj will come to us of its own accord.

RUSKIN

UNTO
THIS
LAST

A PARAPHRASE

M. K. GANDHI

Ruskin

UNTO THIS LAST

A PARAPHRASE

By
M. K. Gandhi

Translated from the Gujarati
By
Valji Govindji Desai

NAVAJIVAN PUBLISHING HOUSE
AHMEDABAD 14

The cover and title page of *Unto This Last: A Paraphrase* (2016)

1862 – *Unto This Last* by John Ruskin

This is the first edition of John Ruskin's *Unto This Last: Four Essays on the First Principles of Political Economy* which was published by Smith, Elder & Company, London. John Ruskin (1819–1900) was a British painter, thinker, writer and philanthropist, and a critic of art, architecture and society.

This is the book that Mahatma Gandhi published in paraphrase under the title *Sarvodaya*. (See 2016 – *Unto This Last: A Paraphrase* by M.K. Gandhi, p. 268.)

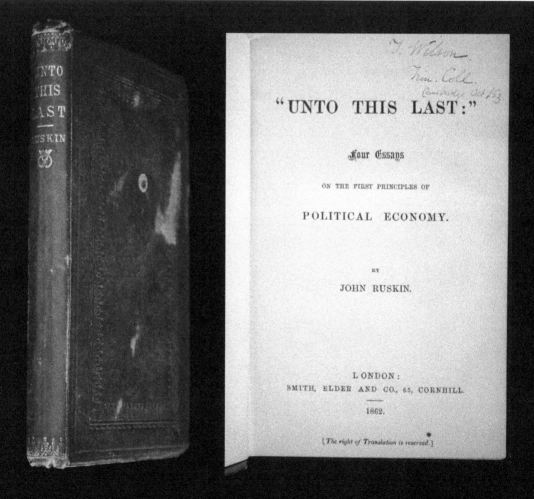

The cover and title page of *Unto This Last* (1862)

1987 – *Mahatma Gandhi and Leo Tolstoy, Letters*

This first US edition of *Mahatma Gandhi and Leo Tolstoy, Letters* was published by Long Beach Publications, Long Beach, California. It was edited with introduction and notes by B. Srinivasa Murthy.

The correspondence between Mohandas K. Gandhi and Count Leo Tolstoy occurred 1909–1910, while Gandhi was in the midst of the campaign for justice for the Indians in South Africa. The first letter was from Gandhi to Tolstoy from London:

Westminster Palace Hotel

4, Victoria Street,

London, S. W.

1st, October, 1909.

To Count Leo Tolstoy

Sir,

I take the liberty of inviting your attention to what has been going on in the Transvaal (South Africa) for nearly three years. …

With respect, I remain,

Your obedient servant,

M. K. Gandhi

Tolstoy immediately replied:

Yasnayá Polyána

Oct. 7, 1909

M. K. Gandhi

Transvaal

Just now I have received your very interesting letter, which gives me great pleasure. May God help all our dear brothers and co-workers in the Transvaal. …

I give my fraternal greetings and am glad to have come into personal contact with you.

Leo Tolstoi

Mahatma Gandhi
and
Leo Tolstoy
Letters

Edited with Introduction and Notes by
B. Srinivasa Murthy

Foreword by
Virginia Hartt Ringer

Long Beach Publications
Post Office Box 14807
Long Beach, California 90803

title page of *Mahatma*
Tolstoy, Letters (1987)

Tolstoy's last letter was:

7th September, 1910.

'KOTCHETY.'

To
M. K. Gandhi,
Johannesburg,
Transvaal, South Africa

I have received your Journal 'Indian Opinion' and I am happy to know all that is written on non-resistance. I wish to communicate to you the thoughts which are aroused in me by the reading of those articles. …

With my perfect esteem,

Leo Tolstoi

Leo Tolstoy died on 20 November 1910.

It is relevant to note that both Tolstoy and Gandhi were inspired by Thoreau's writings. (See 1927 – *Autobiography*, p. 256, and 1887 – *What to Do?*, p. 193.)

1948 – *Kasturba: Wife of Gandhi* by Sushila Nayyar

This first edition of the biography of Kasturba Gandhi, Mahatma Gandhi's wife, written by Dr. Sushila Nayyar, was published by Pendle Hill, Wallingford, PA. Sushila Nayyar was the personal physician for the Gandhis, and later the Minister of Health in independent India. In 1949, she studied at the Johns Hopkins University in Baltimore, Maryland. The book is signed by the author.

The title page has two newspaper clippings attached to it: one is from December 1949 announcing a tea in her honour by the Peace and Social Order Committee of Swarthmore Friends Meeting and the Women's International League. The other is from *Newsweek*, 26 July 1965, reporting that Sushila Nayyar, the Health Minister, "jubilantly held up a slender piece of curved plastic" and said, "It is the IUCD – the loop, with it we shall succeed in controlling births."

> Soon after Kasturba's death in detention, Gandhiji asked me to write down my reminiscences of her. I started writing in prison, but was unable to finish it till after our abrupt release.
>
> From the Foreword by Sushila Nayyar

KASTURBA

WIFE OF GANDHI

by Sushila Nayyar

✦

PENDLE HILL
WALLINGFORD, PENNSLYVANIA

The cover and title page with newspaper clippings of *Kasturba: Wife of Gandhi* (1948)

Contents

(Autographed by Author)

For DS much,
Dec. 1949.

KASTURBA
Wife of Gandhi

By

SUSHILA NAYYAR

Woman — India's Minister of Health.

For DS much.
autographed
1966 Swarthmore, Pa.
at W.I.L.P.F. mtg.

Introduction by the late

MOHANDAS KARAMCHAND GANDHI

PENDLE HILL
WALLINGFORD, PENNSYLVANIA
1948

A Photo Collage of Mahatma Gandhi

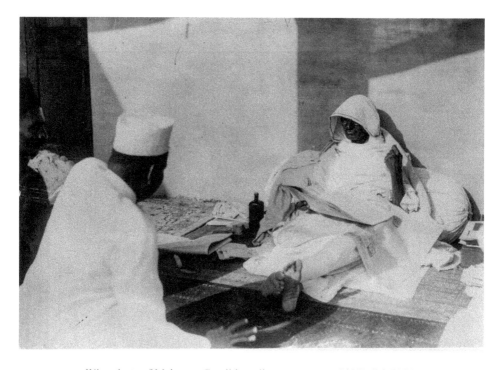

Wire photo of Mahatma Gandhi reading newspaper, Old Delhi (1931)

Verso:

International Newsreel Photo

SLUG (GANDHI – PAPERS)

Gandhi Keeps up with world news

Old Delhi, India … An excellent character study of Mahatma Gandhi, leader of the Indian nationalists, pictured at ease at the home of Dr. Ansari, reading the morning papers with care. With bare feet, sun-protecting cloth over his head, Gandhi doesn't look the native leader he is.

R-3-24-31

Wire photo of Mahatma Gandhi's birthday being celebrated, London (1931)

Verso:

Associated Press From New York

Gandhi feted on his birthday

Mahatma Gandhi's birthday was celebrated in London on October 2, and in honor of the occasion, members of the Indian Women's Association in London met at King George's Hall and wreathed the Indian leader in a garland of flowers. Photo shows Mrs. Nehru presenting Gandhi with a garland of flowers during the birthday celebration.

Associated Press Photo AJE-10/9/31 (MET LST). (KEY OUT)

Wire photo of Congress leaders with Mahatma Gandhi on the dais. Calcutta (undated).

Verso:

A view of the Congress leaders seated in the dais of the Congress. From left to right: Mr. J. M. Sen Gupta Ex-Mayor of Calcutta, 2. Mahatma Gandhi, 3. Pandit Madan Mohan Malyviya a big Congress leader 4. Mr. Subash Chander Bose, Mayor of Calcutta Corporation (extreme left).

N.B. The way the order of persons is written here is confusing. Also, no date is given for when the photo was taken.

Wire photo of Mahatma Gandhi with Jawaharlal Nehru and Vallabhai Patel, Bombay (1939)

Verso:

International News Photo

Bombay, India – Clad only in his usual loin cloth and light scarf, Mahatma Gandhi, great leader of nationalistic India, appears with his entourage outside his new residence 'Birla House' in Bombay, as he waits for his automobile. In spite of his somewhat primitive dress, modern transportation is preferred by the Mahatma. This is the most recent picture of Gandhi since his hunger strike. He seems fully recovered. On his right is pundit Jawaharlal Nehru, and at his left is Vallabhai Patel, both prominent in nationalistic circles.

SM 6-16-39

Wire photo of Mahatma Gandhi with Abha Gandhi and
Sushila Nayyar (1947)

Verso:

Associated Press. New York

Gandhi celebrates birthday

Mahatma Gandhi (center) accompanied by Abha Gandhi (left) and Dr. Sushila
Nayyar (right), one of his attendants during his present illness, walks in the
garden of Birla House, New Delhi, India, October 2, as he celebrates his 78th
birthday. H. S. Suhrawardy, former Chief Minister of Bengal Province, is at
extreme left, rear. Abha Gandhi is the wife of Kanu Gandhi, grandnephew of the
Mahatma.

Associated Press Photo

10/9/1947

Wire photo of Mahatma Gandhi, Delhi (1939)

Verso:

International News

Still Spry

Looking thinner than ever, Mahatma Gandhi, spiritual leader of all Indians, is pictured leaving his Delhi residence to visit the British Viceroy, the Marquess of Linlithgow. The picture was made not long after Gandhi had successfully ended his fifth 'fast unto death' to obtain reforms on behalf of his subjects. Stamped APR 5, 1939

Wire photo of Mahatma Gandhi and Sir Stafford Cripps,
Delhi (1942)

Verso:

Cripps Mission Fails

New Delhi, IND. – The rejection by the All India Congress Party of British proposals for Indian Dominion marked the failure of Sir Stafford Cripps (Left). Here, the British emissary is pictured with Mohandas K. Gandhi, spiritual head of the potent Indian national Congress Party, after a two-hour conference in New Delhi, which bore no fruit. Repercussions of the Indian uprisings were felt in America, many begging Roosevelt to act as intermediary between the British and India's millions.

12/14/42

Wire Photo of Mahatma Gandhi being carried to a prayer meeting, Delhi (1948)

Verso: *10763 A*

From New York

Gandhi carried to prayer

Mohandas K. Gandhi, 78, leader of India's Hindus is carried from his main house to the garden area at New Delhi, India Jan. 21, after halting his five-day fast. Gandhi was shot and killed by an assassin Jan. 30 while attending prayer meeting at New Delhi.

Associate Press Photo

GFR 855 PES 1.30.48 STF MD 63

Autograph of Gandhi

Autograph signature of Mahatma Gandhi

This original signature was probably an autograph given to someone on a piece of paper cut from an envelope. It was characteristic of Gandhi to use envelopes and the blank side of one-sided letters he received for writing his notes.

From Here and There

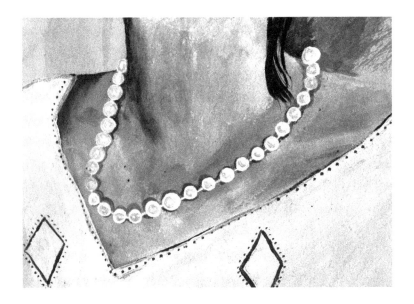

Admiring books for their association
is like celebrating pearls on the maiden who wore them.
Do not forget the mothers who bore them!

This last section contains solitaires from different periods, places, walks
of life and languages that appealed to, or have personal association with,
the curator of the T.G.M. Rare Book Museum – Helen Keller, F. Scott
Fitzgerald, Pearl S. Buck, Jawaharlal Nehru, Robert Frost, Kumaran Asan,
Geevarghese Mar Osthathios, B. Sugathakumari, G. Vijayaraghavan,
Valsamma Mathew, Glory Thomas, G. Kamalamma, Joseph E. Thomas,
Paulos Mar Gregorios and Adoor Gopalakrishnan.

THE
STORY OF MY LIFE

By HELEN KELLER

WITH
HER LETTERS (1887–1901)
AND
A SUPPLEMENTARY ACCOUNT
OF HER EDUCATION, INCLUDING
PASSAGES FROM THE REPORTS
AND LETTERS OF HER TEACHER,
ANNE MANSFIELD SULLIVAN

By JOHN ALBERT MACY

NEW YORK
DOUBLEDAY, PAGE & COMPANY
1903

HELEN KELLER AND MISS SULLIVAN

The cover, title page and facsimile of
Helen Keller's letter from *The Story of
My Life* (1903)

FACSIMILE OF PART OF LETTER TO
PHILLIPS BROOKS

So. Boston,
May 1, 1891.
My dear Mr. Brooks;
Helen
sends you a loving greet
ing this bright May-day.
My teacher has just told
me that you have been
made a bishop, and that
your friends everywhere
are rejoicing because

xiii

1903 – *The Story of My Life* by Helen Keller

This is the first edition of the autobiography of Helen Keller. It was published by Doubleday, Page & Company, New York.

Helen Keller (1880–1968) was born in Tuscumbia, Alabama. At 19 months of age, she lost her hearing and sight to an illness. In 1886, Dr. Julian Chisolm referred her to Alexander Graham Bell who at that time was working with deaf children. Bell arranged for her to join the Perkins Institute for the Blind in Boston. The school's director, Michael Anagnos, helped engage a 20-year-old former student of the school, Anne Sullivan (1866–1936), to be Helen's instructor. The latter was born in Agawam, MA. Their journey together started in 1887, lasted over 40 years, and became one of the most moving and enduring stories of teacher–pupil relationships. Helen Keller was the first deaf and blind person to obtain a BA degree (Radcliffe College of Harvard University, 1904). Her body was cremated and her ashes interred at the Washington National Cathedral, Washington, D.C., alongside those of Anne Sullivan.

Helen Keller dedicated her biography thus:

> To Alexander Graham Bell
>
> WHO has taught the deaf to speak and enabled the listening ear to hear speech from the Atlantic to the Rockies,
>
> I Dedicate this Story of My Life.

Helen Keller inspired people at home and around the world. James Mathew was taught *The Story of My Life* in high-school English class. Helen Keller met Rabindranath Tagore in New York in 1930 and Jawaharlal Nehru in New Delhi in 1955.

> I read from Mark Twain's lips one or two of his good stories. He has his own way of thinking, saying and doing everything. I feel the twinkle of his eye in his handshake. Even while he utters his cynical wisdom in an indescribably droll voice, he makes you feel that his heart is a tender Iliad of human sympathy.
>
> p. 139

THE GREAT GATSBY

BY

F. SCOTT FITZGERALD

Then wear the gold hat, if that will move her;
If you can bounce high, bounce for her too.
Till she cry "Lover, gold-hatted, high-bouncing lover,
I must have you!"
—Thomas Parke D'Invilliers.

NEW YORK
CHARLES SCRIBNER'S SONS
1925

Presented to
Shanti Mariam Mathew
with love and
admiration on
June 5, 2005 on her
Graduation from
Choate Rosemary Hall
Wallingford, CT.
By Dad

The cover, title page and page with
inscription by James Mathew of
The Great Gatsby (1925)

1925 – *The Great Gatsby* by F. Scott Fitzgerald

This landmark American novel by F. Scott Fitzgerald was published by Charles Scribner's & Sons, New York. Shanti Mathew read this novel while in high school, and she introduced it to her father. This first edition was presented to Shanti by her father on her graduation from Choate Rosemary Hall, Wallingford, CT, signed "Dad".

1931 – *The Good Earth* by Pearl S. Buck

This is the first edition of Pearl S. Buck's novel which was awarded the Pulitzer Prize for Literature in 1932. Her parents were American missionaries, and Pearl Sydenstricker Buck lived mostly in Zhenjiang, China, until 1934. She was the first American woman to win the Nobel Prize for Literature (1938). She was born in Hillsboro, WV, in 1892 and died in Danby, VT, in 1973. According to the *Bibliography of American Literature*, the first edition of *The Good Earth* contains the phrase "For the John Day Publishing Company, Inc." on the copyright page, while the second edition has "John Day Company". The first edition was in brown cloth with a tan dust-wrapper, with the scene of a burrowed field topped by a sun, printed in brown ink. It states the copyright date with no mention of subsequent prints.

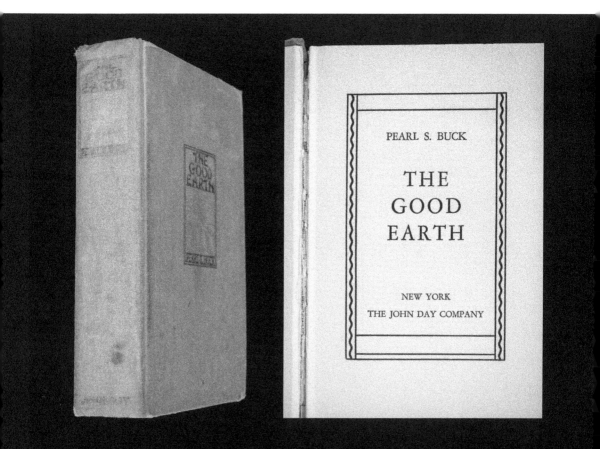

The cover and the title page of *The Good Earth* (1931)

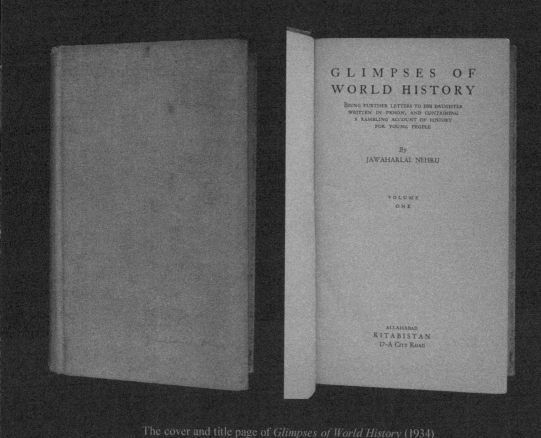

1934 – *Glimpses of World History* by Jawaharlal Nehru

This first edition of *Glimpses of World History* was written by Jawaharlal Nehru and published by *Kitabstan*, Allahabad, in two volumes. The remainder of the title of this book is *Being Further Letters to His Daughter, Written in Prison, and Containing a Rambling Account of History for Young People*.

> After five and half months out of prison my brother, Jawaharlal Nehru, was arrested on February 12, 1934, for 'sedition' and was subsequently sentenced to two years' imprisonment. At the time of his arrest he asked me to take charge of these Letters and to supervise their publication.
>
> From the Foreword by Vijaya Lakshmi Pandit

1936 – *A Further Range* by Robert Frost, Signed by the Author

This first edition of *A Further Range* was published by Henry Holt and Company, New York. This copy is signed by the author. Robert Lee Frost (1874–1963) was born in San Francisco, CA, and died in Boston, MA. He was awarded the Pulitzer Prize for Literature four times (1924, 1931, 1937 for *A Further Range*, and 1943).

Robert Frost was nominated for the Nobel Prize in Literature 31 times, distinguishing him as one of the foremost among the rejected!

BOOK SIX

A FURTHER RANGE BY ROBERT FROST

HENRY HOLT AND COMPANY
NEW YORK

The cover, title page and page with the author's autograph signature
of *A Further Range* (1936)

The cover, title page and the author's autograph signature of *You Come Too* (1962)

1962 – *You Come Too* by Robert Frost, Signed by the Author

This volume is the fifth edition of *You Come Too, Favorite Poems for Young Readers*. It was published by Holt, Rinehart and Winston, New York. It contains wood engravings by Thomas W. Nason. This book is signed by the author. This volume contains his poem "Stopping by Woods on a Snowy Evening", with the moving end:

> The woods are lovely, dark and deep,
> But I have promises to keep,
> And miles to go before I sleep,
> And miles to go before I sleep.

This poem was close to Jawaharlal Nehru's heart. James Mathew has read that Nehru kept it within reach till his death.

1916 – *Rajayogam* (trans. *Rajayoga*) Translated by N. Kumaran Asan

This is the first edition of the first Malayalam translation of the book *Rajayoga*, whose full title is *Yoga Philosophy: Lectures Delivered in New York, Winter of 1895–6 by the Swami Vivekananda on Raja Yoga or Conquering the Internal Nature. Also Patanjali's Yoga Aphorisms, with Commentaries.* (See 1896 – *Yoga Philosophy*, p. 204.)

The translator was *Mahakavi* ("great-poet") N. Kumaran Asan (1873–1924). It was published by Sarada Book Depot, Trivandrum. Asan, as the poet is affectionately known, was one of the triumvirate of modern Malayalam literature along with Ulloor S. Parameswara Iyer (1877–1949) and Vallathol Narayana Menon (1878–1958). Asan transformed his society, which was rotting under superstition and cast system. His spiritual teacher was the saintly reformer Sri Narayana Guru (1856–1928).

This volume was the personal copy of the Sanskrit scholar M.K. Govindan (1901–1968). His older son, who received the book from his father, presented it to his brother, Govindan Viyayaraghavan. The latter is married to Kumaran Asan's granddaughter Nalini. In 2020, the Vijayaraghavans gifted this family heirloom to James Mathew.

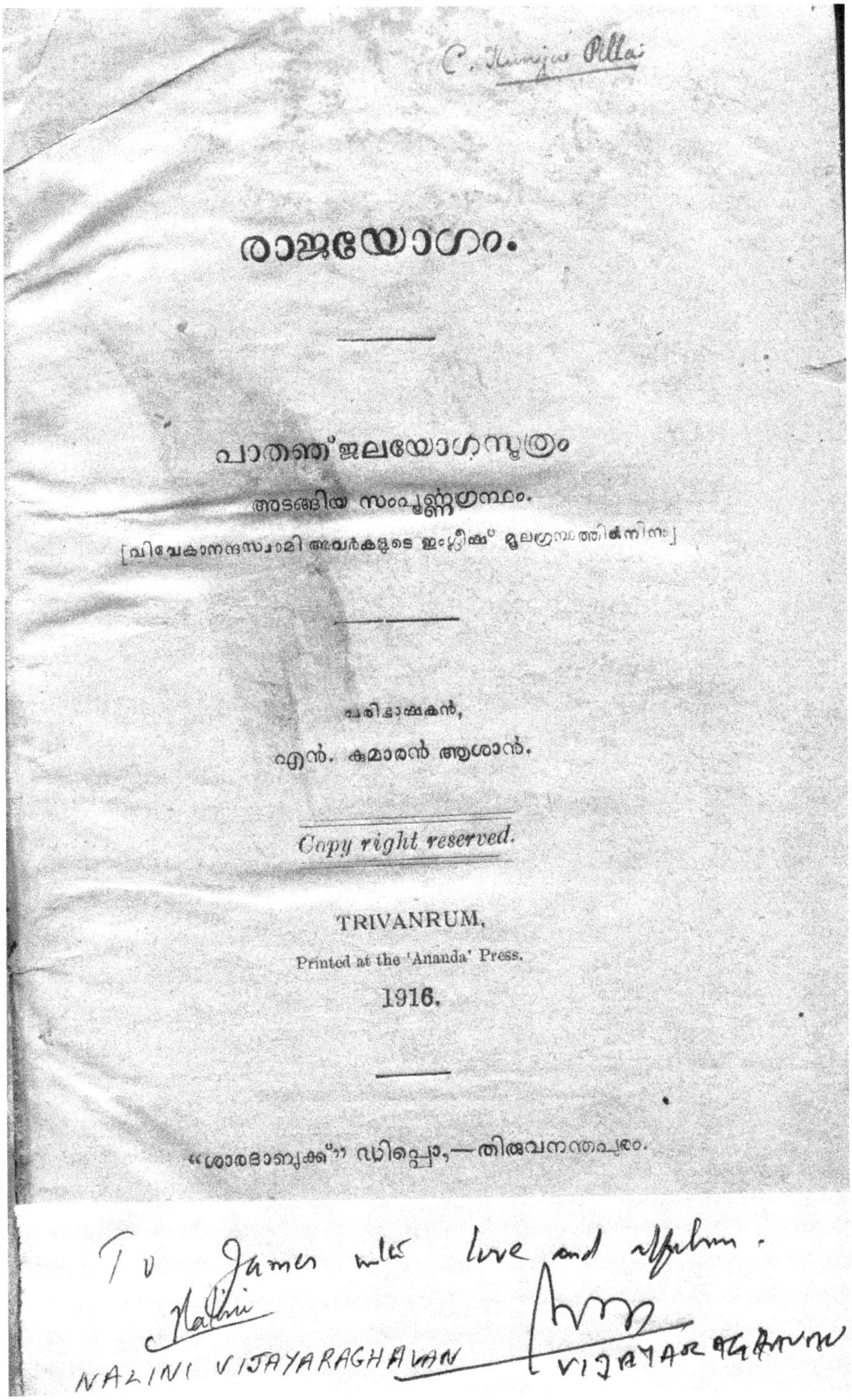

C. Kunju Pillai

രാജയോഗം.

പാതഞ്ജലയോഗസൂത്രം
അടങ്ങിയ സമ്പൂർണ്ണഗ്രന്ഥം.
[വിവേകാനന്ദസ്വാമി അവർകളുടെ ഇംഗ്ലീഷ് മൂലഗ്രന്ഥത്തിൽനിന്നു]

വിവർത്താകൻ,
എൻ. കുമാരൻ ആശാൻ.

Copy right reserved.

TRIVANRUM,
Printed at the 'Ananda' Press.
1916.

"ശാരദാബുക്ക്" ഡിപ്പോ,—തിരുവനന്തപുരം.

To James with love and affection.
Nalini
NALINI VIJAYARAGHAVAN   VIJAYARAGHAVAN

The title page and a presentation note of *Rajayogam* (1916)

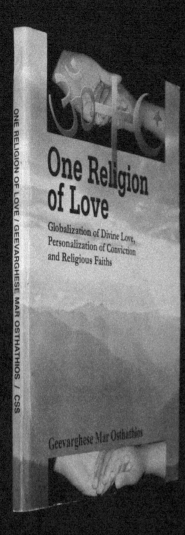

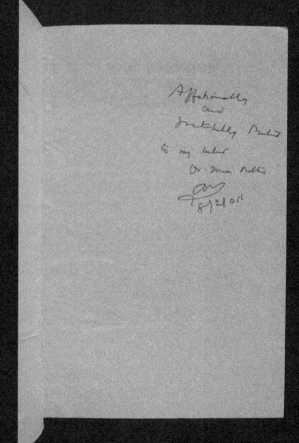

The cover and page with author's
inscription of *One religion of
Love* (2003)

Geevarghese Mar Osthathios

2003 – *One Religion of Love*

This volume is the second edition of *One Religion of Love*, written by Metropolitan Geevarghese Mar Osthathios. It was published by Christava Sahitya Samathi, Thiruvalla, Kerala, India. This presentation copy is inscribed by the author, "Affectionately and gratefully presented to my beloved Dr. James Mathew", signed 8 February 2011.

Metropolitan Geevarghese Mar Osthathios (1918–2012), senior bishop of the Indian Orthodox Church, was a world-renowned theologian, teacher, missionary and humanitarian. He was President of the Mission Board of the Indian Orthodox Church and a Member of the Faith and Order Commission of the World Council of Churches. He represented the Indian Orthodox Church in numerous international forums. He was the founding director of St. Paul's Mission Training Center, Mavelikara, Kerala State, India. He established several orphanages and other charitable centres in India. He taught at the Orthodox Theological Seminary for over half a century. Mar Osthathios has authored over 50 books on theology, orthodox faith, missionary work and social justice.

2007 – *Atraita Theology and One Religion of Love*

This first edition of *Atraita Theology and One Religion of Love*, written by Metropolitan Geevarghese Mar Osthathios, was published by Christava Sahitya Samithy, Thiruvella, Kerala, India.

This volume is a presentation copy inscribed by the author:

> Affectionately presented to Dr. James [Mathew], Valsamma [his sister] and
> mother/for deep [unclear] and the joy of sharing love/with prayers and blessings
> to all, January 8, 2008/MTC [Mission Training Center]/Per Manoj [a nephew of
> James Mathew]

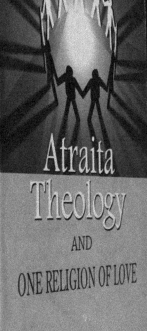

The cover and page with
author's inscription of *Atraita
Theology* (2007)

2008 – *Daridralokathil Dhanavanayirikkunnathu Papam* (trans. *In a World with Poverty It is a Sin to be Rich*)

This is the first edition of the book written by Geevarghese Mar Osthathios Metropolitan and published by Christava Sahitya Samathi, Thiruvalla, in December 2008. (ISBN 978-81-7821-098-6)

This is a presentation copy by the author and it is inscribed, "Affectionately presented to my beloved son Dr. James Mathew and family/esp. daughter Shanti with/love, prayers & blessings/February 14, 2009."

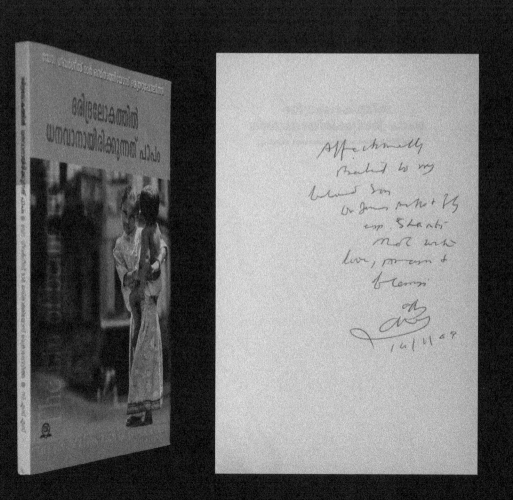

The cover and the page with author's inscription of
Daridralokathil Dhanavanayirikkunnathu Papam (2008)

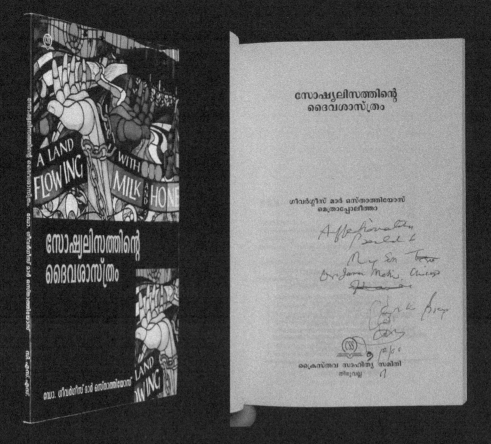

The cover and page with author's inscription of *Socialisathinte Daivasasthram* (2011)

2011 – *Socialisathinte Daivasasthram* (trans. *The Biblical Basis of Socialism*)

This is a first edition of this book written by Metropolitan Geevarghese Mar Osthathios and published by Christava Sahitya Samathi, Thiruvalla, Kerala, India. (ISBN 978-81-7821-313-2) This copy was inscribed and signed by the author, "Affectionately presented to my son Dr. James Mathew, Chicago." (The date is not clear.) This book was presented by the Bishop the last time James Mathew met him.

Geevarghese Mar Osthathios Metropolitan passed away on 16 February 2012, aged 93.

സുഗതകുമാരി
കാവു തീണ്ടല്ലേ

The cover and page with
author's inscription of
Kavu Theendalle (2014)

ഡി സി ബുക്സ്

2014 – *Kavu Theendalle* by B. Sugathakumari (trans. *Do Not Desecrate the Grove*)

This book by B. Sugathakumari contains 25 essays on the environment. The book was first published by DC Books, Kottayam, Kerala, India, in 1993. This fifth impression was made in July 2014. (ISBN 81-7130-283-1)

This presentation copy was inscribed in Malayalam by the author, "To Dr. James Mathew/with affection and respect/Sugathakumari/December 30, 2015." (Inscription translated from the original Malayalam by J.M.)

B. Sugathakumari (1934–2020) was a distinguished Malayalam poet, environmentalist and social activist. In the 1970s, she successfully led the "Save Silent Valley Movement" and saved its namesake, an evergreen forest in Kerala, from being purposefully flooded by the proposed construction of a hydroelectric project. As a result, it was declared a national park in 1985. Founder of the Prakriti Samrakshana Samati (Organization for the Protection of Nature), she has been a powerful advocate for the preservation of nature in her native state of Kerala. She is the founding Secretary of Abhaya ("Refuge") in Trivandrum, a project to rehabilitate neglected or abused women and children. She was the Chairperson of Kerala State Women's Commission. She has been honoured with several state and national awards for her contribution to the fields of literature, the environment and social justice.

On 23 December 2020, Sugathakumari became a victim of the present pandemic. Ironically, the poet's parting plea to the people of Kerala not to waste flowers and money placing wreaths on her body after she died came to pass. Instead of placing them on her body, they piled up flowers far from her body, not out of respect for her wishes but because they were afraid of the virus!

2010 – *Hrudrogam Keraleeyaril* by G. Vijayaraghavan (trans. *Heart Disease in Keralites*)

This book written by Govindan Vijayaraghavan was first published by Sankeerthanam Press, Kollam, Kerala, India, in 2003. It is a guide to the public on the prevention and treatment of heart disease. This volume is a 2010 impression and is stamped, "Author's Copy". The author presented this copy to James Mathew with the inscription, "To Dear James/11/11/10."

Govindan Vijayaraghavan is the Vice-Chairman and founding Director of the Kerala Institute of Medical Sciences in Trivandrum, Kerala, India. He was Professor of Cardiology at the Medical College, Trivandrum, when James Mathew was a student there. In 2002, the government of India honoured him with a civilian award for his contribution to the field of Medicine. (For more on Vijayaraghavan, see 1916 – *Rajayogam*, p. 296.)

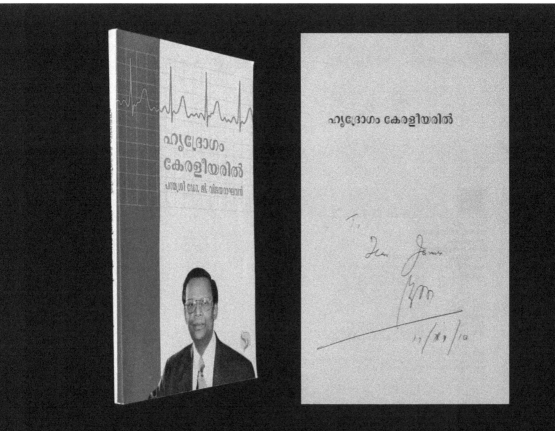

The cover and page with author's inscription of *Hrudrogam Keraleeyaril* (2010)

കൂട്ടുകാരേ! വരൂ...

വത്സമ്മ മാത്യു
നരിയാപുരം

2007 – *Koottukare! Varoo ...* by Valsamma Mathew (trans. *Come on Friends! ...*)

This book is a collection of moral tales for children written by Valsamma Mathew, Nariyapuram. The full title of this book may be translated as *Come on Friends! ... I will Tell You Stories*.

The cover for *Come on Friends* was designed by Ashna Jacob, Thamaravelil Geevarghese Mathai's great granddaughter, when she was in her early teens. She is also the designer of this *Book of Books*.

Valsamma Mathew (1951–2014) was the sixth child of T.G. Mathai. She frequently contributed essays and letters to *Malankara Sabha*, the official monthly magazine of the Indian Orthodox Church. She gave Bible lessons to ladies' and children's groups, taught at Sunday school and earned the affectionate nickname "Bible Aunti" among her students and readers. *Come on Friends* contains the story "Remember the Crows", based on the interaction between T.G. Mathai and the flock of crows, mentioned in "Seedlings/Gleanings" (pp. 18–20).

2021 – *Kalathinte Kanalvazhikaliloode Sancharicha Thamaravelil T.G. Mathai* (trans. *The Travels of T.G. Mathai on Time's Path of Hot Coals*)

This book is a collection of memoirs about the life of T.G. Mathai (see Seedlings/Gleanings, pp. 1–24). The book was edited by Thomas Neelarmadam. The publisher was Glory Thomas, the third daughter of T.G. Mathai, who along with her husband, A.V. Thomas, in 1988, founded the Holy Trinity Vidyabhavan ("The Trinity School") in Karthigapally, Kerala. This book contains an English translation of T.G. Mathai's journal entries from July and August of 1968, about his travels by train to Delhi and Bombay. A portion of this translation by Remi Susan Thomas, daughter of Glory Thomas, is reproduced below:

> 1968 AUGUST   THURSDAY 1
>
> As Leelamma [Leelama Abraham, the second daughter of T.G. Mathai] was taking charge as Atomic Energy Assistant Officer in Trombay, N.B. During the morning prayer (*Mayyalinte prardhana*), I especially prayed to God for all His blessings upon her.
>
> 10.30. A.M. I placed my hand on my daughter and I blessed her. Stayed in the room peacefully. Had lunch.
>
> N.B. Leelamma signs in front of her officer and takes charge. Time 10.45. Especially prayed for her.
>
> N.B. Wrote a postcard for Podiyachen (K.C. Mathew) in Delhi.

This book was released in India on 17 August 2021, the 104th birthday of T.G. Mathai.

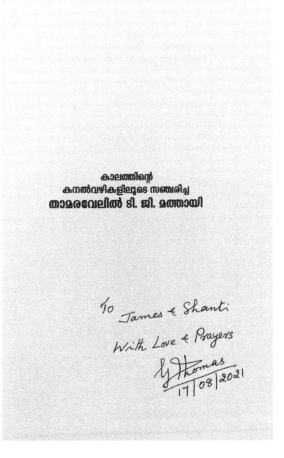

The cover and inscription page of *Kalathinte Kanalvazhikaliloode* ...

2008 – *Kavyāmrutham* (trans. *Poetry-Nectar*) by G. Kamalamma

This book is the first edition of a collection of poems edited by G. Kamalamma. It was published by Rainbow Book Publishers, Kerala, India. This is a presentation copy inscribed by the author, "Merry X'Mas and Happy New Year To Dr. James Mathew and Family", signed 24 December 2011.

G. Kamalamma (1930–2012) was a teacher of the Malayalam language and author of about three dozen books on language, literature and history. She won over half a dozen state and national awards in education and literature. She is the sister of G. Vijayaraghavan. (See 2010 – *Hrudrogam Keraleeyaril*, p. 306.)

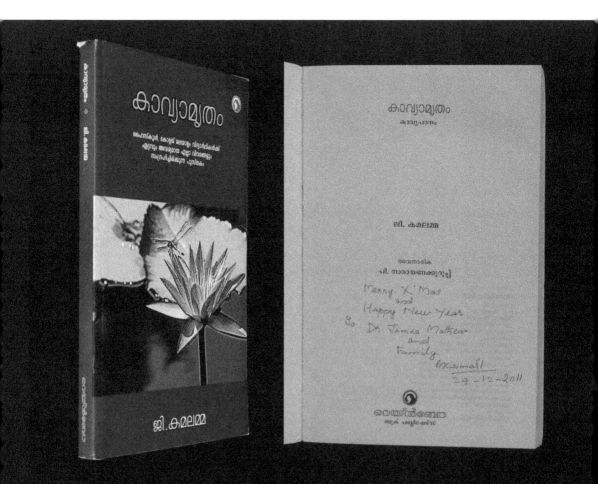

The cover and the page with author's inscription of *Kavyāmrutham* (2008)

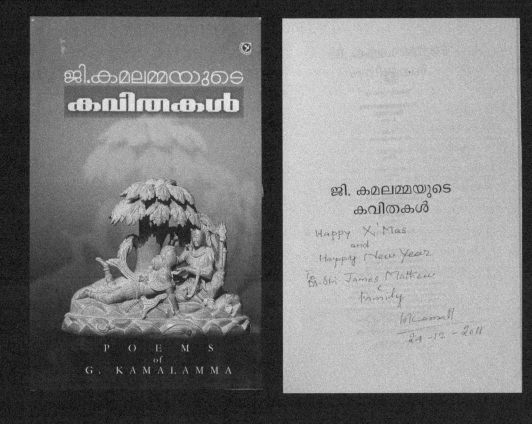

The cover and page with author's inscription of *G. Kamalammayude Kavithakal* (2010)

2010 – *G. Kamalammayude Kavithakal* (trans. *The Poems of G. Kamalamma)*

This is the first edition of a collection of poems written by G. Kamalamma published by Saindhava Books, Kerala, India. This presentation copy was inscribed by the author to James Mathew in 2011. An aerogram letter from the author to James Mathew, damaged during mailing, is retained in this book.

311

2001 – *Metropolitan Dr. Paulos Mar Gregorios: A Personal Reminiscence* by Joseph E. Thomas

Joseph E. Thomas, a life-long friend of Metropolitan Dr. Paulos Mar Gregorios, wrote this book. (For more on Paulos Mar Gregorios, see 1987 – *Science for Sane Societies* below.) This volume is the first edition published by ROY International Providential Foundation, Kottayam, Kerala, India. This volume is a presentation copy from the author inscribed, "To Dr. James & Shanti/With love, signed Babychen" (as he is respectfully addressed by his friends).

Joseph E. Thomas is a clinical psychologist in Chicago, IL. In this book, he relates several incidents which throw light on Mar Gregorios' insights and outlooks.

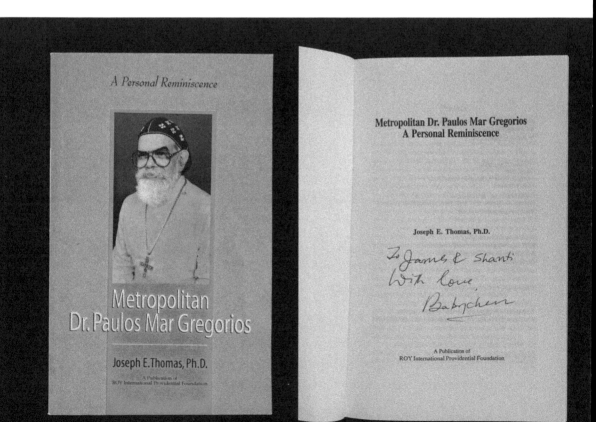

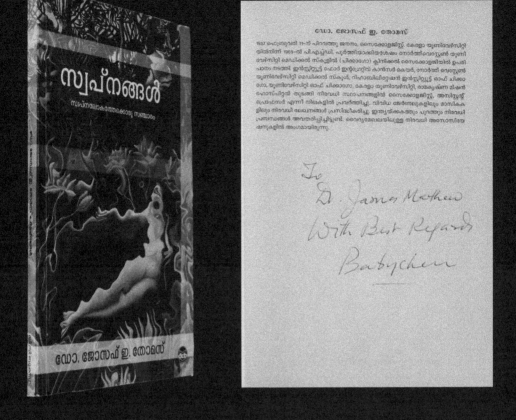

The cover and page with author's inscription of *Swapnangal* (2009)

2009 – *Swapnangal* (trans. *Dreams*) by Joseph E. Thomas

This is the first edition of the book written by Joseph E. Thomas which was published by DC Press, Kottayam, Kerala, India. (ISBN 978-81-264-2545-7) This is a presentation copy from the author with the inscription, "To Dr. James Mathew/With best regards/Babychen." In this book the author, a clinical psychologist, gives the reader a peek into the real world behind dreamland. (For more on Joseph E. Thomas, see 2001 – *Metropolitan Dr. Paulos Mar Gregorios*, opposite.)

The cover and title page of
Science for Sane Societies (1987)

SCIENCE FOR SANE SOCIETIES

by
Paulos Mar Gregorios

PARAGON HOUSE
NEW YORK, NEW YORK

Paulos Mar Gregorios

1987 – *Science for Sane Societies*

This is the first US edition of this book by Metropolitan Dr. Paulos Mar Gregorios, published by Paragon House Publishers, New York. The book was originally published by the Christian Literature Society, Madras, India, in 1980.

Metropolitan Dr. Paulos Mar Gregorios (1922–1996) was a bishop in the Indian Orthodox Church and President of the World Council of Churches for Asia. He was a polymath, a multi-linguist and a visionary. In this book, he gives an analysis of issues related to bio-ethics, genetic engineering and social biology. He also writes about environmental pollution, limits of resources and eco-balance. In this book, he calls for a unique social consciousness, and the need for a new paradigm that includes and transcends both the traditional sciences and religions.

1989 – *Enlightenment: East and West*

This is the first edition of *Enlightenment: East and West* written by
Metropolitan Dr. Paulos Mar Gregorios. It was published by the Indian
Institute of Advanced Study in association with BR Publishing
Corporation, Delhi. (ISBN 81-7018-560-2)

> Here is a thoughtful invitation to take a second look at some of the assumptions
> behind the European Enlightenment civilization from which our elite including
> Pundit Jawaharlal Nehru has borrowed so freely. The author, the Eastern
> Orthodox Metropolitan of Delhi, equally at home in the cultures of the East and
> West, chides us for neglecting our own Enlightenment traditions of which Lord
> Buddha is the outstanding example.
>
> From the publisher

Enlightenment

East & West

PAULOS MAR GREGORIOS

Enlightenment East & West

PAULOS MAR GREGORIOS

The cover and title page of
Enlightenment East and West (1989)

ENLIGHTENMENT:
EAST AND WEST

*Pointers in the Quest for
India's Secular Identity*

PAULOS MAR GREGORIOS

INDIAN INSTITUTE OF ADVANCED STUDY
Shimla
in association with
B.R. PUBLISHING CORPORATION
Delhi

1997 – *Love's Freedom, The Grand Mystery*

This is the first edition of the book *Love's Freedom, The Grand Mystery, A Spiritual Autobiography* of Paulos Mar Gregorios. It was edited by Rev. K.M. George and published by Mar Gregorios Foundation Publications, Kottayam, Kerala, India.

Metropolitan Paulos Mar Gregorios, renowned thinker and theologian, began writing his spiritual autobiography in April 1993 at Oxford. It remained unfinished when he passed away on November 24, 1996.

LOVE'S
FREEDOM
THE
GRAND
MYSTERY

A SPIRITUAL AUTOBIOGRAPHY

PAULOS MAR GREGORIOS

LOVE'S FREEDOM
THE GRAND MYSTERY

A SPIRITUAL AUTOBIOGRAPHY

PAULOS   MAR   GREGORIOS

Edited by
Fr. Dr. K.M. George

MGF PUBLICATIONS
KOTTAYAM, INDIA
1997

The cover, the title page and the author's photo on the back
cover of *Love's Freedom, The Grand Mystery* (1997)

അടൂർ ഗോപാലകൃഷ്ണൻ

സിനിമ
സാഹിത്യം
ജീവിതം

The cover and page with author's
inscription of *Cinema Sahityam
Jeevitham* (2005)

സിനിമ സാഹിത്യം ജീവിതം

ശ്രീമതി ഡോ. ഗ്നുമിംബ്ല
ടെപഹനിപ്,

31-5-2013

Adoor Gopalakrishnan

My attempt is to reflect the sky in a drop of dew.

Adoor Gopalakrishnan

2005 – *Cinema Sahityam Jeevitham* (trans. *Cinema Literature Life*)

This is the first edition of *Cinema Sahityam Jeevitham*, written by Adoor Gopalakrishnan. It was published by Current Books, Thrissur, India. (ISBN 81-226-0473-0) It is a collection of essays on topics implied in the title. This copy was presented by the author to James Mathew. The author wrote the following inscription: "To dear Dr. James, affectionately", signed 31 May 2013. (Trans. by J.M.)

Artist, writer, director and producer Adoor Gopalakrishnan is an internationally acclaimed Indian filmmaker. His works are known for their intellectual content, artistic perfection, sympathetic treatment of sensitive topics, social impact and international appeal. He received the Phalke Award of the Government of India and the British Film Institute Award. India and France honoured him with civic awards. Three major universities gave him honorary doctorate degrees. In 2013, the Peck School of the Arts at the University of Wisconsin-Milwaukee (United States) established the Adoor Gopalakrishnan Film Archive and Research Center.[*] The Center received a gift "in honor of Adoor Gopalakrishnan and in memory of the artist's beloved mother Mrs. Gouri Kunjamma." Adoor Gopalakrishnan's films created over 49 years are preserved here in their original formats. In July 2015, the Center acquired these films in digital format and installed the Sunanda Gopalakrishnan Digital Film Archive in honour of the artist's beloved wife.

---

[*] https://uwm.edu/arts/film/adoor-gopalakrishnan-film-archive-research-center, accessed 13 May 2021

The cover, the title page and page with author's inscription of *Adoor Gopalakrishnan, A Life in Cinema* (2010)

2010 – *Adoor Gopalakrishnan, A Life in Cinema* by Gautaman Bhaskaran

This is the first edition of the authorized biography of Adoor Gopalakrishnan. This book was published by Penguin Books, India. The subject of this biography wrote the following inscription in this book: "To Dr. James Mathew with affection and warm regards,/signed/March 20, 2011."

2011 – *Cinema Samskaaram* (trans. *Cinema Culture*)

This is the first edition of a collection of essays written by Adoor Gopalakrishnan and published by Mathrubhumi Books, Kozhikode, Kerala. The author wrote the following inscription: "To Dear Dr. James/affectionately/Signed/May 31, 2013."

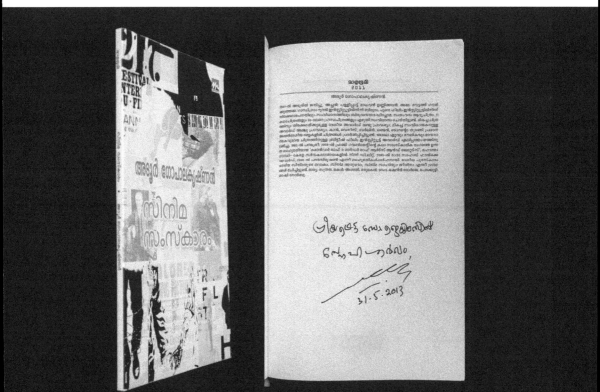

2012 – *Adoor Gopalakrishnante Pathinonnu Thirakkathakal* (trans. *The Eleven Screen Plays of Adoor Gopalakrishnan*)

This is the first edition of the book, written by Adoor Gopalakrishnan and published by DC Books, Kottayam, Kerala, India. (ISBN 978-81-264-3928-7) The book contains the post-production scripts of his first eleven feature films.

This presentation volume is inscribed by the author as follows: "To Dr. James/with warm regards/and deep affection/Adoor." The author presented this copy to James Mathew when the former was in Milwaukee to inaugurate the Adoor Gopalakrishnan Film Archive and Research Center established at the Peck School of the Arts, University of Wisconsin-Milwaukee in 2013.

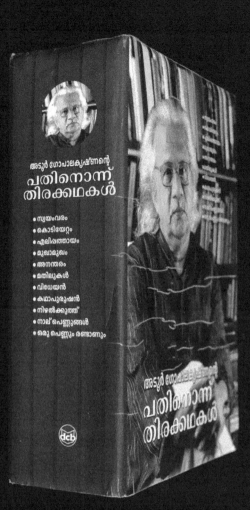

The cover and page with author's
inscription of *Adoor Gopalakrishnante
Pathinonnu Thirakkathakal* (2012)

To
DR. JAMES
WITH WARM REGARDS
AND DEEP AFFECTION

14. 04. 2014

The cover of *Cinemānubhavam* (2013)

2013 – *Cinemānubhavam* (trans. *Cinema Experience*)

This book was first published by the Mathrubhumi Printing and Publishing Company, Kozhikode, Kerala, India, in 2004. It contains 14 essays on the "experience of cinema". This volume is its third printing and is stamped "Author's Copy". The author inscribed the book as follows: "To Dear Dr. James Mathew/affectionately/Signed/December 30, 2013."

ADOOR GOPALAKRISHNAN
DARSANAM TRIVANDRUM 695 017 KERALA INDIA
PHONE + 91- 471-2 551144 + 91- 471-2445567
adoorg@gmail.com

Dr. James Mathew MD,
755 E, Lexington Blvd,
Whitefish Bay,
WI 53217 (USA)

Dear Dr. James Mathew,

Thank you for the photos you have very kindly forwarded.

I really enjoyed that evening at your residence enjoying your warm hospitality and the company of all those good people who joined us.

Let me thank you heartily for all that.

With warm regards,

Adoor Gopalakrishnan   Trivandrum 2-11-2009

A letter from Adoor Gopalakrishnan to James Mathew (2009)

2009 – A Letter from Adoor Gopalakrishnan

This is the letter that Adoor Gopalakrishnan sent to James Mathew following their first meeting, in Milwaukee, WI. This meeting marked the beginning of a lasting friendship between them.

Index

The Authors

James Mathew is a cardiologist who lives in Milwaukee, WI. He has presented papers at the Annual Gatherings of the Thoreau Society in Concord, and the Annual Conference of the American Literature Association in Boston (both in MA). *Book of Books* is his first book.

Kent Bicknell is an educator who lives in New Hampton, NH. He transcribed and published the Gothic thriller by Louisa May Alcott, *A Long Fatal Love Chase*, which became a *New York Times* best-seller.

Endpaper

Pearls are not delivered without labor,
Remember ye the oyster!

CPSIA information can be obtained
at www.ICGtesting.com
Printed in the USA
LVHW070031281221
707313LV00032B/1547